Voyages of
Peter Esprit Radisson

An Account of his Travels and Experiences
among the North American Indians from
1652 to 1684

By Peter Esprit Radisson
Cover Design by Alex Struik

Copyright © 2012 Alex Struik.

Alex Struik retains sole copyright to the cover design of this edition of this book.

All rights reserved. No part of this publication may be reproduced, stored in a retrieval system, or transmitted, in any form or by any means, electronic, mechanical, photocopying, recording or otherwise, without the prior permission of the copyright owner.

The right of Alex Struik to be identified as the author of the cover design of this work has been asserted in accordance with the Copyright, Designs and Patents Act 1988.

ISBN-13: 978-1481187251

ISBN-10: 1481187252

Contents

INTRODUCTION. 4

FIRST VOYAGE OF PETER ESPRIT RADISSON 25

SECOND VOYAGE, MADE IN THE UPPER COUNTRY OF THE IROQUOITS 79

THIRD VOYAGE, MADE TO THE GREAT LAKE OF THE HURONS, UPPER SEA OF THE EAST, AND BAY OF THE NORTH 123

FOURTH VOYAGE OF PETER ESPRIT RADISSON .158

A VOYAGE TO THE NORTH PARTS OF AMERICA IN THE YEARS 1682 AND 1683 224

THE VOYAGE ANNO 1684 282

INTRODUCTION.

The author of the narratives contained in this volume was Peter Esprit Radisson, who emigrated from France to Canada, as he himself tells us, on the 24th day of May, 1651. He was born at St. Malo, and in 1656, at Three Rivers, in Canada, married Elizabeth, the daughter of Madeleine Hainault. [Footnote: Vide History of the Ojibways, by the Rev. E. D. Neill, ed. 1885.] Radisson says that he lived at Three Rivers, where also dwelt "my natural parents, and country-people, and my brother, his wife and children." [Footnote: The Abbe Cyprian Tanguay, the best genealogical authority in Canada, gives the following account of the family: Francoise Radisson, a daughter of Pierre Esprit, married at Quebec, in 1668, Claude Volant de St. Claude, born in 1636, and had eight children. Pierre and Claude, eldest sons, became priests. Francoise died in infancy: Marguerite married Noel le Gardeur; Francoise died in infancy; Etienne, born October 29, 1664, married in 1693 at Sorel, but seems to have had no issue. Jean Francois married Marguerite Godfrey at Montreal in 1701. Nicholas, born in 1668, married Genevieve Niel, July 30, 1696, and both died in 1703, leaving two of their five sons surviving.

There are descendants of Noel le Gardeur who claim Radisson as their ancestor, and also descendants of Claude Volant, apparently through Nicholas. Among these descendants of the Volant family is the Rt. Rev. Joseph Thomas Duhamel, who was consecrated Bishop of Ottawa, Canada, October 28, 1874.

Of Medard Chouart's descendants, no account of any of the progeny of his son Jean Baptiste, born July 25, 1654, can be found.] This brother, often alluded to in Radisson's narratives as his companion on his journeys, was Medard Chouart, "who was the son of Medard and Marie Poirier, of Charly St. Cyr, France, and in 1641, when only sixteen years old, came to Canada." [Footnote: Chouart's daughter Marie Antoinette, born June 7, 1661, married first Jean Jalot in 1679. He was a surgeon, born in 1648, and killed by the Iroquois, July 2, 1690. He was called Des Groseilliers. She had nine children by Jalot, and there are descendants from them in Canada. On the 19th December, 1695, she married, secondly, Jean Bouchard, by whom she had six children. The Bouchard-Dorval family of Montreal descends from this marriage. Vide Genealogical Dictionary of Canadian Families, Quebec, 1881.] He was a pilot, and married, 3rd September, 1647, Helen, the daughter of Abraham Martin, and widow of Claude Etienne. Abraham Martin left his name to the celebrated Plains of Abraham, near Quebec. She dying in 1651, Chouart married, secondly, at Quebec, August 23, 1653, the sister of Radisson, Margaret Hayet, the widow of John Veron Grandmenil. In Canada, Chouart acted as a donne, or lay assistant, in the Jesuit mission near Lake Huron. He left the service of the mission about 1646, and commenced trading with the Indians for furs, in which he was very successful. With his gains he is supposed to have purchased some land in Canada, as he assumed the seigneurial title of "Sieur des Groseilliers."

Radisson spent more than ten years trading with the Indians of Canada and the far West, making long and perilous journeys of from two to three years each, in company with his brother-in-law, Des Groseilliers. He carefully made notes during his wanderings from 1652 to 1664, which he afterwards copied out on his voyage to England in 1665. Between these years he made four journeys, and heads his first narrative with this title: "The Relation of my Voyage, being in Bondage in the Lands of the Irokoits, which was the next year after my coming into Canada, in the yeare 1651, the 24th day of May." In 1652 a roving band of Iroquois, who had gone as far north as the Three Rivers, carried our author as a captive into their country, on the banks of the Mohawk River. He was adopted into the family of a "great captayne who had killed nineteen men with his own hands, whereof he was marked on his right thigh for as many as he had killed." In the autumn of 1653 he accompanied the tribe in his village on a warlike incursion into the Dutch territory. They arrived "the next day in a small brough of the Hollanders," Rensselaerswyck, and on the fourth day came to Fort Orange. Here they remained several days, and Radisson says: "Our treaty's being done, overladened with bootyes abundantly, we putt ourselves in the way that we came, to see again our village."

At Fort Orange Radisson met with the Jesuit Father, Joseph Noncet, who had also been captured in Canada by the Mohawks and taken to their country. In September he was taken down to Fort Orange by his captors, and it is mentioned in the Jesuit "Relations" of 1653, chapter iv., that he "found there a young man captured near Three Rivers, who had been ransomed by the Dutch and acted as interpreter." A few weeks after the return of the Indians to their village, Radisson made his escape alone, and found his way again to Fort Orange, from whence he was sent to New Amsterdam, or Menada, as he calls it. Here he remained three weeks, and then embarked for Holland, where he arrived after a six weeks' voyage, landing at Amsterdam "the 4/7 of January, 1654. A few days after," he says, "I imbarqued myself for France, and came to Rochelle well and safe." He remained until Spring, waiting for "the transport of a shipp for New France."

The relation of the second journey is entitled, "The Second Voyage, made in the Upper Country of the Irokoits." He landed in Canada, from his return voyage from France, on the 17th of May, 1654, and on the 15th set off to see his relatives at Three Rivers. He mentions that "in my absence peace was made betweene the French and the Iroquoits, which was the reson I stayed not long in a place. The yeare before the ffrench began a new plantation in the upper country of the Iroquoits, which is distant from the Low Iroquoits country some four score leagues, wher I was prisoner and been in the warrs of that country.... At that very time the Reverend Fathers Jesuits embarked themselves for a second time to dwell there and teach Christian doctrine. I offered myself to them and was, as their custome is, kindly accepted. I prepare meselfe for the journey, which was to be in June, 1657." Charlevoix [Footnote: Charlevoix's History of New France, Shea's ed., Vol. II. p. 256.] says: "In 1651 occurred the almost complete destruction of the Huron nation. Peace was concluded in 1653. Father Le Moyne went in 1654, to ratify the treaty of peace, to Onondaga, and told the Indians there he wished to have his cabin in their canton. His offer was accepted, and a site marked out of which he took possession. He left Quebec July 2, 1654, and returned September 11. In 1655 Fathers Chaumont and Dablon were sent to Onondaga, and arrived there November 5, and began at once to build a chapel. [Footnote: Charlevoix's Hist. of New France, Shea's ed., Vol. II. p. 263.]

"Father Dablon, having spent some months in the service of the mission at Onondaga, was sent back to Montreal, 30 March, 1656, for reinforcements. He returned with Father Francis le Mercier and other help. They set out from Quebec 7 May, 1656, with a force composed of four nations: French, Onondagas, Senecas, and a few Hurons. About fifty men composed the party. Sieur Dupuys, an officer of the garrison, was appointed commandant of the proposed settlement at Onondaga. On their arrival they at once proceeded to erect a fort, or block-house, for their defence.

"While these things were passing at Onondaga, the Hurons on the Isle Orleans, where they had taken refuge from the Iroquois, no longer deeming themselves secure, sought an asylum in Quebec, and in a moment of resentment at having been abandoned by the French, they sent secretly to propose to the Mohawks to receive them into their canton so as to form only one people with them. They had no sooner taken this step than they repented; but the Mohawks took them at their word, and seeing that they endeavored to withdraw their proposition, resorted to secret measures to compel them to adhere to it." [Footnote: Ibid., Vol. II. p.278.] The different families of the Hurons held a council, and "the Attignenonhac or Cord family resolved to stay with the French; the Arendarrhonon, or Rock, to go to Onondaga; and the Attignaonanton, or Bear, to join the Mohawks." [Footnote: Relation Nouvelle France, 1657 and Charlevoix, Shea's ed., Vol. II. p 280.] "In 1657 Onondagas had arrived at Montreal to receive the Hurons and take them to their canton, as agreed upon the year previous." [Footnote: Charlevoix, Shea's ed., Vol. III. p. 13.] Some Frenchmen and two Jesuits were to accompany them. One of the former was Radisson, who had volunteered; and the two Jesuits were Fathers Paul Ragueneau and Joseph Inbert Duperon. The party started on their journey in July, 1657.

The relation of this, the writer's second voyage, is taken up entirely with the narrative of their journey to Onondaga, his residence at the mission, and its abandonment on the night of the 20th of March, 1658. On his way thither he was present at the massacre of the Hurons by the Iroquois, in August, 1657. His account of the events of 1657 and 1658, concerning the mission, will be found to give fuller details than those of Charlevoix, [Footnote: Ibid., Vol. III. p. 13.] and the Jesuit relations written for those years by Father Ragueneau. Radisson, in concluding his second narrative, says: "About the last of March we ended our great and incredible dangers. About fourteen nights after we went downe to the Three Rivers, where most of us stayed. A month after, my brother and I resolves to travell and see countreys. Wee find a good opportunity in our voyage. We proceeded three years; during that time we had the happiness to see very faire countreys." He says of the third voyage: "Now followeth the Auxoticiat, or Auxotacicae, voyage into the great and filthy lake of the hurrons upper sea of the East and bay of the North." He mentions that "about the middle of June, 1658, we began to take leave of our company and venter our lives for the common good."

Concerning the third voyage, Radisson states above, "wee proceeded three years." The memory of the writer had evidently been thrown into some confusion when recording one of the historical incidents in his relation, as he was finishing his narrative of the fourth journey. At the close of his fourth narrative, on his return from the Lake Superior country, where he had been over three years, instead of over two, as he mentions, he says: "You must know that seventeen ffrenchmen made a plott with four Algonquins to make a league with three score Hurrons for to goe and wait for the Iroquoits in the passage." This passage was the Long Sault, on the Ottawa river, where the above seventeen Frenchmen were commanded by a young officer of twenty-five, Adam Dollard, Sieur des Ormeaux. The massacre of the party took place on May 21, 1660, and is duly recorded by several authorities; namely, Dollier de Casson [Footnote: Histoire de Montreal, Relation de la Nouvelle France, 1660, p. 14.], M. Marie [Footnote: De l'Incarnation, p. 261.], and Father Lalemont [Footnote: Journal, June 8,

1660.]. As Radisson has placed the incident in his manuscript, he would make it appear as having occurred in May, 1664. He writes: "It was a terrible spectacle to us, for wee came there eight dayes after that defeat, which saved us without doubt." He started on this third journey about the middle of June, 1658, and it would therefore seem he was only absent on it two years, instead of over three, as he says. Charlevoix gives the above incident in detail. [Footnote: Shea's edition, Vol. III. p. 33, n.]

During the third voyage Radisson and his brother-in-law went to the Mississippi River in 1658/9. He says, "Wee mett with severall sorts of people. Wee conversed with them, being long time in alliance with them. By the persuasion of som of them wee went into the great river that divides itself in two where the hurrons with some Ottanake and the wild men that had warrs with them had retired.... The river is called the forked, because it has two branches: the one towards the West, the other towards the South, which we believe runs towards Mexico, by the tokens they gave." They also made diligent inquiry concerning Hudson's Bay, and of the best means to reach that fur-producing country, evidently with a view to future exploration and trade. They must have returned to the Three Rivers about June 1, 1660. Radisson says: "Wee stayed att home att rest the yeare. My brother and I considered whether we should discover what we have seen or no, and because we had not a full and whole discovery which was that we have not ben in the bay of the north (Hudson's Bay), not knowing anything but by report of the wild Christinos, we would make no mention of it for feare that those wild men should tell us a fibbe. We would have made a discovery of it ourselves and have an assurance, before we should discover anything of it."

In the fourth narrative he says: "The Spring following we weare in hopes to meet with some company, having ben so fortunat the yeare before. Now during the winter, whether it was that my brother revealed to his wife what we had seene in our voyage and what we further intended, or how it came to passe, it was knowne so much that the ffather Jesuits weare desirous to find out a way how they might gett downe the castors from the bay of the North, by the Sacques, and so make themselves masters of that trade. They resolved to make a tryall as soone as the ice would permitt them. So to discover our intentions they weare very earnest with me to ingage myselfe in that voyage, to the end that my brother would give over his, which I uterly denied them, knowing that they could never bring it about." They made an application to the Governor of Quebec for permission to start upon this their fourth voyage; but he refused, unless they agreed to certain hard conditions which they found it impossible to accept. In August they departed without the Governor's leave, secretly at midnight, on their journey, having made an agreement to join a company of the nation of the Sault who were about returning to their country, and who agreed to wait for them two days in the Lake of St. Peter, some six leagues from Three Rivers. Their journey was made to the country about Lake Superior, where they passed much of their time among the nations of the Sault, Fire, Christinos (Knisteneux), Beef, and other tribes.

Being at Lake Superior, Radisson says they came "to a remarkable place. It's a banke of Rocks that the wild men made a Sacrifice to,... it's like a great portall by reason of the beating of the waves. The lower part of that opening is as bigg as a tower, and grows bigger in the going up. There is, I believe, six acres of land above it; a shipp of 500 tuns could passe by, soe bigg is the arch. I gave it the name of the portail of St. Peter, because my name is so called, and that I was the first Christian that ever saw it." Concerning Hudson's Bay, whilst they were among the Christinos at Lake Assiniboin, Radisson mentions in his narrative that "being resolved to know what we heard before, we waited untill the Ice should vanish."

The Governor was greatly displeased at the disobedience of Radisson and his brother-in-law in going on their last voyage without his permission. On their return, the narrative states, "he made my brother prisoner for not having obeyed his orders; he fines us L. 4,000 to make a fort at the three rivers, telling us for all manner of satisfaction that he would give us leave to put our coat of armes upon it; and moreover L. 6,000 for the country, saying that wee should not take it so strangely and so bad, being wee were inhabitants and did intend to finish our days in the same country with our relations and friends.... Seeing ourselves so wronged, my brother did resolve to go and demand justice in France." Failing to get restitution, they resolved to go over to the English. They went early in 1665 to Port Royal, Nova Scotia, and from thence to New England, where they engaged an English or New England ship for a trading adventure into Hudson's Straits in 61 deg. north.

This expedition was attempted because Radisson and Des Groseilliers, on their last journey to Lake Superior, "met with some savages on the lake of Assiniboin, and from them they learned that they might go by land to the bottom of Hudson's Bay, where the English had not been yet, at James Bay; upon which they desired them to conduct them thither, and the savages accordingly did it. They returned to the upper lake the same way they came, and thence to Quebec, where they offered the principal merchants to carry ships to Hudson's Bay; but their project was rejected. Des Groseilliers then went to France in hopes of a more favorable hearing at Court; but after presenting several memorials and spending a great deal of time and money, he was answered as he had been at Quebec, and the project looked upon as chimerical." [Footnote: Oldmixon, Vol. I. p. 548.] This voyage to Hudson's Straits proved unremunerative. "Wee had knowledge and conversation with the people of those parts, but wee did see and know that there was nothing to be done unlesse wee went further, and the season of the year was far spent by the indiscretion of our Master." Radisson continues: "Wee were promised two shipps for a second voyage." One of these ships was sent to "the Isle of Sand, there to fish for Basse to make oyle of it," and was soon after lost.

In New England, in the early part of the year 1665, Radisson and Des Groseilliers met with two of the four English Commissioners who were sent over by Charles II in 1664 to settle several important questions in the provinces of New York and New England. They were engaged in the prosecution of their work in the different governments from 1664 to 1665/6. The two Frenchmen, it appears, were called upon in Boston to defend themselves in a lawsuit instituted against them in the courts there, for the annulling of the contract in the trading adventure above mentioned, whereby one of the two ships contracted for was lost. The writer states, that "the expectation of that ship made us loose our second voyage, which did very much discourage the merchants with whom wee had to do; they went to law with us to make us recant the bargaine that wee had made with them. After wee had disputed a long time, it was found that the right was on our side and wee innocent of what they did accuse us. So they endeavoured to come to an agreement, but wee were betrayed by our own party.

"In the mean time the Commissioners of the King of Great Britain arrived in that place, & one of them would have us goe with him to New York, and the other advised us to come to England and offer ourselves to the King, which wee did." The Commissioners were Colonel Richard Nicolls, Sir Robert Carr, Colonel George Cartwright, and Samuel Mavericke. Sir Robert Carr wished the two Frenchmen to go with him to New York, but Colonel George Cartwright, erroneously called by Radisson in his manuscript "Cartaret," prevailed upon them to embark with him from Nantucket, August 1, 1665. On this voyage Cartwright carried with him "all the original papers of the transactions of the Royal Commissioners, together with the maps of the several colonies." They had also as a fellow passenger George Carr, presumably the brother of Sir Robert, and probably the acting secretary to the Commission. Colonel Richard Nicolls, writing to Secretary Lord Arlington, July 31, 1665, Says, "He supposes Col. Geo. Cartwright is now at sea." George Carr, also writing to Lord Arlington, December 14, 1665, tells him that "he sends the transactions of the Commissioners in New England briefly set down, each colony by itself. The papers by which all this and much more might have been demonstrated were lost in obeying His Majesty's command by keeping company with Captain Pierce, who was laden with masts; for otherwise in probability we might have been in England ten days before we met the Dutch 'Caper,' who after two hours' fight stripped and landed us in Spain. Hearing also some Frenchmen discourse in New England of a passage from the West Sea to the South Sea, and of a great trade of beaver in that passage, and afterwards meeting with sufficient proof of the truth of what they had said, and knowing what great endeavours have been made for the finding out of a North Western passage, he thought them the best present he could possibly make His Majesty, and persuaded them to come to England. Begs His Lordship to procure some consideration for his loss, suffering, and service." Colonel Cartwright, upon his capture at Sea by the Dutch "Caper," threw all his despatches and papers overboard.

No doubt the captain of the Dutch vessel carefully scrutinized the papers of Radisson and his brother-in-law, and, it may be, carried off some of them; for there is evidence in one part at least of the former's narration of his travels, of some confusion, as the writer has transposed the date of one important and well-known event in Canadian history. It is evident that the writer was busy on his voyage preparing his narrative of travels for presentation to the King. Towards the conclusion of his manuscript he says: "We are now in the passage, and he that brought us, which was one of the Commissioners called Collonell George Cartaret, was taken by the Hollanders, and wee arrived in England in a very bad time for the plague and the warrs. Being at Oxford, wee went to Sir George Cartaret, who spoke to His Majesty, who gave good hopes that wee should have a shipp ready for the next Spring, and that the King did allow us forty shillings a week for our maintenance, and wee had chambers in the town by his order, where wee stayed three months. Afterwards the King came to London and sent us to Windsor, where wee stayed the rest of the winter."

Charles II., with his Court, came to open Parliament and the Courts of Law at Oxford, September 25, 1665, and left for Hampton Court to reside, January 27, 1666. Radisson and Des Groseilliers must have arrived there about the 25th of October. DeWitt, the Dutch statesman, and Grand Pensionary of the States of Holland from 1652, becoming informed by the captain of the Dutch "Caper" of the errand of Radisson and his companion into England, despatched an emissary to that country in 1666 to endeavor to entice them out of the English into the service of the Dutch. Sir John Colleton first brought the matter before the notice of

Lord Arlington in a letter of November 12th. The agent of DeWitt was one Elie Godefroy Touret, a native of Picardy, France, and an acquaintance of Groseilliers. Touret had lived over ten years in the service of the Rhinegrave at Maestricht. Thinking it might possibly aid him in his design, he endeavored to pass himself off in London as Groseilliers' nephew. One Monsieur Delheure deposed that Groseilliers "always held Touret in suspicion for calling himself his nephew, and for being in England without employment, not being a person who could live on his income, and had therefore avoided his company as dangerous to the State. Has heard Touret say that if his uncle Groseilliers were in service of the States of Holland, he would be more considered than here, where his merits are not recognised, and that if his discovery were under the protection of Holland, all would go better with him."

On the 21st of November a warrant was issued to the Keeper of the Gate House, London, "to take into custody the person of Touret for corresponding with the King's enemies." On the 23d of December Touret sent in a petition to Lord Arlington, bitterly complaining of the severity of his treatment, and endeavored to turn the tables upon his accuser by representing that Groseilliers, Radisson, and a certain priest in London tried to persuade him to join them in making counterfeit coin, and for his refusal had persecuted and entered the accusation against him.

To Des Groseilliers and Radisson must be given the credit of originating the idea of forming a settlement at Hudson's Bay, out of which grew the profitable organization of the Hudson's Bay Company. They obtained through the English Ambassador to France an interview with Prince Rupert, and laid before him their plans, which had been before presented to the leading merchants of Canada and the French Court. Prince Rupert at once foresaw the value of such an enterprise, and aided them in procuring the required assistance from several noblemen and gentlemen, to fit out in 1667 two ships from London, the "Eagle," Captain Stannard, and the "Nonsuch," ketch, Captain Zechariah Gillam. This Gillam is called by Oldmixon a New Englander, and was probably the same one who went in 1664/5 with Radisson and Groseilliers to Hudson's Strait on the unsuccessful voyage from Boston.

Radisson thus alludes to the two ships that were fitted out in London by the help of Prince Rupert and his associates. The third year after their arrival in England "wee went out with a new Company in two small vessels, my brother in one and I in another, and wee went together four hundred leagues from the North of Ireland, where a sudden greate storme did rise and put us asunder. The sea was soe furious six or seven hours after, that it did almost overturne our ship. So that wee were forced to cut our masts rather then cutt our lives; but wee came back safe, God be thanked; and the other, I hope, is gone on his voyage, God be with him."

Captain Gillam and the ketch "Nonsuch," with Des Groseilliers, proceeded on their voyage, "passed thro Hudson's Streights, and then into Baffin's Bay to 75 deg. North, and thence Southwards into 51 deg., where, in a river afterwards called Prince Rupert river, He had a friendly correspondence with the natives, built a Fort, named it Charles Fort, and returned with Success." [Footnote: Oldmixon, British Empire, ed. 1741, Vol. I. p. 544] When Gillam and Groseilliers returned, the adventurers concerned in fitting them out "applied themselves to Charles II. for a patent, who granted one to them and their successors for the Bay called Hudson's Streights." [Footnote: Ibid., Vol. I. p. 545.] The patent bears date the 2d of May, in the twenty-second year of Charles II., 1670.

In Ellis's manuscript papers [Footnote: Ibid., Vol. V. p.319] has been found the following original draft of an "answer of the Hudson's Bay Company to a French paper entitled Memoriall justifieing the pretensions of France to Fort Bourbon." 1696/7.

"The French in this paper carrying their pretended right of Discovery and settlement no higher then the year 1682, and their being dispossessed in 1684. Wee shall briefly shew what sort of possession that was, and how those two actions were managed. Mr. Radisson, mentioned in the said paper to have made this settlement for the French at Port Nelson in 1682, was many years before settled in England, and marryed an English wife, Sir John Kirke's daughter, and engaged in the interest and service of the English upon private adventure before as well as after the Incorporation of the Hudson's Bay Company. In 1667, when Prince Rupert and other noblemen set out two shipps, Radisson went in the Eagle, Captain Stannard commander, and in that voyage the name of Rupert's river was given. Again in 1668 and in 1669, and in this voyage directed his course to Port Nelson, and went on shore with one Bayly (designed Governor for the English), fixed the King of England's arms there, & left some goods for trading. In 1671 three ships were set out from London by the Hudson's Bay Company, then incorporated, and Radisson went in one of them in their service, settled Moose River, & went to Port Nelson, where he left some goods, and wintered at Rupert's River. In 1673, upon some difference with the Hudson's Bay Company, Radisson returned into France and was there persuaded to go to Canada. He formed severall designs of going on private accounts for the French into Hudson's Bay, which the Governor, Monsr. Frontenac, would by no means permitt, declaring it would break the union between the two Kings."

Oldmixon says [Footnote: Oldmixon, Vol. I. p. 549.] that the above-mentioned Charles Baily, with whom went Radisson and ten or twenty men, took out with him Mr. Thomas Gorst as his secretary, who at his request kept a journal, which eventually passed into the possession of Oldmixon. The following extracts give some idea of the life led by the fur-traders at the Fort: "They were apprehensive of being attacked by some Indians, whom the French Jesuits had animated against the English and all that dealt with them. The French used many artifices to hinder the natives trading with the English; they gave them great rates for their goods, and obliged Mr Baily to lower the price of his to oblige the Indians who dwelt about Moose river, with whom they drove the greatest trade. The French, to ruin their commerce with the natives, came and made a settlement not above eight days' journey up that river from the place where the English traded. 'Twas therefore debated whether the Company's Agents should not remove from Rupert's to Moose river, to prevent their traffick being interrupted by the French. On the 3d of April, 1674, a council of the principal persons in the Fort was held, where Mr Baily, the Governor, Captain Groseilliers, and Captain Cole were present and gave their several opinions. The Governor inclined to move. Captain Cole was against it, as dangerous, and Captain Groseilliers for going thither in their bark to trade. [Footnote: Oldmixon, Vol. I. p. 552.] ... The Governor, having got everything ready for a voyage to Moose river, sent Captain Groseilliers, Captain Cole, Mr Gorst, and other Indians to trade there. They got two hundred and fifty skins, and the Captain of the Tabittee Indians informed them the French Jesuits had bribed the Indians not to deal with the English, but to live in friendship with the Indian nations in league with the

French.... The reason they got no more peltry now was because the Indians thought Groseilliers was too hard for them, and few would come down to deal with him." [Footnote: Oldmixon, Vol. I. p. 554.] After Captain Baily [Footnote: Ibid., Vol. I. p. 555.] had returned from a voyage in his sloop to trade to the fort, "on the 30th Aug a missionary Jesuit, born of English parents, arrived, bearing a letter from the Governor of Quebec to Mr Baily, dated the 8th of October, 1673.

"The Governor of Quebec desired Mr Baily to treat the Jesuit civilly, on account of the great amity between the two crowns. Mr Baily resolved to keep the priest till ships came from England. He brought a letter, also, for Capt Groseilliers, which gave jealousy to the English of his corresponding with the French. His son-in-law lived in Quebec, and had accompanied the priest part of the way, with three other Frenchmen, who, being afraid to venture among strange Indians, returned.... Provisions running short, they were agreed, on the 17th Sept, they were all to depart for Point Comfort, to stay there till the 22d, and then make the best of their way for England. In this deplorable condition were they when the Jesuit, Capt Groseilliers, & another papist, walking downwards to the seaside at their devotions, heard seven great guns fire distinctly. They came home in a transport of joy, told their companions the news, and assured them it was true. Upon which they fired three great guns from the fort to return the salute, though they could ill spare the powder upon such an uncertainty." The ship "Prince Rupert" had arrived, with Captain Gillam, bringing the new Governor, William Lyddel, Esq.

Groseilliers and Radisson, after remaining for several years under the Hudson's Bay Company, at last in 1674 felt obliged to sever the connection, and went over again to France. Radisson told his nephew in 1684 that the cause was "the refusal, that showed the bad intention of the Hudson's Bay Company to satisfy us." Several influential members of the committee of direction for the Company were desirous of retaining them in their employ; among them the Duke of York, Prince Rupert their first Governor, Sir James Hayes, Sir William Young, Sir John Kirke, and others; but it is evident there was a hostile feeling towards Radisson and his brother-in-law on the part of several members of the committee, for even after his successful expedition in 1684 they found "some members of the committee offended because I had had the honour of making my reverence to the King and to his Royal Highness."

From 1674 to 1683, Radisson seems to have remained stanch in his allegiance to Louis XIV. In his narrative of the years 1682 and 1683 he shews that Colbert endeavored to induce him to bring his wife over into France, it would appear to remain there during his absence in Hudson's Bay, as some sort of security for her husband's fidelity to the interests of the French monarch. After his return from this voyage in 1683 he felt himself again unfairly treated by the French Court, and in 1684, as he relates in his narrative, he "passed over to England for good, and of engaging myself so strongly to the service of his Majesty, and to the interests of the Nation, that any other consideration was never able to detach me from it."

We again hear of Radisson in Hudson's Bay in 1685; and this is his last appearance in public records or documents as far as is known. A Canadian, Captain Berger, states that in the beginning of June, 1685, "he and his crew ascended four leagues above the English in Hudson's Bay, where they made a Small Settlement. On the 15th of July they set out to return to Quebec. On the 17th they met with a vessel of ten or twelve guns, commanded by Captain Oslar, on board of which was the man named Bridgar, the Governor, who was going to relieve the Governor at the head of the Bay. He is the same that Radisson brought to Quebec three years ago in the ship Monsieur de la Barre restored to him. Berger also says he asked a parley with the captain of Mr Bridgar's bark, who told him that Radisson had gone with Mr Chouart, his nephew, fifteen days ago, to winter in the River Santa Theresa, where they wintered a year." [Footnote: New York Colonial Documents, Vol. IX.]

After this date the English and the French frequently came into hostile collision in Hudson's Bay. In 1686 King James demanded satisfaction from France for losses inflicted upon the Company. Then the Jesuits procured neutrality for America, and knew by that time they were in possession of Fort Albany. In 1687 the French took the "Hayes" sloop, an infraction of the treaty. In 1688 they took three ships, valued, in all, at L. 15,000; L. 113,000 damage in time of peace. In 1692 the Company set out four ships to recover Fort Albany, taken in 1686. In 1694 the French took York, alias Fort Bourbon. In 1696 the English retook it from them. On the 4th September, 1697, the French retook it and kept it. The peace was made September 20, 1697. [Footnote: Minutes Relating to Hudson's Bay Company.] In 1680 the stock rose from L. 100 to near L. 1,000. Notwithstanding the losses sustained by the Company, amounting to L. 118,014 between 1682 and 1688, they were able to pay in 1684 the shareholders a dividend of fifty per cent. Radisson brought home in 1684 a cargo of 20,000 beaver skins. Oldmixon says, "10,000 Beavers, in all their factories, was one of the best years of Trade they ever had, besides other peltry." Again in 1688 a dividend of fifty per cent was made, and in 1689 one of twenty-five per cent. In 1690, without any call being made, the stock was trebled, while at the same time a dividend of twenty-five per cent was paid on the increased or newly created stock.

At the Peace of Utrecht, in 1713, the forts captured by the French in 1697 were restored to the Company, who by 1720 had again trebled their capital, with a call of only ten per cent. After a long and fierce rivalry with the Northwest Fur Company, the two companies were amalgamated in 1821. [Footnote: Encyclopaedia Britannica.]

Radisson commences his narrative of 1652 in a reverent spirit, by inscribing it "a la plus grande gloire de Dieu." All his manuscripts have been handed down in perfect preservation. They are written out in a clear and excellent handwriting, showing the writer to have been a person of good education, who had also travelled in Turkey and Italy, and who had been in London, and perhaps learned his English there in his early life. The narrative of travels between the years 1652 and 1664 was for some time the property of Samuel Pepys, the well-known diarist, and Secretary of the Admiralty to Charles II. and James II. He probably received it from Sir George Cartaret, the Vice-Chamberlain of the King and Treasurer of the Navy, for whom it was no doubt carefully copied out from his rough notes by the author, So that it might, through him, be brought under the notice of Charles II. Some years after the death of Pepys, in 1703, his collection of manuscripts was dispersed and fell into the hands of various London tradesmen, who bought parcels of it to use in their shops as waste-paper. The most valuable portions were carefully reclaimed by the celebrated collector, Richard Rawlinson, who in writing to his friend T. Rawlins, from. "London house, January 25th, 1749/50," says: "I have purchased the best part of the fine collection of Mr Pepys, Secretary to the Admiralty during the reigns of Charles 2d and James 2d. Some are as old as King Henry VIII. They were collected with a design for a Lord High Admiral such as he should approve; but those times are not yet come, and so little care was taken of them that they were redeemed from thus et adores vendentibus."

The manuscript containing Radisson's narrative for the years 1682 and 1683 was "purchased of Rodd, 8th July, 1839," by the British Museum. The narrative in French, for the year 1684, was bought by Sir Hans Sloane from the collection of "Nicolai Joseph Foucault, Comitis Consistoriani," as his bookplate informs us. With the manuscript this gentleman had bound up in the same volume a religious treatise in manuscript, highly illuminated, in Italian, relating to some of the saints of the Catholic Church. [Footnote: I am under obligations to Mr. John Gilmary Shea for valuable information.]

FIRST VOYAGE OF PETER ESPRIT RADISSON

The Relation of my Voyage, being in Bondage in the Lands of the Irokoits, which was the next yeare after my coming into Canada, in the yeare 1651, the 24th day of May.

Being persuaded in the morning by two of my comrades to go and recreat ourselves in fowling, I disposed myselfe to keepe them Company; wherfor I cloathed myselfe the lightest way I could possible, that I might be the nimbler and not stay behinde, as much for the prey that I hoped for, as for to escape the danger into which wee have ventered ourselves of an enemy the cruelest that ever was uppon the face of the Earth. It is to bee observed that the french had warre with a wild nation called Iroquoites, who for that time weare soe strong and so to be feared that scarce any body durst stirre out either Cottage or house without being taken or kill'd, [Footnote: In 1641-1645 Father Vimont writes: "I had as lief be beset by goblins as by the Iroquois. The one are about as invisible as the other. Our people on the Richelieu and at Montreal are kept in a closer confinement than ever were monks or nuns in our smallest convents in France."] saving that he had nimble limbs to escape their fury; being departed, all three well armed, and unanimiously rather die then abandon one another, notwithstanding these resolutions weare but young mens deboasting; being then in a very litle assurance and lesse security.

At an offspring of a village of three Rivers we consult together that two should go the watter side, the other in a wood hardby to warne us, for to advertise us if he accidentaly should light [upon] or suspect any Barbars in ambush, we also retreat ourselves to him if we should discover any thing uppon the River. Having comed to the first river, which was a mile distant from our dwellings, wee mett a man who mett a man who kept cattell, and asked him if he had knowne any appearance of Ennemy, and likewise demanded which way he would advise us to gett better fortune, and what part he spied more danger; he guiding us the best way he could, prohibiting us by no means not to render ourselves att the skirts of the mountains; ffor, said he, I discovered oftentimes a multitude of people which rose up as it weare of a sudaine from of the Earth, and that doubtless there weare some enemys that way; which sayings made us looke to ourselves and charge two of our fowling peeces with great shot the one, and the other with small. Priming our pistols, we went where our fancy first lead us, being impossible for us to avoid the destinies of the heavens; no sooner tourned our backs, but my nose fell ableeding without any provocation in the least. Certainly it was a warning for me of a beginning of a yeare and a half of hazards and of miseryes that weare to befall mee. We did shoot sometime and killed some Duks, which made one of my fellow travellers go no further. I seeing him taking such a resolution, I proffered some words that did not like him, giving him the character of a timourous, childish humor; so this did nothing prevaile with him, to the Contrary that had with him quite another isue then what I hoped for; ffor offending him with my words he prevailed so much with the others that he persuaded them to doe the same. I lett them goe, laughing them to scorne, beseeching them to help me to my fowles, and that I would tell them the discovery of my designes, hoping to kill meat to make us meate att my retourne.

I went my way along the wood some times by the side of the river, where I finde something to shute att, though no considerable quantitie, which made me goe a league off and more, so I could not go in all further then St. Peeter's, which is nine mile from the plantation by reason of the river Ovamasis, which hindered me the pasage. I begun'd to think att my retourne how I might transport my fowle. I hide one part in a hollow tree to keep them from the Eagles and other devouring fowles, so as I came backe the same way where before had no bad incounter. Arrived within one halfe a mile where my comrades had left me, I rested awhile by reason that I was looden'd with three geese, tenn ducks, and one crane, with some teales.

After having layd downe my burden uppon the grasse, I thought to have heard a noise in the wood by me, which made me to overlook my armes; I found one of my girdle pistols wette. I shott it off and charged it againe, went up to the wood the soffliest I might, to discover and defend myselfe the better against any surprise. After I had gone from tree to tree some 30 paces off I espied nothing; as I came back from out of the wood to an adjacent brooke, I perceived a great number of Ducks; my discovery imbouldened me, and for that there was a litle way to the fort, I determined to shute once more; coming nigh preparing meselfe for to shute, I found another worke, the two young men that I left some tenne houres before heere weare killed. Whether they came after mee, or weare brought thither by the Barbars, I know not. However [they] weare murthered. Looking over them, knew them albeit quite naked, and their hair standing up, the one being shott through with three boulletts and two blowes of an hatchett on the head, and the other runne thorough in severall places with a sword and smitten with an hatchett. Att the same instance my nose begun'd to bleed, which made me afraid of my life; but withdrawing myselfe to the watter side to see if any body followed mee, I espied twenty or thirty heads in a long grasse. Mightily surprized att the view, I must needs passe through the midst of them or tourne backe into the woode. I slipped a boullet uppon the shott and beate the paper into my gunne. I heard a noise, which made me looke on that side; hopeing to save meselfe, perswading myselfe I was not yet perceived by them that weare in the medow, and in the meane while some gunns weare lett off with an horrid cry.

Seeing myselfe compassed round about by a multitude of dogges, or rather devils, that rose from the grasse, rushesse, and bushesse, I shott my gunne, whether un warrs or purposly I know not, but I shott with a pistolle confidently, but was seised on all sids by a great number that threw me downe, taking away my arme without giving mee one blowe; ffor afterwards I felt no paine att all, onely a great guidinesse in my heade, from whence it comes I doe not remember. In the same time they brought me into the wood, where they shewed me the two heads all bloody. After they consulted together for a while, retired into their boats, which weare four or five miles from thence, and wher I have bin a while before. They layed mee hither, houlding me by the hayre, to the imbarking place; there they began to errect their cottages, which consisted only of some sticks to boyle their meate, whereof they had plenty, but stuncke, which was strange to mee to finde such an alteration so sudaine. They made [me] sitt downe by. After this they searched me and tooke what I had, then stripped me naked, and tyed a rope about my middle, wherin I remained, fearing to persist, in the same posture the rest of the night. After this they removed me, laughing and howling like as many wolves, I knowing not the reason, if not for my skin, that was soe whit in respect of theirs. But their gaping did soone cease because of a false alarme, that their Scout who stayed behind gave them, saying that the ffrench and the wild Algongins, friends to the ffrench, came with all speed. They presently put out the fire, and tooke hould of the most advantageous passages, and sent 25 men to discover what it meant, who brought certaine tydings of assurance and liberty.

In the meanewhile I was garded by 50 men, who gave me a good part of my cloathes. After kindling a fire againe, they gott theire supper ready, which was sudenly don, ffor they dresse their meat halfe boyled, mingling some yallowish meale in the broath of that infected stinking meate; so whilst this was adoing they combed my head, and with a filthy grease greased my head, and dashed all over my face with redd paintings. So then, when the meat was ready, they feeded me with their hod-pot, forcing me to swallow it in a maner. My heart did so faint at this, that in good deede I should have given freely up the ghost to be freed from their clawes, thinking every moment they would end my life. They perceived that my stomach could not beare such victuals. They tooke some of this stinking meate and boyled it in a cleare watter, then mingled a litle Indian meale put to it, which meale before was tossed amongst bourning sand, and then made in powder betwixt two rocks. I, to shew myselfe cheerfull att this, swallowed downe some of this that seemed to me very unsavoury and clammie by reason of the scume that was upon the meat. Having supped, they untyed mee, and made me lye betwixt them, having one end of one side and one of another, and covered me with a red Coverlet, thorough which I might have counted the starrs. I slept a sound sleep, for they awaked me upon the breaking of the day. I dreamed that night that I was with the Jesuits at Quebuc drinking beere, which gave me hopes to be free sometimes, and also because I heard those people lived among Dutch people in a place called Menada [Footnote: Menada, Manhattan, or New Netherlands, called by the French of Canada "Manatte."], and fort of Orang, where without doubt I could drinke beere. I, after this, finding meselfe somewhat altered, and my body more like a devil then anything else, after being so smeared and burst with their filthy meate that I could not digest, but must suffer all patiently.

Finally they seemed to me kinder and kinder, giving me of the best bitts where lesse wormes weare. Then they layd [me] to the watter side, where there weare 7 and 30 boats, ffor each of them imbark'd himselfe. They tyed me to the barre in a boat, where they tooke at the same instance the heads of those that weare killed the day before, and for to preserve them they cutt off the flesh to the skull and left nothing but skin and haire, putting of it into a litle panne wherein they melt some grease, and gott it dry with hot stones. They spread themselves from off the side of the river a good way, and gathered together againe and made a fearfull noise and shott some gunns off, after which followed a kind of an incondit singing after nots, which was an oudiousom noise. As they weare departing from thence they injoyned silence, and one of the Company, wherein I was, made three shouts, which was answered by the like maner from the whole flocke; which done they tooke their way, singing and leaping, and so past the day in such like. They offered mee meate; but such victuals I reguarded it litle, but could drinke for thirst. My sperit was troubled with infinite deale of thoughts, but all to no purpose for the ease of my sicknesse; sometimes despairing, now againe in some hopes. I allwayes indeavoured to comfort myselfe, though half dead. My resolution was so mastered with feare, that at every stroake of the oares of these inhumans I thought it to be my end.

By sunsett we arrived att the Isles of Richelieu, a place rather for victors then for captives most pleasant. There is to be seen 300 wild Cowes together, a number of Elks and Beavers, an infinit of fowls. There we must make cottages, and for this purpose they imploy all together their wits and art, ffor 15 of these Islands are drowned in Spring, when the floods begin to rise from the melting of the snow, and that by reason of the lowness of the land. Here they found a place fitt enough for 250 men that their army consisted [of]. They landed mee & shewed mee great kindnesse, saying Chagon, which is as much [as] to say, as I understood afterwards, be cheerfull or merry; but for my part I was both deafe and dumb. Their behaviour made me neverthelesse cheerfull, or att least of a smiling countenance, and constraine my aversion and feare to an assurance, which proved not ill to my thinking; ffor the young men tooke delight in combing my head, greasing and powdering out a kinde of redd powder, then tying my haire with a redd string of leather like to a coard, which caused my haire to grow longer in a short time.

The day following they prepared themselves to passe the adjacent places and shoote to gett victualls, where we stayed 3 dayes, making great cheere and fires. I more and more getting familiarity with them, that I had the liberty to goe from cottage, having one or two by mee. They untyed mee, and tooke delight to make me speake words of their language, and weare earnest that I should pronounce as they. They tooke care to give me meate as often as I would; they gave me salt that served me all my voyage. They also tooke the paines to put it up safe for mee, not taking any of it for themselves. There was nothing else but feasting and singing during our abode. I tooke notice that our men decreased, ffor every night one other boate tooke his way, which persuaded mee that they went to the warrs to gett more booty.

The fourth day, early in the morning, my Brother, viz., he that tooke me, so he called me, embarked me without tying me. He gave me an oare, which I tooke with a good will, and rowed till I sweate againe. They, perceaving, made me give over; not content with that I made a signe of my willingnesse to continue that worke. They consent to my desire, but shewed me how I should row without putting myselfe into a sweat. Our company being considerable hitherto, was now reduced to three score. Mid-day wee came to the River of Richlieu, where we weare not farre gon, but mett a new gang of their people in cottages; they began to hoop and hollow as the first day of my taking. They made me stand upright in the boat, as they themselves, saluting one another with all kindnesse and joy. In this new company there was one that had a minde to doe me mischiefe, but prevented by him that tooke me. I taking notice of the fellow, I shewed him more friendshipe. I gott some meate roasted for him, and throwing a litle salt and flower over it, which he finding very good tast, gave it to the rest as a rarity, nor did afterwards molest mee.

They tooke a fancy to teach mee to sing; and as I had allready a beginning of their hooping, it was an easy thing for me to learne, our Algonquins making the same noise. They tooke an exceeding delight to heare mee. Often have I sunged in French, to which they gave eares with a deepe silence. We passed that day and night following with litle rest by reason of their joy and mirth. They lead a dance, and tyed my comrades both their heads att the end of a stick and hopt it; this done, every one packt and embarked himselfe, some going one way, some another. Being separated, one of the boats that we mett before comes backe againe and approaches the boat wherein I was; I wondered, a woman of the said company taking hould on my haire, signifying great kindnesse. Shee combs my head with her fingers and tyed my wrist with a bracelett, and sunged. My wish was that shee would proceed in our way. After both companys made a shout wee separated, I was sorry for this woman's departure, ffor having shewed me such favour att her first aspect, doubtlesse but shee might, if neede required, saved my life.

Our journey was indifferent good, without any delay, which caused us to arrive in a good and pleasant harbour. It was on the side of the sand where our people had any paine scarce to errect their cottages, being that it was a place they had sejourned [at] before. The place round about [was] full of trees. Heare they kindled a fire and provided what was necessary for their food. In this place they cutt off my hair in the front and upon the crowne of the head, and turning up the locks of the haire they dab'd mee with some thicke grease. So done, they brought me a looking-glasse. I viewing myselfe all in a pickle, smir'd with redde and black, covered with such a cappe, and locks tyed up with a peece of leather and stunked horridly, I could not but fall in love with myselfe, if not that I had better instructions to shun the sin of pride. So after repasting themselves, they made them ready for the journey with takeing repose that night. This was the time I thought to have escaped, ffor in vaine, ffor I being alone feared least I should be apprehended and dealt with more violently. And moreover I was desirous to have seene their country.

Att the sun rising I awaked my brother, telling him by signes it was time to goe. He called the rest, but non would stirre, which made him lye downe againe. I rose and went to the water side, where I walked awhile. If there weare another we might, I dare say, escape out of their sight. Heere I recreated myselfe running a naked swoord into the sand. One of them seeing mee after such an exercise calls mee and shews me his way, which made me more confidence in them. They brought mee a dish full of meate to the water side. I began to eat like a beare.

In the mean time they imbark'd themselves, one of them tooke notice that I had not a knife, brings me his, which I kept the rest of the voyage, without that they had the least feare of me. Being ready to goe, saving my boat that was ammending, which was soone done. The other boats weare not as yett out of sight, and in the way my boat killed a stagg. They made me shoot att it, and not quite dead they runed it thorough with their swoords, and having cutt it in peeces, they devided it, and proceeded on their way. At 3 of the clock in the afternoone we came into a rappid streame, where we weare forced to land and carry our Equipages and boats thorough a dangerous place. Wee had not any encounter that day. Att night where we found cottages ready made, there I cutt wood as the rest with all dilligence. The morning early following we marched without making great noise, or singing as accustomed. Sejourning awhile, we came to a lake 6 leagues wide, about it a very pleasant country imbellished with great forests. That day our wild people killed 2 Bears, one monstrous like for its biggnesse, the other a small one. Wee arrived to a fine sandy bancke, where not long before many Cabbanes weare errected and places made where Prisoners weare tyed.

In this place our wild people sweated after the maner following: first heated stones till they weare redd as fire, then they made a lantherne with small sticks, then stoaring the place with deale trees, saving a place in the middle whereinto they put the stoanes, and covered the place with severall covers, then striped themselves naked, went into it. They made a noise as if the devil weare there; after they being there for an hour they came out of the watter, and then throwing one another into the watter, I thought veryly they weare insensed. It is their usual Custome. Being comed out of this place, they feasted themselves with the two bears, turning the outside of the tripes inward not washed. They gave every one his share; as for my part I found them [neither] good, nor savory to the pallet. In the night they heard some shooting, which made them embark themselves speedily. In the mean while they made me lay downe whilst they rowed very hard. I slept securely till the morning, where I found meselfe in great high rushes. There they stayed without noise.

From thence wee proceeded, though not without some feare of an Algonquin army. We went on for some dayes that lake. Att last they endeavoured to retire to the woods, every one carrying his bundle. After a daye's march we came to a litle river where we lay'd that night. The day following we proceeded on our journey, where we mett 2 men, with whome our wild men seemed to be acquainted by some signes. These 2 men began to speake a longe while. After came a company of women, 20 in number, that brought us dry fish and Indian corne. These women loaded themselves, after that we had eaten, like mules with our baggage. We went through a small wood, the way well beaten, untill the evening we touched a place for fishing, of 15 Cabbans. There they weare well received but myselfe, who was stroaken by a yong man. He, my keeper, made a signe I should to him againe. I tourning to him instantly, he to me, taking hould of my haire, all the wild men came about us, encouraging with their Cryes and hands, which encouraged me most that non helpt him more then mee. Wee clawed one another with hands, tooth, and nailes. My adversary being offended I have gotten the best, he kick't me; but my french shoes that they left mee weare harder then his, which made him [give up] that game againe. He tooke me about the wrest, where he found himselfe downe before he was awarre, houlding him upon the ground till some came and putt us asunder. My company seeing mee free, began to cry out, giving me watter to wash me, and then fresh fish to relish me. They encouraged me so much, the one combing my head, the other greasing my haire. There we stayed 2 dayes, where no body durst trouble me.

In the same Cabban that I was, there has bin a wild man wounded with a small shott. I thought I have seen him the day of my taking, which made me feare least I was the one that wounded him. He knowing it to be so had shewed me as much charity as a Christian might have given. Another of his fellowes (I also wounded) came to me att my first coming there, whom I thought to have come for reveng, contrarywise shewed me a cheerfull countenance; he gave mee a box full of red paintings, calling me his brother. I had not as yett caryed any burden, but meeting with an ould man, gave me a sacke of tobacco of 12 pounds' weight, bearing it uppon my head, as it's their usuall custome. We made severall stayes the day by reason of the severall encounters of their people that came from villages, as warrs others from fishing and shooting. In that journey our company increased, among others a great many Hurrons that had bin lately taken, and who for the most part are as slaves. We lay'd in the wood because they would not goe into their village in the night time.

The next day we marched into a village where as wee came in sight we heard nothing but outcryes, as from one side as from the other, being a quarter of a mile from the village. They satt downe and I in the midle, where I saw women and men and children with staves and in array, which put me in feare, and instantly stripped me naked. My keeper gave me a signe to be gone as fast as I could drive. In the meane while many of the village came about us, among which a good old woman, and a boy with a hatchet in his hand came near mee. The old woman covered me, and the young man tooke me by the hand and lead me out of the company. The old woman made me step aside from those that weare ready to stricke att mee. There I left the 2 heads of my comrades, and that with comforted me yet I escaped the blowes. Then they brought me into their Cottage; there the old woman shewed me kindnesse. Shee gave me to eate. The great terror I had a litle before tooke my stomack away from me. I stayed an hower, where a great company of people came to see mee. Heere came a company of old men, having pipes in their mouthes, satt about me.

After smoaking, they lead me into another cabban, where there weare a company all Smoaking; they made [me] sitt downe by the fire, which made [me] apprehend they should cast me into the said fire. But it proved otherwise; for the old woman followed mee, Speaking aloud, whom they answered with a loud ho, then shee tooke her girdle and about mee shee tyed it, so brought me to her cottage, and made me sitt downe in the same place I was before. Then shee began to dance and sing a while, after [she] brings downe from her box a combe, gives it to a maide that was neare mee, who presently comes to greas and combe my haire, and tooke away the paint that the fellows stuck to my face. Now the old woman getts me some Indian Corne toasted in the fire. I tooke paines to gether it out of the fire; after this shee gave me a blew coverlett, stokins and shoos, and where with to make me drawers. She looked in my cloathes, and if shee found any lice shee would squeeze them betwixt her teeth, as if they had ben substantiall meate. I lay'd with her son, who tooke me from those of my first takers, and gott at last a great acquaintance with many. I did what I could to gett familiarity with them, yeat I suffered no wrong att their hands, taking all freedom, which the old woman inticed me to doe. But still they altered my face where ever I went, and a new dish to satisfy nature.

I tooke all the pleasures imaginable, having a small peece at my command, shooting patriges and squerells, playing most part of the day with my companions. The old woman wished that I would make meselfe more familiar with her 2 daughters, which weare tolerable among such people. They weare accustomed to grease and combe my haire in the morning. I went with them into the wilderness, there they would be gabling which I could not understand. They wanted no company but I was shure to be of the number. I brought all ways some guifts that I received, which I gave to my purse-keeper and refuge, the good old woman. I lived 5 weeks without thinking from whence I came. I learned more of their maners in 6 weeks then if I had bin in ffrance 6 months. Att the end I was troubled in minde, which made her inquire if I was Anjonack, a Huron word. Att this I made as if I weare subported for speaking in a strang language, which shee liked well, calling me by the name of her son who before was killed, Orinha, [Footnote: Called Orimha, over-leaf.] which signifies ledd or stone, without difference of the words. So that it was my Lordshippe. Shee inquired [of] mee whether I was Asserony, a french. I answering no, saying I was Panugaga, that is, of their nation, for which shee was pleased.

My father feasted 300 men that day. My sisters made me clean for that purpos, and greased my haire. My mother decked me with a new cover and a redd and blew cappe, with 2 necklace of porcelaine. My sisters tyed me with braceletts and garters of the same porcelaine. My brother painted my face, and [put] feathers on my head, and tyed both my locks with porcelaine. My father was liberall to me, giving me a garland instead of my blew cap and a necklace of porcelaine that hung downe to my heels, and a hattchet in my hand. It was hard for me to defend myselfe against any encounter, being so laden with riches. Then my father made a speech shewing many demonstrations of vallor, broak a kettle full of Cagamite [Footnote: Cagamite, Cagaimtie, Sagamite, a mush made of pounded Indian corn boiled with bits of meat or fish.] with a hattchett So they sung, as is their usual coustom. They weare waited on by a sort of yong men, bringing downe dishes of meate of Oriniacke, [Footnote: Oriniacke, Auriniacks, horiniac, the moose, the largest species of deer. Called by the French writers— Sagard-Theodat, La Hontan, and Charlevoix— Eslan, Orinal, or Orignal.] of Castors, and of red deer mingled with some flowers. The order of makeing was thus: the corne being dried between 2 stones into powder, being very thick, putt it into a kettle full of watter, then a quantity of Bear's grease. This banquett being over, they cryed to me Shagon, Orimha, that is, be hearty, stone or ledd. Every one withdrew into his quarters, and so did I.

But to the purpose of my history. As I went to the fields once, where I mett with 3 of my acquaintance, who had a designe for to hunt a great way off, they desired me to goe along. I lett them know in Huron language (for that I knew better then that of the Iroquoits) I was content, desiring them to stay till I acquainted my mother. One of them came along with mee, and gott leave for me of my kindred. My mother gott me presently a sack of meale, 3 paire of shoos, my gun, and tourned backe where the 2 stayed for us. My 2 sisters accompanied me even out of the wildernesse and carried my bundle, where they tooke leave.

We marched on that day through the woods till we came by a lake where we travelled without any rest. I wished I had stayed att home, for we had sad victualls. The next day about noone we came to a River; there we made a skiffe, so litle that we could scarce go into it. I admired their skill in doing of it, ffor in lesse then 2 hours they cutt the tree and pulled up the Rind, of which they made the boat. We embarked ourselves and went to the lower end of the river, which emptied it selfe into a litle lake of about 2 miles in length and a mile in breadth. We passed this lake into another river broader then the other; there we found a fresh track of a stagge, which made us stay heere a while. It was five of the clock att least when 2 of our men made themselves ready to looke after that beast; the other and I stayed behind. Not long after we saw the stagge crosse the river, which foarding brought him to his ending. So done, they went on their cours, and came backe againe att 10 of the clocke with 3 bears, a castor, and the stagge which was slaine att our sight. How did wee rejoice to see that killed which would make the kettle boyle. After we have eaten, wee slept.

The next day we made trappes for to trapp castors, whilst we weare bussie, one about one thing, one about another. As 3 of us retourned homewards to our cottage we heard a wild man singing. He made us looke to our selves least he should prove an ennemy, but as we have seene him, called to him, who came immediately, telling us that he was in pursuite of a Beare since morning, and that he gave him over, having lost his 2 doggs by the same beare. He came with us to our Cottage, where we mett our companion after having killed one beare, 2 staggs, and 2 mountain catts, being 5 in number. Whilst the meat was a boyling that wild man spoake to me the Algonquin language. I wondred to heare this stranger; he tould me that he was taken 2 years agoe; he asked me concerning the 3 rivers and of Quebuck, who wished himselfe there, and I said the same, though I did not intend it. He asked me if I loved the french. I inquired [of] him also if he loved the Algonquins? Mary, quoth he, and so doe I my owne nation. Then replyed he, Brother, cheare up, lett us escape, the 3 rivers are not a farre off. I tould him my 3 comrades would not permitt me, and that they promised my mother to bring me back againe. Then he inquired whether I would live like the Hurrons, who weare in bondage, or have my owne liberty with the ffrench, where there was good bread to be eaten. Feare not, quoth he, shall kill them all 3 this night when they will bee a sleepe, which will be an easy matter with their owne hatchetts.

Att last I consented, considering they weare mortall ennemys to my country, that had cutt the throats of so many of my relations, burned and murdered them. I promissed him to succour him in his designe. They not understanding our language asked the Algonquin what is that that he said, but tould them some other story, nor did they suspect us in the least. Their belly full, their mind without care, wearyed to the utmost of the formost day's journey, fell a sleepe securely, leaning their armes up and downe without the least danger. Then my wild man pushed me, thinking I was a sleepe. He rises and sitts him downe by the fire, behoulding them one after an other, and taking their armes a side, and having the hattchetts in his hand gives me one; to tell the truth I was loathsome to do them mischif that never did me any. Yett for the above said reasons I tooke the hattchet and began the Execution, which was soone done. My fellow comes to him that was nearest to the fire (I dare say he never saw the stroake), and I have done that like to an other, but I hitting him with the edge of the hattchett could not disingage [it] presently, being so deep in his head, rises upon his breast, butt fell back sudainly, making a great noise, which almost waked the third; but my comrade gave him a deadly blow of a hattchet, and presently after I shott him dead.

Then we prepared our selves with all speed, throwing their dead corps, after that the wild man took off their heads, into the watter. We tooke 3 guns, leaving the 4th, their 2 swoords, their hattchetts, their powder and shott, and all their porselaine; we tooke also some meale and meate. I was sorry for to have ben in such an incounter, but too late to repent. Wee tooke our journey that night alongst the river. The break of day we landed on the side of a rock which was smooth. We carryed our boat and equippage into the wood above a hundred paces from the watter side, where we stayed most sadly all that day tormented by the Maringoines; [Footnote: Musquetos.] we tourned our boat upside downe, we putt us under it from the raine. The night coming, which was the fitest time to leave that place, we goe without any noise for our safty. Wee travelled 14 nights in that maner in great feare, hearing boats passing by. When we have perceaved any fire, left off rowing, and went by with as litle noise as could [be] possible. Att last with many tournings by lande and by watter, wee came to the lake of St. Peeter's.

We landed about 4 of the clock, leaving our skiff in among rushes farr out of the way from those that passed that way and doe us injury. We retired into the wood, where we made a fire some 200 paces from the river. There we roasted some meat and boyled meale; after, we rested ourselves a while from the many labours of the former night. So, having slept, my companion awaks first, and stirrs me, saying it was high time that we might by day come to our dweling, of which councel I did not approve. [I] tould him the Ennemys commonly weare lurking about the river side, and we should doe very well [to] stay in that place till sunnsett. Then, said he, lett us begon, we [are] passed all feare. Let us shake off the yoake of a company of whelps that killed so many french and black-coats, and so many of my nation. Nay, saith he, Brother, if you come not, I will leave you, and will go through the woods till I shall be over against the french quarters. There I will make a fire for a signe that they may fetch me. I will tell to the Governor that you stayed behind. Take courage, man, says he. With this he tooke his peece and things. Att this I considered how if [I] weare taken att the doore by meere rashnesse; the next, the impossibility I saw to go by myselfe if my comrad would leave me, and perhaps the wind might rise, that I could [only] come to the end of my journey in a long time, and that I should be accounted a coward for not daring to hazard myselfe with him that so much ventured for mee. I resolved to go along through the woods; but the litle constancy that is to be expected in wild men made me feare he should [take] to his heels, which approved his unfortunate advice; ffor he hath lost his life by it, and I in great danger have escaped by the helpe of the Almighty. I consent to goe by watter with him.

In a short time wee came to the lake. The watter very calme and cleare. No liklyhood of any storme. We hazarded to the other side of the lake, thinking ffor more security. After we passed the third part of the lake, I being the foremost, have perceaved as if it weare a black shaddow, which proved a real thing. He at this rises and tells mee that it was a company of buzards, a kinde of geese in that country. We went on, where wee soone perceaved our owne fatall blindnesse, ffor they weare ennemys. We went back againe towards the lande with all speed to escape the evident danger, but it was too late; ffor before we could come to the russhes that weare within halfe a league of the waterside we weare tired. Seeing them approaching nigher and nigher, we threw the 3 heads in the watter. They meet with these 3 heads, which makes them to row harder after us, thinking that we had runn away from their country. We weare so neere the lande that we saw the bottom of the watter, but yett too deepe to step in. When those cruel inhumans came within a musquett shott of us, and fearing least the booty should gett a way from them, shott severall times att us, and deadly wounding my comrade, [who] fell dead. I expected such another shott. The litle skiff was pierced in severall places with their shooting, [so] that watter ran in a pace. I defended me selfe with the 2 arms. Att last they environed me with their boats, that tooke me just as I was a sinking. They held up the wild man and threw him into one of their boats and me they brought with all diligence to land. I thought to die without mercy.

They made a great fire and tooke my comrade's heart out, and choped off his head, which they put on an end of a stick and carryed it to one of their boats. They cutt off some of the flesh of that miserable, broyled it and eat it. If he had not ben so desperately wounded they had don their best to keepe him alive to make him suffer the more by bourning him with small fires; but being wounded in the chin, and [a] bullet gon through the troat, and another in the shoulder that broake his arme, making him incurable, they burned some parte of his body, and the rest they left there. That was the miserable end of that wretch.

Lett us come now to the beginning of my miseries and calamities that I was to undergo. Whilst they weare bussie about my companion's head, the others tyed me safe and fast in a strang maner; having striped me naked, they tyed me above the elbows behind my back, and then they putt a collar about me, not of porcelaine as before, but a rope wrought about my midle. So [they] brought me in that pickle to the boat. As I was imbarqued they asked mee severall questions. I being not able to answer, gave me great blowes with their fists. [They] then pulled out one of my nailes, and partly untied me.

What displeasure had I, to have seen meselfe taken againe, being almost come to my journey's end, that I must now goe back againe to suffer such torments, as death was to be expected. Having lost all hopes, I resolved alltogether to die, being a folly to think otherwise. I was not the [only] one in the clawes of those wolves. Their company was composed of 150 men. These tooke about Quebucq and other places 2 frenchmen, one french woman, 17 Hurrons, men as [well as] women. They had Eleven heads which they sayd weare of the Algonquins, and I was the 33rd victime with those cruels.

The wild men that weare Prisners sang their fatal song, which was a mornfull song or noise. The 12 couleurs (which weare heads) stood out for a shew. We prisoners weare separated, one in one boat, one in an other. As for me, I was put into a boat with a Huron whose fingers weare cutt and bourned, and very [few] amongst them but had the markes of those inhuman devils. They did not permitt me to tarry long with my fellow prisoner, least I should tell him any news, as I imagine, but sent me to another boat, where I remained the rest of the voyage by watter, which proved somewhat to my disadvantage.

In this boat there was an old man, who having examined me, I answered him as I could best; tould him how I was adopted by such an one by name, and as I was a hunting with my companions that wildman that was killed came to us, and after he had eaten went his way. In the evening [he] came back againe and found us all a sleepe, tooke a hattchett and killed my 3 companions, and awaked me, and so embarked me and brought me to this place. That old man believed me in some measure, which I perceived in him by his kindnesse towards me. But he was not able to protect me from those that [had] a will to doe me mischief. Many slandred me, but I tooke no notice.

Some 4 leagues thence they erected cottages by a small river, very difficult to gett to it, for that there is litle watter on a great sand [bank] a league wide. To this very houre I tooke notice how they tyed their captives, though all my owne cost. They planted severall poastes of the bignesse of an arme, then layd us of a length, tyed us to the said poasts far a sunder from one another. Then tyed our knees, our wrists, and elbows, and our hairs directly upon the crowne of our heads, and then cutt 4 barrs of the bignesse of a legge & used thus. They tooke 2 for the necke, puting one of each side, tying the 2 ends together, so that our heads weare fast in a hole like a trappe; likewayes they did to our leggs. And what tormented us most was the Maringoines and great flyes being in abundance; did all night but puff and blow, that by that means we saved our faces from the sting of those ugly creatures; having no use of our hands, we are cruelly tormented. Our voyage was laborious and most miserable, suffering every night the like misery.

When we came neere our dwellings we mett severall gangs of men to our greatest disadvantage, for we weare forced to sing, and those that came to see us gave porcelaine to those that most did us injury. One cutt of a finger, and another pluck'd out a naile, and putt the end of our fingers into their bourning pipes, & burned severall parts in our bodyes. Some tooke our fingers and of a stick made a thing like a fork, with which [they] gave severall blowes on the back of the hands, which caused our hands to swell, and became att last insensible as dead. Having souffred all these crueltyes, which weare nothing to that they make usually souffer their Prisoners, we arrived att last to the place of execution, which is att the coming in to their village, which wheere not [long] before I escaped very neere to be soundly beaten with staves and fists. Now I must think to be no lesse traited by reason of the murder of the 3 men, but the feare of death takes away the feare of blowes.

Nineteen of us prisoners weare brought thither, and 2 left behind with the heads. In this place we had 8 coulours. Who would not shake att the sight of so many men, women, and children armed with all sorte of Instruments: staves, hand Irons, heelskins wherein they putt halfe a score [of] bullets? Others had brands, rods of thorne, and all suchlike that the Crueltie could invent to putt their Prisoners to greater torments. Heere, no help, no remedy. We must passe this dangerous passage in our extremity without helpe. He that is the fearfullest, or that is observed to stay the last, getts nothing by it butt more blowes, and putt him to more paine. For the meanest sort of people commonly is more cruell to the fearfullest then to the others that they see more fearfull, being att last to suffer chearfuly and with constancy.

They begun to cry to both sides, we marching one after another, environed with a number of people from all parts to be witnesse to that hidious sight, which seriously may be called the Image of hell in this world. The men sing their fatall song, the women make horrible cryes, the victores cryes of joy, and their wives make acclamations of mirth. In a word, all prepare for the ruine of these poore victims who are so tyed, having nothing saving only our leggs free, for to advance by litle and litle according [to] the will of him that leades; ffor as he held us by a long rope, he stayed us to his will, & often he makes us falle, for to shew them cruelty, abusing you so for to give them pleasure and to you more torment.

As our band was great, there was a greater crew of people to see the prisoners, and the report of my taking being now made, and of the death of the 3 men, which afflicted the most part of that nation, great many of which came through a designe of revenge and to molest me more then any other. But it was altogether otherwise, for among the tumult I perceaved my father & mother with their 2 daughters. The mother pushes in among the Crew directly to mee, and when shee was neere enough, shee clutches hould of my haire as one desperat, calling me often by my name; drawing me out of my ranck, shee putts me into the hands of her husband, who then bid me have courage, conducting me an other way home to his Cabban, when he made me sitt downe. [He] said to me: You senselesse, thou was my son, and thou rendered thyselfe enemy, and thou rendered thyself enemy, thou lovest not thy mother, nor thy father that gave thee thy life, and thou notwithstanding will kill me. Bee merry; Conharrassan, give him to eate. That was the name of one of the sisters. My heart shook with trembling and feare, which tooke away my stomach. Neverthelesse to signifie a bould countenance, knowing well a bould generous minde is allwayes accounted among all sort of nations, especially among wariors, as that nation is very presumptious and haughty. Because of their magnanimity and victories opposing themselves into all dangers and incounters what ever, running over the whole land for to make themselves appeere slaining and killing all they meete in exercising their cruelties, or else shewing mercy to whom they please to give liberty. God gave mee the grace to forgett nothing of my duty, as I tould my father the successe of my voyage in the best tearme I could, and how all things passed, mixturing a litle of their languag with that of the Hurrons, which I learned more fluently then theirs, being longer and more frequently with the Hurrons.

Every one attentively gave ears to me, hoping by this means to save my life. Uppon this heere comes a great number of armed men, enters the Cabban, where finding mee yett tyed with my cords, fitting by my parents, made their addresses to my father, and spak to him very loud. After a while my father made me rise and delivers me into their hands. My mother seeing this, cryes and laments with both my sisters, and I believing in a terrible motion to goe directly on to the place of execution. I must march, I must yeeld wheere force is predominant att the publique place.

I was conducted where I found a good company of those miserable wretches, alltogether beaten with blowes, covered with blood, and bourned. One miserable frenchman, yett breathing, having now ben consumed with blowes of sticks, past so through the hands of this inraged crew, and seeing he could [bear] no more, cutt off his head and threw it into the fire. This was the end of this Execrable wofull body of this miserable.

They made me goe up the scaffold where weare 5 men, 3 women, and 2 children captives, and I made the Eleventh. There weare severall scaffolds nigh one an other, where weare these wretches, who with dolefull singings replenished the heavens with their Cryes. For I can say that an houre before the weather approved very faire, and in an instant the weather changed and rayned Extremely. The most part retired for to avoid this hayle, and now we must expect the full rigour of the weather by the retiration of those perfidious [persons], except one part of the Band of hell who stayed about us for to learn the trade of barbary; ffor those litle devils seeing themselves all alone, continued [a] thousand inventions of wickednesse. This is nothing strang, seeing that they are brought up, and suck the crueltie from their mother's brest.

I prolong a litle from my purpose of my adventure for to say the torments that I have seen souffred att Coutu, after that they have passed the sallett, att their entering in to the village, and the rencounters that they meet ordinarily in the wayes, as above said. They tie the prisoners to a poast by their hands, their backs tourned towards the hangman, who hath a bourning fire of dry wood and rind of trees, which doth not quench easily. They putt into this fire hattchets, swords, and such like instruments of Iron. They take these and quench them on human flesh. They pluck out their nailes for the most part in this sort. They putt a redd coale of fire uppon it, and when it is swolen bite it out with their teeth. After they stop the blood with a brand which by litle and litle drawes the veines the one after another from off the fingers, and when they draw all as much as they can, they cutt it with peeces of redd hott Iron; they squeeze the fingers between 2 stones, and so draw the marrow out of the boanes, and when the flesh is all taken away, they putt it in a dishfull of bourning sand. After they tye your wrist with a corde, putting two for this effect, one drawing him one way, another of another way. If the sinews be not cutt with a stick, putting it through & tourning it, they make them come as fast as they can, and cutt them in the same way as the others. Some others cutt peeces of flesh from all parts of the body & broyle them, gett you to eat it, thrusting them into yor mouth, puting into it a stick of fire. They breake your teeth with a stoane or clubbs, and use the handle of a kettle, and upon this do hang 5 or 6 hattchetts, red hott, which they hang about their neck and roast your leggs with brands of fire, and thrusting into it some sticks pointed, wherein they put ledd melted and gunnepowder, and then give it fire like unto artificiall fire, and make the patient gather it by the stumps of his remaining fingers. If he cannot sing they make him quack like a henne.

I saw two men tyed to a rope, one att each end, and hang them so all night, throwing red coales att them, or bourning sand, and in such like bourne their feet, leggs, thighs, and breech. The litle ones doe exercise themselves about such cruelties; they deck the bodyes all over with hard straw, putting in the end of this straw, thornes, so leaves them; now & then gives them a litle rest, and sometimes gives them fresh watter and make them repose on fresh leaves. They also give them to eat of the best they have that they come to themselves againe, to give them more torments. Then when they see that the patient can no more take up his haire, they cover his head with a platter made of rind full of bourning sand, and often getts the platter a fire. In the next place they cloath you with a suit made of rind of a tree, and this they make bourne out on your body. They cutt off your stones and the women play with them as with balles. When they See the miserable die, they open him and pluck out his heart; they drink some of his blood, and wash the children's heads with the rest to make them valient. If you have indured all the above said torments patiently and without moanes, and have defied death in singing, then they thrust burning blades all along your boanes, and so ending the tragedie cutt off the head and putt it on the end of a stick and draw his body in quarters which they hawle about their village. Lastly [they] throw him into the watter or leave [him] in the fields to be eaten by the Crowes or doggs.

Now lett me come to our miserable poore captives that stayed all along [through] the raine upon the scaffold to the mercy of 2 or 300 rogues that shott us with litle arrowes, and so drew out our beards and the haire from those that had any. The showre of rayne being over, all come together againe, and having kindled fires began to burne some of those poore wretches. That day they pluckt 4 nailes out of my fingers, and made me sing, though I had no mind att that time. I became speechlesse oftentimes; then they gave me watter wherin they boyled a certain herbe that the gunsmiths use to pollish their armes. That liquour brought me to my speech againe. The night being come they made me come downe all naked as I was, & brought to a strang Cottage. I wished heartily it had ben that of my parents. Being come, they tyed me to a poast, where I stayed a full houre without the least molestation.

A woman came there with her boy, inticed him to cutt off one of my fingers with a flint stoan. The boy was not 4 yeares old. This [boy] takes my finger and begins to worke, but in vaine, because he had not the strength to breake my fingers. So my poore finger escaped, having no other hurt don to it but the flesh cutt round about it. His mother made him suck the very blood that runn from my finger. I had no other torment all that day. Att night I could not sleepe for because of the great paine. I did eat a litle, and drunk much watter by reason of a feaver I caught by the cruel torment I suffred.

The next morning I was brought back againe to the scaffold, where there were company enough. They made me sing a new, but my mother came there and made [me] hould my peace, bidding me be cheerfull and that I should not die. Shee brought mee some meate. Her coming comforted me much, but that did not last long; ffor heare comes severall old people, one of which being on the scaffold, satt him downe by me, houlding in his mouth a pewter pipe burning, tooke my thumb and putt it on the burning tobacco, and so smoaked 3 pipes one after another, which made my thumb swell, and the nayle and flesh became as coales. My mother was allwayes by me to comfort me, but said not what I thought. That man having finished his hard worke, but I am sure I felt it harder to suffer it. He trembled, whether for feare or for so much action I cannot tell. My mother tyed my fingers with cloath, and when he was gon shee greased my haire and combed my haire with a wooden comb, fitter to combe a horse's tayle then anything else. Shee goes back againe.

That day they ended many of those poore wretches, flinging some all alive into the midle of a great fire. They burned a frenchwoman; they pulled out her breasts and tooke a child out of her belly, which they broyled and made the mother eat of it; so, in short, [she] died. I was not abused all that day till the night. They bourned the soales of my feet and leggs. A souldier run through my foot a swoord red out of the fire, and plucked severall of my nailes. I stayed in that maner all night. I neither wanted in the meane while meate nor drinke. I was supplied by my mother and sisters. My father alsoe came to see me & tould me I should have courage. That very time there came a litle boy to gnaw with his teeth the end of my fingers. There appears a man to cutt off my thumb, and being about it leaves me instantly & did no harme, for which I was glad. I believe that my father dissuaded him from it.

A while after my father was gon 3 came to the scaffold who swore they would me a mischiefe, as I thinke, for yet he tied his leggs to mine, called for a brand of fire, and layd it between his leggs and mine, and sings: but by good lucke it was out on my side, and did no other effect then bourne my skin, but bourned him to some purpos. In this posture I was to follow him, & being not able to hould mee, draweth mee downe. One of the Company Cutt the rope that held us with his knife, and makes mee goe up againe the scaffold and then went their way.

There I stayed till midday alone. There comes a multitude of people who make me come downe and led mee into a cottage where there weare a number of sixty old men smoaking tobacco. Here they make mee sitt downe among them and stayed about halfe an houre without that they asked who and why I was brought thither, nor did I much care. For the great torments that I souffred, I knew not whether I was dead or alive. And albeit I was in a hott feavor & great pain, I rejoyced att the sight of my brother, that I have not seene since my arrivement. He comes in very sumptuously covered with severall necklaces of porcelaine,[Footnote: Porcelaine, the French for wam-pum, or shell beads.] & a hattchett in his hand, satt downe by the company and cast an eye on me now and then. Presently and comes in my father with a new and long cover, and a new porcelaine about him, with a hatchett in his hands, likewise satt downe with the company. He had a calumet of red stoane in his hands, a cake [Footnote: Cake, meaning a medicine-bag.] upon his shoulders, that hanged downe his back, and so had the rest of the old men. In that same cake are incloased all the things in the world, as they tould me often, advertising mee that I should [not] disoblige them in the least nor make them angry, by reason they had in their power the sun, and moone, and the heavans, and consequently all the earth. You must know in this cake there is nothing but tobacco and roots to heale some wounds or sores; some others keepe in it the bones of their deceased friends; most of them wolves' heads, squirrels', or any other beast's head. When there they have any debatement among them they sacrifice to this tobacco, that they throw into the fire, and make smoake, of that they puff out of their pipes; whether for peace or adversity or prosperity or warre, such ceremonies they make very often.

My father, taking his place, lights his pipe & smoaks as the rest. They held great silence. During this they bring 7 prisoners; to wit, 7 women and 2 men, more [then] 10 children from the age of 3 to 12 years, having placed them all by mee, who as yett had my armes tyed. The others all att liberty, being not tyed, which putt me into some despaire least I should pay for all. Awhile after one of the company rises and makes a long speech, now shewing the heavens with his hands, and then the earth, and fire. This good man putt himselfe into a sweate through the earnest discours. Having finished his panigerique, another begins, and also many, one after another.

They gave then liberty to some, butt killed 2 children with hattchetts, and a woman of 50 years old, and threw them out of the cottage (saving onely myselfe) att full liberty. I was left alone for a stake, they contested together [upon] which my father rose and made a speech which lasted above an houre, being naked, having nothing on but his drawers and the cover of his head, and putt himselfe all in a heate. His eyes weare hollow in his head; he appeared to me like [as if] mad, and naming often the Algonquins in their language [that is, Eruata], which made me believe he spoake in my behalfe. In that very time comes my mother, with two necklaces of porcelaine, one in her armes, and another about her like a belt. As soone as shee came in shee began to sing and dance, and flings off one of her necklaces in the midle of the place, having made many tourns from one end to the other. Shee takes the other necklace and gives it mee, then goes her way. Then my brother rises and holding his hattchett in his hand sings a military song. Having finished [he] departs. I feared much that he was first to knock me in the head; and happy are those that can escape so well, rather then be bourned. My father rises for a second time and sings; so done, retired himselfe. I thought all their guifts, songs, and speeches should prevaile nothing with mee.

Those that stayed held a councell and spoake one to an other very long, throwing tobacco into the fire, making exclamations. Then the Cottage was open of all sides by those that came to view, some of the company retires, and place was made for them as if they weare Kings. Forty staye about me, and nigh 2000 about my cottage, of men, women, and children. Those that went their way retourned presently. Being sett downe, smoaked againe whilest my father, mother, brother, and sisters weare present. My father sings a while; so done, makes a speech, and taking the porcelaine necklace from off me throws it att the feet of an old man, and cutts the cord that held me, then makes me rise. The joy that I receaved att that time was incomparable, for suddenly all my paines and griefs ceased, not feeling the least paine. He bids me be merry, makes me sing, to which I consented with all my heart. Whilst I did sing they hooped and hollowed on all sids. The old man bid me "ever be cheerfull, my son!" Having don, my mother, sisters, and the rest of their friends [sung] and danced.

Then my father takes me by the arme and leads me to his cabban. As we went along nothing was heard but hooping and hollowing on all parts, biding me to take great courage. My mother was not long after me, with the rest of her friends. Now I see myselfe free from death. Their care att this was to give me meate. I have not eaten a bitt all that day, and for the great joy I had conceaved, caused me to have a good stomach, so that I did eat lustily. Then my mother begins to cure my sores and wounds. Then begins my paines to [break out] a new; ffor shee cleans my wounds and scrapes them with a knife, and often thrusts a stick in them, and then takes watter in her mouth, and spouts it to make them cleane. The meanwhile my father goes to seeke rootes, and my sister chaws them, and my mother applyes them to my sores as a plaster. The next day the swelling was gone, but worse then before; but in lesse then a fortnight my sores weare healed, saving my feete, that kept [me] more then a whole month in my Cabban. During this time my nailes grewed a pace. I remained onely lame of my midle finger, that they have Squeezed between two stoanes. Every one was kind to mee as beforesaid, and [I] wanted no company to be merry with.

I should [be] kept too long to tell you the particulars that befell me during my winter. I was beloved of my Parents as before. My exercise was allwayes a hunting without that any gave me the least injury. My mother kept me most brave, and my sisters tooke great care of mee. Every moneth I had a white shirt, which my father sent for from the Flemeings, who weare not a farr off our village. I could never gett leave to goe along with my brother, who went there very often. Finally, seeing myselfe in the former condition as before, I constituted as long as my father and fortune would permitt mee to live there. Dayly there weare military feasts for the South nations, and others for the Algonquins and for the French. The exclamations, hoopings and cryes, songs and dances, signifies nothing but the murdering and killing, and the intended victory that they will have the next yeare, which is in the beginning of Spring. In those feasts my father heaves up his hattchett against the Algonquins. For this effect [he] makes great preparations for his next incamping. Every night [he] never failes to instruct and encourage the young age to take armes and to reveng the death of so many of their ennemy that lived among the french nation. The desire that I had to make me beloved, for the assurance of my life made me resolve to offer myselfe for to serve, and to take party with them. But I feared much least he should mistrust me touching his advis to my resolution. Neverthelesse I finding him once of a good humour and on the point of honnour encourages his son to break the kettle and take the hattchett and to be gon to the forraigne nations, and that was of courage and of great renowne to see the father of one parte and the son of another part, & that he should not mispraise if he should seperat from him, but that it was the quickest way to make the world tremble, & by that means have liberty everywhere by vanquishing the mortall enemy of his nation; uppon this I venture to aske him what I was. [He] presently answers that I was a Iroquoite as himselfe. Lett me revenge, said I, my kindred. I love my brother. Lett me die with him. I would die with you, but you will not because you goe against the ffrench. Lett me a gaine goe with my brother, the prisoners & the heads that I shall bring, to the joy of my mother and sisters, will make me undertake att my retourne to take up the hattchett against those of Quebecq, of the 3 rivers, and Monteroyall in declaring them my name, and that it's I that kills them, and by that you shall know I am your son, worthy to beare that title that you gave me when you adopted me. He sett [up] a great crye, saying, have great courage, son Oninga, thy brother died in the warrs not in the Cabban; he was of a courage not of a woman. I goe to aveng his death. If I die, aveng you mine. That one word was my leave, which made me hope that one day I might escape, having soe great an opportunity; or att least I should have the happinesse to see their country, which I heard so much recommended by the

Iroquoites, who brought wondrous stories and the facilitie of killing so many men.

Thus the winter was past in thoughts and preparing for to depart before the melting of the snow, which is very soone in that Country. I began to sett my witts together how I should resolve this my voyage; for my mother opposed against it mightily, saying I should bee lost in the woods, and that I should gett it [put] off till the next yeare. But at last I flattered with her and dissembled; besides, my father had the power in his hands. Shee daring not to deny him any thing because shee was not borne in my father's country, but was taken [when] little in the Huronit's Country. Notwithstanding [she was] well beloved of her husband, having lived together more then fourty years, and in that space brought him 9 children, 4 males and 5 females. Two girls died after a while, and 3 sons killed in the warrs, and one that went 3 years before with a band of 13 men to warre against a fiery nation which is farre beyonde the great lake. The 5th had allready performed 2 voyages with a greate deale of successe. My father was a great Captayne in warrs, having ben Commander in all his times, and distructed many villages of their Ennemy, having killed 19 men with his owne hands, whereof he was marked [on] his right thigh for as many [as] he killed. He should have as many more, but that you must know that the Commander has not amused himselfe to kille, but in the front of his army to encourage his men. If by chance he tooke any prisoners, he calles one of his men and gives him the captives, saying that it's honour enough to command the conquerors, and by his example shews to the yong men that he has the power as much as the honour. He receaved 2 gunn shots and 7 arrows shotts, and was runne through the shoulders with a lance. He was aged 3 score years old, he was talle, and of an excellent witt for a wild man.

When our baggage was ready, my father makes a feast to which he invites a number of people, & declares that he was sorry he had resolved to go to warre against an Ennemy which was in a cold country, which hindred him to march sooner then he would, but willing to see his sonnes before him, and that this banquett was made for his 2 sons' farewell. Then he tould that his adopted son was ready to go with his owne son to be revenged of the death of their brothers, and desired the Commander to have a care of us both. This Commander loved us both, said that the one which [was] meselfe should be with him to the end. If anything should oppose he would make me fight him. I was not att home when he spoke those words, but my mother toald me it att my retourne. I was a fishing by with my sisters & brother. When wee came back wee found all ready, butt with a heart broken that our mother and sisters lett us goe. Few days after I was invited to a military banquett where was the Captayne, a yong gallant of 20 years old, with a company of 8, and I made the 10th. We all did sing and made good cheare of a fatt beare. We gave our things to slaves, we carried only our musquetts. Our kindred brought us a great way. My sister could not forbeare crying, yett tould me to be of a stout heart. We tooke att last [leave and] bid them adieu. We tooke on our journey over great snowes for to come to the great Lake before the Spring. We travelled 7 days through woods and indifferent country, easie in some places and others difficult. The Rivers weare frozen, which made us crosse with a great deale of ease.

Wee arrived the 7th day in a village called Nojottga [Footnote: Nojottga, or Oneioutga, Oneida.], where we stayed 2 days. From thence came a young man with us. We arrived into another village, Nontageya [Footnote: Nontageya, Onontaguega, or Onondaga.], where we stayed foure days. Wee had allways great preparations, and weare invited 9 or tenne times a day. Our bellyes had not tyme to emptie themselves, because we feeded so much, and that what was prepared for us weare severall sortes, Stagg, Indian corne, thick flower, bears, and especially eels. We have not yett searched our baggs wheare our provision was. In this place wee mended them. For my part I found in myne 6 pounds of powder and more then 15 pounds of shott, 2 shirts, a capp, 8 pairs of shoes, and wherewith to make a paire of breeches, and about 1000 graines of black and white porcelaine, and my brother as many. Wee had new covers, one to our body, another hung downe from our shoulders like a mantle. Every one [had] a small necklace of porcelaine and a collar made with a thread of nettles to tye the Prisoners. I had a gunne, a hattchett, and a dagger. That was all we had. Our slaves brought the packs after us.

After we marched 3 dayes, we came to a village, Sononteeonon,[Footnote: Sononteeonon, Tionnontonan, or Seneca.] there we layd a night. The next day, after a small journey, we came to the last village of their confederates. Heere they doe differ in their speech though of [our] nation. It's called Oiongoiconon. [Footnote: Oiongoiconon is Cayuga.] Here we stay 2 dayes, and sent away our slaves and carryed our bundles ourselves, going allwayes through the woods. We found great plaines of 2 leagues and a halfe journey without a tree. We saw there stagges, but would not goe out of our way to kill them. We went through 3 villages of this nation neare one another. They admired to see a frenchman accompanying wild men, which I understood by their exclamations. I thought I grewed leane to take litle voyage, but the way seemed tedious to all. The raquett alwayes with the feet and sometimes with the hands, which seemed to me hard to indure, yett have I not complained. Att the parting of the slaves, I made my bundle light as the rest. We found snowes in few places, saving where the trees made a shaddow, which hindred the snow to thaw, which made us carry the raquetts with our feete, and sometimes with the hands.

After 10 days' march [we completed our journey] through a country covered with water, and where also are mountaines and great plaines. In those plaines wee kill'd stagges, and a great many Tourquies. Thence we came to a great river of a mile wide which was not frozen, which made us stay there 10 or 12 dayes making skiffs of the rind of walnut trees. We made good cheere and wished to stay there longer. We made 3 skiffs to hould 3 men, and one to hould two. We imbarked though there weare ice in many places, and yett no hinderance to us going small journeys, fearing least what should befall us. In 4 dayes we came to a lake much frozen; covered in some places with ice by reason of the tossing of the wind, and the ground all covered with snow. Heere we did our best to save us from the rigour of the aire, and must stay 15 dayes. The wild men admired that the season of the yeare was so backward. Att the end the wind changes southerly, which made the lake free from Ice and cleare over all the skirts of it, without either snow or ice. There was such a thawing that made the litle brookes flow like rivers, which made us imbarque to wander [over] that sweet sea. The weather lovely, the wind fayre, and nature satisfied. Tending forwards, singing and playing, not considering the contrary weather past, continued so 6 days upon the lake and rested the nights ashore.

The more we proceeded in our journey, the more the pleasant country and warmer. Ending the lake, we entered into a beautifull sweet river, a stoan-cast wide. After halfe a day we rid on it, weare forced to bring both barks and equipage uppon our backs to the next streame of that river. This done above 20 times, hawling our boats after us all laden. We went up that river att least 30 or 40 leagues. Att last [it] brought us to a lake of some 9 miles in length.

Being comed to the highest place of the lake, we landed and hid our boats farr enough in the woods, [and] tooke our bundles. We weare 3 dayes going through a great wildernesse where was no wood, not so much as could make us fire. Then the thickned flower did serve us instead of meate, mingling it with watter. We foorded many litle rivers, in swiming & sayling. Our armes, which we putt uppon some sticks tyed together of such wood as that desolat place could afford, to keepe them from the weatt. The evening we came on the side of a violent river, uppon which we made bridges of trees that we [made] to meet, to go over.

We left this place after being there 3 dayes. We went up that river in 2 dayes; there we killed stagges. After we came to a mouth of another river. We made a litle fort, where it was commanded by our captayne to make no noise. They desired me to be very quiet, which I observed strictly. After refreshment we imbarked, though unseasonably, in the night, for to make som discovery. Some went one way, some another. We went a great way, but not farr off our fort. The next day we meet altogether & made some Councell, where it was decreed that 2 should go to the furthermost part of a small river in a boat, to make a discovery, and see if there weare tracks of people there, whilst the other 9 should take notice of a villag, that they knew'd to be nigh, and because it was lesse danger to make there a discovery. The youngest of the company and me are pitched [upon] to goe into the river. We tooke the lightest boat. It was well, [for] that in some places of the river there was not watter enough to carry us. We weare fained to draw the boat after us. I believe not that ever a wild man went that way because of the great number of trees that stops the passage of the river.

After we have gon the best part of the day, we found ourselves att the end of a small lake some 4 mile in length, and seeing the woods weare not so thick there as wheare wee passed, we hid our boat in some bushes, taking onely our armes along, intending on still to pretend some discovery. We scarce weare in the midle of the lake when we perceave 2 persons goeing on the watter side, att the other side of the lake; so my comrade getts him up a tree to discerne better if there weare any more. After he stayed there a while [he] comes [down] & tells me that he thought they weare 2 women, and that we might goe kill them. Doubtlesse, said I, if they are women the men are not afarre from them, and we shall be forced to shoote. Wee are alone, and should runne the hazzard of 2 women for to be discovered. Our breethren also would be in danger that knowes nothing. Moreover it's night; what dost thou intend to doe? You say well, replyes he; lett us hide ourselves in the wood, for we cannot goe downe in the river in the night time. Att breake of day we will [goe] back to our companions where we will finde them in the fort.

Here we came without any provisions, where we must lie under a rotten tree. That night it rayned sadly. We weare wett; but a naturall Exercise is good fire. We weare in our boat early in the morning, and with great diligence we came back better then we went up, for the river grewed mighty high by reason of so much that fell of raine. I will not omitt a strange accident that befell us as we came. You must know that as we past under the trees, as before mentioned, there layd on one of the trees a snake with foure feete, her head very bigg, like a Turtle, the nose very small att the end, the necke of 5 thumbs wide, the body about 2 feet, and the tayle of a foot & a halfe, of a blackish collour, onto a shell small and round, with great eyes, her teeth very white but not long. That beast was a sleepe upon one of the trees under which wee weare to goe; neither of us ever seeing such a creature weare astonished. We could not tell what to doe. It was impossible to carry our boat, for the thicknesse of the wood; to shoot att her wee would att least be discovered, besides it would trouble our Company. Att last we weare resolved to goe through att what cost soever, and as we weare under that hellish beast, shee started as shee awaked, and with that fell'd downe into our boat, there weare herbes that served [to secure] us from that dreadfull animal. We durst not ventur to kill her, for feare of breaking of our boat. There is the question who was most fearfull? As for me, I quaked. Now seeing shee went not about to doe us hurt, and that shee was fearfull, we lett her [be] quiet, hoping shortly to land and to tourne upsid downe of our boat to be rid of such a devill. Then my comrad began to call it, and before we weare out of the litle river our feare was over; so we resolved to bring her to the fort, and when once arrived att the great river, nothing but crosse over it to be neare our fort. But in the mean while a squirrell made us good spoart for a quarter of an houre. The squirrell would not leap into the water; did but runne, being afraid of us, from one end of the boat to the other; every time he came nearer, the snake opened her wide mouth & made a kind of a noise, & rose up, having her 2 fore feet uppon the side of the boat, which persuaded us that shee would leave us. We leaned on that side of the boat, so with our owers thrusted her out; we seeing her swime so well, hasted to kill her with our owers, which shee had for her paines. [Footnote: Radisson's description of this reptile has been shown to one of the most eminent herpetologists in America, who writes that "no such reptile has ever been described by scientific writers."] The squirrell tooke the flight, soe we went, longing to be with our comrades to tell them of what we have seene. We found one of our company watching for us att the side of a woode, for they weare in feare least wee should be taken, & expected us all night long. As for their part they neither have seen nor heard anything. Wherefore resolved to goe further, but the news we brought them made them alter their resolution. Wee layd all night in our fort, where we made good cheare and great fires, fearing nothing, being farr enough in the wood.

The next day before the breaking of the day we foorded the river, & leaving our 3 boats in the wood, went a foot straight towards the place where we have seene the 2 persons; & before we came to the lake we tooke notice of some fresh trakes which made us look to ourselves, and followed the trakes, which brought us to a small river, where no sooner came but we saw a woman loaden with wood, which made us believ that some cottage or village was not afar off. The Captaine alone takes notice of the place where abouts the discovery was, who soone brought us [to see] that there weare 5 men & 4 women a fishing. We wagged [sic] att this the saffest [way] to come unawarre uppon them, and like starved doggs or wolves devoured those poore creatures who in a moment weare massacred. What we gott by this was not much, onely stagges' skins with some guirdles made of goate's hair, of their owne making. These weare in great estime among our wild men. Two of ours goes to the cabban which was made of rushes, where they founde an old woman. They thought it charity to send her into the other world, with two small children whome also they killed; so we left that place, giving them to the fishes their bodyes. Every one of us had his head, and my brother two; our share being considerable [we] went on along the river till we came to a small lake. Not desiring to be discovered, we found a faire road close by a wood, withtooke ourselves out of it with all haste, and went towards a village. There we came by night, where we visited the wildernesse to find out a secure place for security to hide ourselves; but [finding] no conveniencies we [went] into the wood in a very cleare place. Heere we layd downe uppon our bellies. We did eat, among other things, the fish we gott in the cabban of the fishermen. After dispatching one of the Company bouldly into the village, being thirsty after eating, for heere we had no water, [which] brings us [so] that we are all very quiett. The great desire we had to catch and take made us to controule the Buissinesse.

Early in the morning we came to the side of the wildernesse, where we layd in an ambush, but could see nobody that morning. Att two of the clock in the after non we see 20, as well men as women, a great way from us. We went to the wood, whence we perceived many att worke in the fields. Att evening [they] passed by very nigh us, but they neither see nor perceived us. They went to cutt wood; whilst they weare att worke there comes foure men and three women, that tooke notice of our ambush. This we could not avoid, so weare forced to appeare to their ruine. We tooke the 3 women and killed 2 men. The other 2 thought to escape, but weare stayed with our peeces; the other 2 that weare aworking would runne away, but one was taken, the other escaped. The news was brought over all those parts. Thence we runne away with our 4 prisoners and the 4 new heads with all speed. The women could not goe fast enough, and therefore killed them after they went a whole night; their corps we threwed into the river; heere we found a boat which Served us to goe over. We marched all that day without any delay; being come to an open field we hid ourselves in bushes till thee next day. We examined our Prisoners, who tould us no news; non could understand them, although many Huron words weare in their language. In this place we perceived 2 men a hunting afarre off; we thought [it] not convenient to discover ourselves, least we should be discovered and passe our aime. We tooke another day, 2 before and the rest after, thee prisoners in the midle. We speedily went the rest of thee day through a burned country, and the trees blowne downe with some great windes. The fire over came all, over 15 leagues in length and 10 in breadth. We layd in the very midle of that country upon a faire sandy place where we could see 3 or 4 leagues off round about us, and being secure we made the prisoners sing which is their Acconroga before death. There we made a litle fire to make our Kettle boyle a tourkey, with some meale that was left. Seeing no body persued, we resolved to goe thence before daylight to seeke for more booty. We stayed 14 nights before we turned back to the village, during which time we mett with nothing, and having gon on all sides with great paines without victualls. Att last we came to kill 2 Stagges, but did not suffice 12 of us. We weare forced to gather the dung of the stagges to boyle it with the meat, which made all very bitter. But good stomachs make good favour. Hunger forced us to kill our Prisoners, who weare chargeable in eating our food, for want of which have eaten the flesh. So by that means we weare freed from the trouble.

The next day we came neere a Village. Att our coming we killed a woman with her child, & seeing no more for us that way we tourned backe againe for feare of pursueing, and resolved to goe backe to the first village that was 3 days' journey; but on the way we mett with 5 and 20 or 30 men and women, who discovered us, which made [us] go to it. They fought & defended themselves lustily; but [there is] no resisting the Strongest party, for our guns were a terrour to them, and made them give over. During the fight the women ranne away. Five of the men weare wounded with arrowes and foure escaped, but he that was sent with me att first to make a discovery was horribly wounded with 2 arrowes and a blow of a club on the head. If he had stuck to it as we, he might proceed better. We burned him with all speed, that he might not languish long, to putt ourselves in safty. We killed 2 of them, & 5 prisoners wee tooke, and came away to where we left our boats, where we arrived within 2 days without resting, or eating or drinking all the time, saveing a litle stagge's meate. We tooke all their booty, which was of 2 sacks of Indian corne, stagges' skins, some pipes, some red and green stoanes, and some tobacco in powder, with some small loaves of bread, and some girdles, garters, necklaces made of goats' haire, and some small coyne of that country, some bowes and arrowes, and clubbs well wrought. The tournes of their heads weare of snakes' skin with bears' pawes. The hayre of some of them very long, & all proper men. We went on the other side of the river the soonest we could, and came to our fort. After we looked about us least we should be surprised, and perceiving nothing, we went about to gett meat for our wants & then to sleepe.

Att midnight we left that place. Six of us tooke a boate, 5 an other, and 2 the litle one. We row the rest of the night with all strength, & the breaking of the day hid ourselves in very long rushes & our boats. The litle boat went att the other side of the river, those hid it in the wood. One of them went up a tree to spie about, in case he could perceive any thing, to give notice to his comrades, & he was to come within sight of us to warne us. We weare in great danger going downe the streame of that river in the night time. We had trouble enough to carry all our baggage without the least noise. Being come to the end of the river which empties it selfe into a lake of some 8 or 9 leagues in compasse, we went into a small river to kill salmons, as in deed we tooke great many with staves, and so sturgeons, of which we made provision for a long while. Att last finding our selves out of all feare & danger, we went freely a hunting about the lake, where we tarried 3 dayes, and 2 of our Company mett with 2 women that runned away from the Sanoutin's country, which is of the Iroquoit nation. Those poore creatures having taken so much paines to sett themselves att liberty to goe to their native country, found themselves besett in a greater slavery then before, they being tyed [and] brought to us.

The next day we went from thence with the 5 prisoners & the 22 heads. So much for the litlenesse of our boats as for the weight we had to putt upon them, being in danger, which made us make the more hast to the place where we intended to make new boats. For 9 days we went through dangerous places which weare like so many precipices with horrible falling of watters. We weare forced to carry our boats after the same maner as before, with great paines. We came att last to a lake where we contrived other boats, and there we parted our acquisited booty, and then each had care of his owne. We ordered the biggest boat should hould 4 men and 2 prisoners; the next 3 men and the 2 women that last weare taken; the 3d should hould 3 and the other prisoner. My brother and I had a man & woman with 4 heads to our share, and so the rest accordingly without dispute or noise.

We wandered severall dayes on that lake. It was a most delightfull place, and a great many islands. Here we killed great many bears. After we came to a most delightfull place for the number of stagges that weare there. Thence into a straight river. From thence weare forced to make many carriages through many stony mountains, where we made severall trappes for castors. We tooke above 200 castors there, and fleaced off the best skins. There weare some skins so well dressed that [they] held the oyle of beares as pure bottles. During that time we mett severall huntsmen of our country; so we heard news of our friends. Only our father was not yett retourned from the warrs against the french and algonquins. We left our small boats, that weare purposely confected for our hunting, & tooke our great boats that could carry us and all our luggage.

69

We went up the same river againe, not without great labour. Att last with much ado we arrived at the landing place where wee made a stay of 4 days; where many Iroquoites women came, and among others my 2 sisters, that received me with great joy, with a thousand kindnesses and guifts, as you may think. I gave them the 2 heads that I had, keeping the woman for my mother, to be her slave. There was nothing but singing & dancing out of meere joy for our safe retourne. I had 20 castors for my share, with 2 skins full of oyle of beare and another full of oriniack and stagge's grease. I gave to each of my sisters 6 stagges' skins to make them coats. I kept the grease for my mother, to whome it is convenient to give what is necessary for the family. We made our slaves carry all our booty, & went on to litle journeys through woods with ease, because the woods weare not thick and the earth very faire and plaine. All the way the people made much of me, till we came to the village, and especially my 2 sisters, that in all they shewed their respects, giveing me meate every time we rested ourselves, or painting my face or greasing my haire or combing my head. Att night they tooke the paines to pull off my stokins, & when I supped they made me lay downe by them and cover me with their coats, as if the weather had ben cold.

This voyage being ended, albeit I came to this village, & twice with feare & terror, the 3d time notwithstanding with joy & contentment. As we came neare the village, a multitude of people came to meete us with great exclamations, and for the most part for my sake, biding me to be cheerfull & qualifying me dodcon, that is, devil, being of great veneration in that country to those that shew any vallour. Being arrived within halfe a league of the village, I shewed a great modesty, as usually warriors use to doe. The whole village prepares to give the scourge to the captives, as you [have] heard before, under which I myselfe I was once to undergoe. My mother comes to meet mee, leaping & singing. I was accompanied with both [of] my sisters. Shee takes the woman, slave that I had, and would not that any should medle with her. But my brother's prisoner, as the rest of the captives, weare soundly beaten. My mother accepted of my brother's 2 heads. My brother's prisoner was burned the same day, and the day following I received the sallery of my booty, which was of porcelaine necklaces, Tourns of beads, pendants, and girdles.

There was but banqueting for a while. The greatest part of both young men & women came to see me, & the women the choicest of meats, and a most dainty and cordiall bit which I goe to tell you; doe not long for it, is the best that is among them. First when the corne is greene they gather so much as need requireth, of which leaves they preserve the biggest leaves for the subject that followes. A dozen more or lesse old women meet together alike, of whome the greatest part want teeth, and seeth not a jott, and their cheeks hange downe like an old hunting-dogg, their eyes full of watter and bloodshott. Each takes an eare of corne and putts in their mouths, which is properly as milke, chawes it, and when their mouths are full, spitts it out in their hands, which possibly they wash not once one yeare; so that their hands are white inside by reason of the grease that they putt to their haire & rubbing of it with the inside of their hands, which keeps them pretty clean, but the outside in the rinknesse of their rinkled hands there is a quarter of an ounze of filth and stinking grease.

And so their hands being full of that mince meate minced with their gumms and [enough] to fill a dish. So they chaw chestnutts; then they mingle this with bear's grease or oyle of flower (in french we call it Tourne Sol) with their hands. So made a mixture, they tye the leaves att one end & make a hodgepot & cover it with the same leaves and tye the upper end so that what is within these leaves becomes a round ball, which they boile in a kettle full of watter or brouth made of meate or fish. So there is the description of the most delicious bitt of the world. I leave you taste of their Salmi gondy, which I hope to tell you in my following discourses of my other voyages in that country, and others that I frequented the space of tenne years.

To make a period of this my litle voyage. After I stayed awhile in this village with all joy & mirth, for feasts, dances, and playes out of meere gladnesse for our small victorious company's hapy retourne, so after that their heads had sufficiently danced, they begin to talke [of going] to warre against the hollanders. Most of us are traited againe for the castors we bestowed on them. They resolve unanimously to goe on their designe. Every thing ready, we march along. The next day we arrived in a small brough [Footnote: Brough probably means borough, used, as the French applied it to "bourgade," for a town of Indians or whites.] of the hollanders, where we masters them, without that those beere-bellies had the courage to frowne att us. Whether it was out of hope of lucre or otherwise, we with violence tooke the meate out of their potts, and opening their coubards [cupboards] we take and eat what we [can] gett. For drinking of their wine we weare good fellowes. So much that they fought with swords among themselves without the least offer of any misdeed to me. I drunk more then they, but more soberly, letting them make their quarrells without any notice.

The 4th day we come to the fort, of Orange, wher we weare very well received, or rather our Castors, every one courting us; and was nothing but pruins and reasins and tobbacco plentifully, and all for ho, ho, which is thanks, adding nianonnha, thanke you. We went from house to house. I went into the fort with my brother, and have not yett ben knowne a french. But a french souldier of the fort speaks to me in Iroquois language, & demanded if I was not a stranger, and did veryly believe I was french, for all that I was all dabbled over with painting and greased. I answered him in the same language, that no; and then he speaks in swearing, desiring me [to tell him] how I fell in the hands of those people. And hearing him speake french, amazed, I answered him, for which he rejoyced very much. As he embraces me, he cryes out with such a stirre that I thought him senselesse. He made a shame for all that I was wild but to blush red. I could be no redder then what they painted me before I came there. All came about me, ffrench as well as duch, every one makeing [me] drink out of the bottles, offering me their service; but my time yett was not out, so that I wanted not their service, for the onely rumour of my being a frenchman was enough. The flemish women drawed me by force into their houses, striving who should give, one bread, other meate, to drinke and to eate, and tobacco. I wanted not for those of my nation, Iroquois, who followed me in a great squadroon through the streets, as if I had bin a monster in nature or a rare thing to be seen.

I went to see the Governor, & talked with me a long time, and tould him the life that I lead, of which he admired. He offred me to buy me from them att what prise so ever, or else should save me, which I accepted not, for severall reasons. The one was for not to be behoulding to them, and the other being loathsome to leave such kind of good people. For then I began to love my new parents that weare so good & so favourable to me. The 3d reason was to watch a better opportunity for to retyre to the french rather then make that long circuit which after I was forced to doe for to retyre to my country more then 2,000 leagues; and being that it was my destiny to discover many wild nations, I would not to strive against destinie. I remitted myselfe to fortune and adventure of time, as a thing ordained by God for his greatest glorie, as I hope it will prove. Our treatis being done, overladend with bootyes abundantly, we putt ourselves in the way that we came to see againe our village, and to passe that winter with our wives, and to eat with them our Cagaimtie in peece, hoping that nobody should trouble us during our wintering, and also to Expect or finde our fathers retourning home.

Leaving that place, many cryed to see me among a company of wolves, as that souldier tould me who knowed me the first houre; and the poore man made the tears come to my eyes. The truth is, I found many occasions to retire for to save me, but have not yett souffred enough to have merited my deliverence. In 2 dayes' journey we weare retourned to our cabbans, where every one of us rendered himself to his dearest kindred or master. My sisters weare charged of porcelaine, of which I was shure not to faile, for they weare too liberall to mee and I towards them. I was not 15 dayes retourned, but that nature itselfe reproached me to leade such a life, remembering the sweet behaviour and mildnesse of the french, & considered with meselfe what end should I expect of such a barbarous nation, enemy to God and to man. The great effect that the flemings shewed me, and the litle space was from us there; can I make that journey one day? The great belief that that people had in me should make them not to mistrust me, & by that I should have greater occasion to save me without feare of being pursued.

All these reasons made one deliberat to take a full resolution, without further delay, of saving meselfe to the flemings; ffor I could be att no safty among such a nation full of reveng. If in case the ffrench & algonquins defeats that troupe of theirs, then what spite they will have will reveng it on my boanes; ffor where is no law, no faith to undertake to goe to the ffrench. I was once interrupted, nor have I had a desire to venture againe for the second time. I should delight to be broyled as before in pitifull torments. I repented of a good occasion I lett slippe, finding meselfe in the place with offers of many to assist me. But he that is of a good resolution must be of strong hopes of what he undertakes; & if the dangers weare considered which may be found in things of importancy, you ingenious men would become cooks. Finally, without expecting my father's retourne, putting away all feare & apprehension, I constituted to deliver meselfe from their hands at what ever rate it would come too. For this effect I purposed to faine to goe a hunting about the brough; & for to dissemble the better, I cutt long sticks to make handles for a kind of a sword they use, that thereby they might not have the least suspition.

One day I tooke but a simple hattchett & a knife, if occasion presented to cutt some tree, & for to have more defence, if unhappily I should be rencountred, to make them believe that I was lost in the woods. Moreover, as the whole nation tooke me for proud, having allways great care to be guarnished with porcelaine, & that I would fly away like a beggar, a thing very unworthy, in this deliberation I ventured. I inquired [of] my brother if he would keepe me company. I knewed that he never thought, seeing that he was courting of a young woman, who by the report of many was a bastard to a flemish. I had no difficulty to believe, seeing that the colour of her hayre was much more whiter then that of the Iroquoits. Neverthelesse, shee was of a great familie. I left them to their love. In shorte, that without any provision I tooke journey through the forests guided by fortune. No difficulty if I could keepe the highway, which is greatly beatten with the great concours of that people that comes & goes to trade with the flemings; but to avoid all encounters I must prolong a farre off. Soe being assisted by the best hope of the world, I made all diligence in the meene while that my mother nor kindred should mistrust me in the least.

I made my departure att 8 of the clock in the morning the 29th 8bre, 1663 [1653]. I marched all that journey without eating, but being as accustomed to that, without staying I continued my cours att night. Before the breaking of the day I found myselfe uncapable because of my feeblenesse and faintnesse for want of food and repose after such constraint. But the feare of death makes vertu of necessity. The morning commanded me to goe, for it's faire and could ayre, which [was] somewhat advantageous to keepe [me] more cheerfull. Finally the resolution reterning my courage, att 4 of the clocke att evening, the next daye I arrived in a place full of trees cutt, which made mee looke to myselfe, fearing to approach the habitation, though my designe was such. It is a strange thing that to save this life they abhorre what they wish, & desire which they apprehend. Approaching nigher and nigher untill I perceived an opening that was made by cutting of wood where was one man cutting still wood, I went nearer and called him. [He] incontinently leaves his work & comes to me, thinking I was Iroquoise. I said nothing to him to the contrary. I kept him in that thought, promising him to treat with him all my castors att his house, if he should promise me there should be non of my brother Iroquoise there, by reson we must be liberall to one another. He assured me there was non then there. I tould him that my castors were hidden and that I should goe for them to-morrow. So satisfied [he] leads me to his cabban & setts before me what good cheare he had, not desiring to loose time because the affaire concerned me much. I tould him I was savage, but that I lived awhile among the ffrench, & that I had something valuable to communicate to the governor. That he would give me a peece of paper and Ink and pen. He wondered very much to see that, what he never saw before don by a wildman. He charges himself with my letter, with promise that he should tell it to nobody of my being there, and to retourne the soonest he could possible, having but 2 litle miles to the fort of Orange.

In the meane while of his absence shee shews me good countenance as much as shee could, hoping of a better imaginary profit by me. Shee asked me if we had so much libertie with the ffrench women to lye with them as they; but I had no desire to doe anything, seeing myselfe so insnared att death's door amongst the terrible torments, but must shew a better countenance to a worse game. In the night we heard some wild men singing, which redoubled my torments and apprehension, which inticed me to declare to that woman that my nation would kill [me] because I loved the ffrench and the flemings more than they, and that I resolved hereafter to live with the flemings. Shee perceiving my reason hid me in a corner behind a sack or two of wheat. Nothing was to me but feare. I was scarcely there an houre in the corner, but the flemings came, 4 in number, whereof that french man [who] had knowne me the first, who presently getts me out & gives me a suite that they brought purposely to disguise me if I chanced to light upon any of the Iroquoits. I tooke leave of my landlady & landlord, yett [it] grieved me much that I had nothing to bestow upon them but thanks, being that they weare very poore, but not so much [so] as I.

I was conducted to the fort of Orange, where we had no incounter in the way, where I have had the honnour to salute the Governor, who spoake french, and by his speech thought him a french man. The next day he caused an other habit to be given me, with shoos & stokins & also linnen. A minister that was a Jesuit [Footnote: "A minister that was a Jesuit." This was the Jesuit father, Joseph Noncet. See

77

Introduction, page 3.] gave me great offer, also a Marchand, to whom I shall ever have infinit obligations, although they weare satisfied when I came to france att Rochel. I stayed 3 dayes inclosed in the fort & hidden. Many came there to search me, & doubt not but my parents weare of the party. If my father had ben there he would venture hard, & no doubt but was troubled att it, & so was my mother, & my parents who loved me as if I weare their owne naturall son. My poore sisters cryed out & lamented through the town of the flemings, as I was tould they called me by my name, ffor they came there the 3rd day after my flight. Many flemings wondered, & could not perceive how those could love me so well; but the pleasure caused it, as it agrees well with the Roman proverbe, "doe as they doe." I was imbarked by the governor's order; after taking leave, and thanks for all his favours, I was conducted to Menada, a towne faire enough for a new country, where after some 3 weekes I embarked in one of their shipps for holland, where we arrived after many boisterous winds and ill weather, and, after some six weeks' sayle and some days, we landed att Amsterdam the 4th of January, 1664 [1654]. Some days after I imbarked myselfe for france and came to Rochelle well & safe, not without blowing my fingers many times as well as I [had] done before [when] I arrived in holland. I stayed till spring, expecting the transporte of a shippe for new france.

SECOND VOYAGE, MADE IN THE UPPER COUNTRY OF THE IROQUOITS

The 15th day of may I embarked in a fisherboat to go for peerce Island, which is 6 score leagues off Quebecq, being there arrived the 7th of may. I search diligently the means possible for to end my voyage & render meselfe neere my naturall parents & country people. Att last I found an occasion to goe by some shallops & small boats of the wildernesse, which went up as farre as the ffrench habitation, there to joyne with the Algonquins & Mountaignaies to warre against the Iroquoits from all times, as their histories mentions. Their memory is their Chronicle, for it [passes] from father to son, & assuredly very excellent for as much as I know & many others has remarked. I embarked into one of their shallops & had the wind favorable for us N. E. In 5 dayes came to Quebecq, the first dwelling place of the ffrench. I mean not to tell you the great joy I perceivd in me to see those persons that I never thought to see more, & they in like maner with me thought I was dead long since. In my absence peace was made betweene the french & the Iroquoits, which was the reason I stayed not long in a place. The yeare before, the French began a new plantation [Footnote: "Began a new plantation," at Onondaga.] in the upper Country of the Iroquoits, which is distant from the Low Iroquois Country som fourscore leagues, where I was prisoner, & been in the warrs of that country. I tooke great notice of it, as I mentioned in my formest voyage, which made me have mind to goe thither againe, by the reason peace was concluded among them.

Friends, I must confesse I loved those poore people entirely well; moreover, nothing was to be feared by reason of the great distance which causes a difference in their speech, yett they understand one another. At that very time the Reverend fathers Jesuits embarked themselves for a second time to dwell there and teach Christian doctrin. I offered myselfe to them, and was, as their custome is, kindly accepted. I prepare meselfe for the journey, which was to be in June. You must know that the Hurrons weare contained in the article of peace, but not the Algonquins, which caused more difficulty; for those Iroquoits who imbarqued us durst not come downe the 3 rivers where the french should embarque, because it is the dwelling place of the Algonquin. To remedy this the ffrench and the barbarrs that weare to march, must come to Mont Royall, the last french inhabitation, in shalopps.

It will not be amisse to leave the following of the voyage for to repeat the reasons why those poor hurrons ventured themselves into their hands, who have bin ennemy one to another all their life time, and that naturally. You must know that the Hurrons, so called by the ffrench, have a bush of a hair rised up artificially uppon the heads like to a cock's comb. Those people, I say, weare 20 or 30,000 by report of many not 20 years ago. Their dwelling is neere the uper lake, so called by name of the ffrench. That people tell us of their pedegree from the beginning, that their habitation above the Lake, many years agoe, and as they increased, many, great many, began to search out another country. For to tend towards the South they durst not, for the multitude of people that was there, and besides some of their owne nations had against them. Then [they] resolved to goe to the north parts, for westward there was much watter, which was without end. Moreover many inhabitants, monstruous for the greatnesse of body. We will speake about this in another place more att large, where will give an exact account of what came to our knowledge dureing our travells, and the land we have discovered since. If eastward, they had found the Iroquoits who possessed some parts of the river of Canada, and their dwelling was where Quebecq is situated, and about that place, & att the upper end of Montmerency 2 leagues from Quebecq, where was a great village where now is seene a desolat country, that is, for woods and forests, nor more nor lesse then what small bushes nigh the river's side in the place called the Cape de Magdelaine. It's such a country that the ffrench calls it the burned country 20 miles about, and in many places the same is to be seene where there weare forests.

So seeing that the north regions weare not so peopled, they pursued [their] route of that way, and for the purpose provided themselves provision for a twelvemonth to live, with all their equipage imbarqued in the begining of the Spring. After that they passed great wayes, coming to a lake which conducts them into a great river, [Footnote: "Coming to a lake which conducts them into a great river." Moose River, which leads into Hudson's Bay.] which river leads them to a great extent of salt watter; so as they being good fishers want no fish. They coasted this great watter for a long time, finding allways some litle nation whose language they knew not, haveing great feare of one another. Finally, finding but a fearfull country full of mountains and rocks, they made great boats that might hould some 30 men to traverse with more assurance the great bay for to decline from the tediousnesse of the highway, which they must doe, having but small boats; whence they came to a country full of mountains of ice, which made us believe that they descended to the goulden arme.

So, fearing the winter should come on, they made sayles wherein they made greate way when the wind was behind; otherwyse they could not make use of their sayles, and many of their boats weare lost, but still went on, hoping of a better country. They wandered so many moons with great danger and famine, ffor they began to misse such plenty as they [were] used [to]. Att last [they] gott out, and coasting the skirts of the sea, and enters as it weare into a country where the sumer begins againe, they weare incouraged to greater hopes, insomuch that the poore people became from their first origine to lead another life. Being only conducted by their imaginary idea or instinct of nature ffor steering, they knewed nothing but towards the roote of the Sun, and likewise by some starrs. Finally the coast brings them to the great river St. Lawrence, river of Canada; knowing not that it was a river till they came just opposit against the mounts of our blessed lady, where they then perceaved to [be] betwixt 2 lands, albeit that litle summer was past, and that the season of the yeare growing on somewhat sharpe, which made them think to search for winter. [They] mounted allways up the river, and finding one side most beautifull for the eye, they passed it over, and planted their cabbans in many parts by reason of the many streams there flowing with quantity of fish, whereof they made a good store for their wintering. After a while that upon this undertaking they made cognicence and commerced with the highlanders, inhabitants of that country, who gave them notice that there weare a nation higher who should understand them, being that they weare great travellers, that they should goe on the other side and there should find another river named Tatousac.

They seeing the winter drawing on they made a fort and sent to discover the said place a band of their men to Tatousac. They finde a nation that understands them not more then the first, but by chance some that escaped the hands of their ennemy Iroquoits, and doubts that there is great difference of language between the Iroquoits and the Hurrons. They weare heard; & further you must note that neere the lake of the Hurrons some 40 leagues eastward there is another lake belonging to the nation of the Castors, which is 30 miles about. This nation have no other trafick nor industry then huntsmen. They use to goe once a yeare to the furthest place of the lake of the Hurrons to sell their Castors for Indian Corne, for some collors made of nettles, for sacks, & such things, for which they weare curious enough. So coming backe to their small lake againe, those marchandises weare transported to a nation beyond that lake towards N. N. E., and that nation had commerce with a people called the white fish, which is norwest to the 3 rivers some 150 leagues in the land. That nation had intelligence with the Saguenes, who are those that liveth about Tadousac, so that the 2 nations have great correspondency with one another because of their mutual language, saving that each one have a particular letter and accent.

Finding that nation of the Castors, who for the most part understands the Hurron idiom, they conversed together & weare supplied with meat by that wandring nation that lives onely by what they may or can gett. Contrary wise the Hurrons are seditious. We shall speak of them more amply in its place. So those miserable adventurers had ayd during that winter, who doubtlesse should souffer without this favor. They consulted together often, seeing themselves renforced with such a succour of people for to make warrs against the Iroqois.

The next spring their warre was conducted with success, ffor they chassed the Iroquois out of their country which they lost some winters before. They march up to the furthest part of the Lake Champlaine, to know if that was their formest dwelling, but they speak no further of it. Those Iroquoits to wander up and downe and spread themselves as you have heard to the lake d'Ontario, of which I will after make mention. I heard all this from frenchmen that knewed the Huron speech better then I myselfe, and after I heard it from the wildmen, & it's strang (being if it be so as the french as [well] as wildmen do already) that those people should have made a circuit of that litle world.

The Iroquoits after being putt out of that country of Quebecq, the Hurrons and Algonquins made themselves masters in it; that is to say, they went up above monmorency after that they left the place of their wintring, which was over against Tadousac, att the height of the Chaudiere (so called in french), and after many years they retourned to live att the gape of their lake, which is 200 Leagues long & 50 or 60 leagues large. Those hurrons lived in a vast country that they found unhabited, & they in a great number builded villages & they multiplied very many. The Iroquoits also gott a great country, as much by sweetnesse as by force. They became warriors uppon their owne dispences and cost. They multiplied so much, but they became better souldiers, as it's seene by the following of this discourse. The hurrons then inhabited most advantageously in that place, for as much as for the abundance of dears and staggs, from whence they have the name since of Staggy. It's certaine that they have had severall other callings, according as they have builded villages. Fishing they have in abundance in his season of every kind; I may say, more then wee have in Europe. In some places in this lake where is an innumerable quantity of fish, that in 2 houres they load their boat with as many as they can carry.

At last [they] became so eminent strong that they weare of a minde to fight against the neighbouring nation. Hearing that their sworne ennemys the Iroquoits retired towards the nation called Andasstoueronom, which is beyond the lake d'Ontario, between Virginia & that lake, they resolved to goe & search them for to warre against them; but they shall find it to their ruine, which I can affirme & assure, because the Iroquoits in the most part of their speeches, which comes from father to son, says, we bears (for it's their name) whilst we scraped the earth with our pawes, for to make the wheat grow for to maintain our wives, not thinking that the deare shall leape over the lake to kill the Beare that slept; but they found that the beare could scratch the stagge, for his head and leggs are small to oppose. Such speeches have they commonly together, in such that they have had warrs many years.

The Holanders being com'd to inhabit Menada, furnished that nation with weopens, by which means they became conquerors. The ffrench planters in Newfrance came up to live among this nation. In effect they doe live now many years; but the ambition of the fathers Jesuits not willing to permitt ffrench families to goe there, for to conserve the best to their profitt, houlding this pretext that yong men should frequent the wild women, so that the Christian religion by evil example could not be established. But the time came that they have forsook it themselves. For a while after the Iroquoits came there, the number of seaven hundred, on the snow in the beginning of Spring, where they make a cruell slaughter as the precedent years, where some ghostly fathers or brothers or their servants weare consumed, taken or burnt, as their relation maks mention.

This selfesame yeare they tooke prisoners of 11 or 12,000 of those poore people in a village att [in] sight of the Jesuits' Fort, which had the name Saint, but [from] that houre it might have the name of feare. Heere follows sicknesse, and famine also was gott among these people, flying from all parts to escape the sword. They found a more rude and cruell enemy; for some after being taken gott their lives, but the hunger and their treachery made them kill one another, be it for booty or whatsoever other. None escaped, saving some hundred came to Quebecq to recover their first liberty, but contrary they found their end. So the ffathers left walls, wildernesse, and all open wide to the ennemy and came to Quebecq with the rest of the poore fugitives. They were placed in the wildernesse neere the habitation of Quebecq; but being not a convenient place, they weare putt to the Isle of Orleans, 3 leagues below Quebecq, in a fort that they made with the succour of the ffrench, where they lived some years planting & sowing Indian corne for their nourishment, and greased robes of Castors, of which grease the profit came to the ffathers, the summe of 10,000 livres tournois yearly.

In this place they weare catched when they least thought of it, not without subject of conivance. God knoweth there weare escaped that time about 150 women and some 20 men. The rest are all killed, taken and brought away, of which for the most part weare sett at liberty in the country of their ennemy, where they found a great number of their kindred and relations who lived with all sorte of liberty, and went along with the Iroquois to warre as if they weare natives, in them was no trust to be given, ffor they weare more cruell then the Iroquois even to their proper country, in soe much that the rest resolved to surrender themselves then undergoe the hazard to be taken by force. The peace was made by the instancy of the ffather Jesuits. As before, some weare going there to live, as they have already begun. They seeing our departure & transporting of our goods to Mount Royall for to runne yea the hazard, they also must come. To lett you know [if] our fortune or theirs be better or worse, it should be a hard thing for me to declare; you may judge yourselfe.

Lett us come to our purpose and follow our voyage. Being arrived att the last french habitation, where we must stay above 15 dayes, ffor to pass that place without guide was a thing impossible, but after the time expired, our guides arrived. It was a band of Iroquois that was appointed to fetch us, and conduct us into their country. One day att 10 of the clock in the morning, when we least thought of any, saw severall boats coming from the point of St Louis, directly att the foot of a hill so called some 3 miles from mont Royall. Then rejoycing all to see coming those that they never thought to have seene againe, ffor they promised to come att the beginning of Spring and should arrive 15 dayes before us, but seeing them, every one speakes but of his imbarcation.

The Hurrons that weare present began to make speeches to encourage their wives to make ready with all their stuffe and to feare nothing, being that the heavans would have it so disposed, & that it was better to die in Iroquois Country and peace with their brethren, then stay in the knott of their nativity, that is their country, to be murthered, & better in the Iroquois Country in warre for to be burned. All things so disposed, they prepare themselves to receave the Iroquois, who weare no more then 3,000 in number, [Footnote: "No more than 3,000 in number," meaning, no doubt, that number at Onondaga and its vicinity.] and made a halt for to hold councell to know what they must say that they thought of every one and of the Hurrons. But those Barbars had an other designe, ffor their destiny was to doe, and not to speake; but for to doe this, this must be a treachery in which they are experted. You must know that that bande [of] Irokois [in] descending the last streame or falling watter one of their skiffs made shipwrake in which weare seaven, all drowned without none could souccour them. A thing remarkable, that every one strive to help himselfe without that they will give ayde or assistance to an other; uppon this, that untoward army, those wild barbarous with vengence, held councell, as is before said, for to be revenged of the losse of their Compagnions, where they determined, being that they come to fetch the french and the hurrons, to revenge this uppon them and kill them as soone as they should be in their jurisdiction; but considering after that wee french had a fort in their country with a good strong guard, and that that should cause affairs, it was concluded that there furor should not be discharged but uppon the poore hurrons.

Upon this deliberation they broke councell and arrived att the fort. Their speech was cleare contrary to their designe, and promises inviolably ffriendshipp. There was presents and guifts given of both party, but when they pertooke the death of their Compagnions they must make other presents perhaps that prevailed somewhat in their thoughts, and tourne them from their perfidious undertakings. For often the liberalitie of those savage was seene executed, but the desire brings great booty, and observance causes that covetousnesse will prove deare to the ffrench as to the Hurrons in few days. Presently they procure some boats, ffor the Iroquoits had but eleven and the hurrons none, for they came in the ffrench shallope. So that it must be contrivance for the one and other, which was soone done. In lesse then 8 dayes parted the dwelling we found more then 30 boats, and all very great, we being also so many in company, 80 Iroquoits, some hundred huron women and some 10 or 12 men, 20 ffrench with two ffathers Jesuits. In this manner we departed Mont royall, every one loaded with his burden. Wee passed the same journie. Wee passed the gulfe of St Louis, and made cabbans in the furthermost part of the streame. That day was laborious to us, so much that the Iroquoits resolved to be backe againe, and make a company to fight against the Algonquins of Quebecq. Upon this, 30 left us.

The next day we embarqued though not without confusion, because many weare not content nor satisfied. What a pleasure the two ffathers to see them trott up and downe the rocks to gett their menage into the boat, which with much adoe they gott in. The boats weare so loaden that many could not proceed if bad weather should happen. The journey but small came only to the lake of St Louis, 3 leagues beyond the streame. There the savage threwed the ffathers' bundle on the watter side, and would take no care for them; seeing many of their men gone, the french as well as Hurrons, who would have disputed their lives with them for their lives, and had prevented them if their designe had bin discovered. So that after a great debat we must yeeld to the strongest party for the next embarking.

The ffathers' merchandises weare left behind to oblige the ffrench to stay with it, and seaven of us onely embarqued, one of the ffathers with 6 more, and the rest stayed to bring what was left behind, so that ours weare diminished above 40 men. Wee embarqued indifferently one with another, ffrench, Iroquoits, and Hurrons. After we came to the highest of the Isle of Montroyall; we saw the separation, or rather the great two rivers that of Canada are composed; the one hath its origine from the west and the other from South Southeast. It was the last that wee sayled, coming to the end of that lake, which is 14 or 15 leagues long and 3 in breadth. We must make carriages which are high withall, and the boats by lande because no other way to passe. The trainage is where the watter is not so trepid. We draw the boats loaden after us, and when there is not water enough, every one his bundle by land.

Having proceeded 3 dayes' journey on the river, we entered another lake somewhat bigger; it's called St. francis. This is delightfull to the eye as the formost. I speak not of the goodnesse, for there are many things to be spoaken off. I am satisfied to assure you that it is a delightfull & beautifull country. We wanted nothing to the view passing those skirts, killing staggs, auriniacks & fowles. As for the fish, what a thing it is to see them in the bottom of the watter, & take it biting the hooke or lancing it with lance or cramp iron. In this lake the Hurrons began to suspect the treachery conspirated against them, ffor they observed that the Iroquoits allways consulted privately together, not giving them the least notice, which made a Hurron with 3 men & 2 women goe away & run away to the ffrench of Quebecq; & for this intent one very morning, after being imbarqued as the rest, went in to the midle of the river, where they began to sing & take their leave, to the great astonishment of the rest & to the great discontent of the Iroquoits, that saw themselves so frustrated of so much booty that they exspected. But yett they made no signe att the present, but lett them goe without trouble for feare the rest would doe the same, & so be deprived of the conspiracy layde for the death of their compagnions. To that purpose knowing the place where they weare to land, which was in an island in the midle of the river, a league long & a quarter broade, they resolved to murder them in the said place, which was promptly executed in this maner following:—

They embarqued both hurron men and women in their boats, and among them made up som 20 that embarked themselves in 2 of their boats, in a posture as if they should goe to the warrs, & went before the breake of day. We weare but 7 frenchmen, & they put us 7 [in] several boats. I find meselfe with 3 Iroquoits & one Hurron man. Coming within sight of the Isle where they weare to play their game, one of the Iroquoits in the same boate as I landed, takes his gunne & charges it. The hurron and I saw this, but neither dreamed of the tragedy that was att hand. After goes into the woode, & the Iroquois that governed the boat takes up a hattchett & knocks downe the poore hurron, that never thought to be so ended, and the other that charged his musket in the wood shoots him and fell downe uppon my heels. My feet soone swims in the miserable hurron's bloode. He did quiver as if he had an ague, and was wounded with great many wounds, that still they doubled. Both Iroquoits came to me and bid [me have] courage, ffor they would not hurt me; but [as] for him that was killed, he was a dogg, good for nothing. The small knowledge that I have had of their speech made of a better hope; but one that could not have understood them would have ben certainly in a great terror. This murder could not be committed so but that the rest of the boats should heare it, and therefore in that very time we heard sad moans and cryes horidly by hurron women. They threwed the corps immediately into the water and went the other side of the river into the abovesaid isle. Being landed together, the poore women went in a flock like sheep that sees the wolves ready to devour them. There were 8 hurron men that tooke theire armes. The Iroquoits not hindering them in the least, but contrarily the Captayne of the Iroquoits appeared to defend their cause, giving sharp apprehensions to those that held up armes, and so farr that he did beat those that offered to hurt them.

In this example you may perceive the dissimulation & vengence of this cursed people. So that the Company, reassured in some respects, the affrighted company, made them goe up to the toppe of the hill and there errect cottages some 40 paces from them; during the while I walked on the side where they weare hard at work and firmly believed that the poore hurron was killed by the Iroquoit out of malice, so much trust I putt in the traiterous words. As I was directly coming where the hurrons weare, what should I see? A band of Iroquoits all daubed, rushing out of a wood all painted, which is the signe of warre. I thought they weare those that I have seene in [the] morning before, as effectually they weare. I came to the place where weare all those poore victims. There was the good ffather comforting the poore innocent women. The chief of them satt by a valliant huron who all his life time killed many Iroquoits, and by his vallour acquired the name of great Captayne att home and abroad. The Iroquoit spake to him, as the ffather told us, and as I myself have heard. "Brother, cheare up," says he, "and assure yourselfe you shall not be killed by doggs; thou art both man and captayne, as I myselfe am, and will die in thy defence." And as the afforesaid crew shewed such a horrid noise, of a sudaine the captayne tooke hold of the chaine that was about him, thou shalt not be killed by another hand then by mine. Att that instant the cruell Iroquoits fell upon those hurrons, as many wolves, with hattchetts, swords, and daggers, & killed as many [as] there weare, save onely one man. That hurron captayne seeing himselfe so basly betrayed, he tooke hold of his hattchett that hunged downe his side, and strook downe a Iroquoit; but the infinit deale tooke his courage and life away. This that was saved was an old man, who in his time had ben att the defeat and taking of severall Iroquoits. He in authority by his means saved some. This news brought to them and his name as benefactor, which deed then saved his life. Heere you see a good example, that it is decent to be good to his Ennemy.

After this was done & their corps throwne into the watter, the women weare brought together. I admired att them, seeing them in such a deepe silence, looking on the ground with their coverletts uppon their heads, not a sigh heard, where a litle before they made such a lamentable noise for the losse of their companyion that was killed in my boate. Some 2 howers all was pacified & the kettle almost ready for [to] goe to worke. In this very moment there calls a councell. The ffather was called as a statsman to that councell, where he hears their wild reasons; that what they had done was in reveng of their deare comrades that weare drowned in coming for them, and also to certifie the ffrench of their good will. So done, the meate was dressed, we weare invited. The ffather comes to take his dish, and finds us all 5 in armes, resolving to die valiently, thinking the councell was called to conclud our death as the Hurron's. The 6th was not able to menage armes, being a litle boy. The ffather gave us a brother of his company who had invincible good looke and a stout heart. We waited onely for his shooting. The ffather could not persuade him to draw. We told him if he would not fight, to leave our company; which perceived by the Iroquoits, made them looke to themselves. They came & assured us of their good will. The 4 frenchmen that understood not longed for the schermish & die for it. Att last the ffather prevailed with us, & tould us what was done in Councell. Two Iroquoits came to us with weapons, who signifies there is nothing layd against you, & commanded their compagnions to put by their armes, that they weare our brethren. The agreement was made. Some went to the feast, some stayed. Having eaten, the ffather calls them againe to councell, & for that purpose borrows some porcelaine from the captayne to make 3 guifts.

All being together the ffather begins his speech, throwing the first guift into the midle of the place, desiring that it might be accepted for the conservation of the ffriendshipe that had ben long between them and us, and so was accepted with a ho, ho, which is an assurance & a promise, as thanks. The 2nd was for the lives of the women which weare in their hands, & to conduct them with saftie into their country, which was accepted in like manner. The 3rd was to encourage them to bring us to their owne country & carry our Marchandises in such [manner] that they may not be wett, nor leave them behind, which was, as abovesaid, punctually observed.

The councell being ended, the captaynes made speeches to encourage the masters of the boats to take a bundle to his care & charge, & give an account of it in the country. I wish the lotts weare so distributed before we came from mont royall, but that it is the miserable comfort, better late then never. Att night every one to his cabben, and the women dispersed into every cabban with their children, which was a sight of compassion. The day following being the 8th day of our departure, some went a hunting, some stayed att home. The next day to that we embarqued all a sunder, a boat for each. I was more chearfull then the rest, because I knewed a litle of their language, and many saw me in the low country. Wherefore [they] made me embarque with a yong man, taller & properer then myselfe. We had paines and toyles enough; especially my sperit was grieved, and have souffred much troubles 6 weeks together. I thought we should come to our journey's end & so help one another by things past; ffor a man is glad to drive away the time by honest, ingenuous discours, and I would rejoyce very much to be allwayes in company uppon my journey. It was contrary to me all the voyage, ffor my boat and an other, wherein weare 2 men & a woman Iroquoit, stayed behind without seeing or hearing from one another. I leave with you to think if they weare troubled for me or I for them. There was a great alteration a litle before; a whole fleete of boats, now to be reduced [to] 2 onely. But patience perforce.

We wandered on that gay river by the means of high and low gulfs that are in it; ffor since I made reflection of the quantity of water that comes in that river that comes from off the top of the high mountains with such a torrent that it causes a mighty noise which would make the bouldest men afraid. We went on some journeys with a deale of paines and labour becaus for our weeknesse, and moreover a man of the other boat fell sick of the ague, soe that one of us must helpe him either in the carriag or drawing the boat; and, which was wors, my compagnion was childish and yong as I. The long familiarity we had with one another breeded contempt, so that we would take nothing from one another, which made us goe together by the ears, and fought very often till we weare covered in blood. The rest tooke delight to see us fight; but when they saw us take either gun or sword, then came they to putt us a sunder. When we weare in the boat we could not fight but with our tongues, flying water att one another. I believe if the fathers' packet had ben there, the guift could not keepe it from wetting. As for meat we wanted none, and we had store of large staggs along the watter side. We killed some almost every day, more for sport then for neede. We finding them sometimes in islands, made them goe into the watter and after we killed about a score, we clipped the ears of the rest and hung a bell to it, and then let them loose. What a sporte to see the rest flye from that that had the bell!

As I satt with my compagnion I saw once of an evening a very remarquable thing. There comes out of a vast forest a multitud of bears, 300 att least together, making a horrid noise, breaking small trees, throwing the rocks downe by the watter side. We shot att them but [they] stirred not a step, which frightned us that they slighted our shooting. We knewed not whether we killed any or no, because of the darke, neither dare we venter to see. The wild men tould me that they never heard their father speake of so many together.

We went to the other side to make cabbans, where being arrived, where we made fire & put the kettle on. When it was ready we eat our belly full. After supper the sick wild man tould me a story and confirmed it to be true, which happened to him, being in warre in the upper Country of the Iroquoits neere the great river that divides it self in two. "Brother," says he, "it's a thing to be admired to goe afar to travell. You must know, although I am sick I am [a] man, and fought stoutly and invaded many. I loved alwayes the ffrench for their goodnesse, but they should [have] given us [to] kill the Algonkins. We should not warre against the ffrench, but traited with them for our castors. You shall know I am above 50 years (yett the fellow did not looke as if he had 40). I was once a Captayne," says he, "of 13 men, against the nation of the fire & against the Stairing hairs, our Ennemys. We stayed 3 whole winters from our country, and most of that time among our ennemy, but durst not appeare because of the small number we had against a multitude, which made us march in the night and hide ourselves in the daytime in forests. Att last we are weary to be so long absent from our wives & countrey. We resolved some more execution, & take the first nation that we should incountre. We have allready killed many. We went some dayes on that river, which is bordered of fine sands; no rocks there to be seene. Being landed one morning to goe out of the way least we should be discovered, and for [to] know the place that we weare, sent two of our men to make a discovery, who coming back brought us [word] that they have seen devils, and could not believe that they weare men. We presently putt ourselves on our gards, and looke to our armes, thought to have ben lost, but tooke a strong resolution to die like men, and went to meet those monsters. We weare close to one an other, saveing they that made a discovery, that went just before us, tould us, being neere the waterside, that they have seene afar off (as they thought) a great heape of stoanes. We needing them mightily we went to gett some. Within 200 paces nigh we found them converted into men, who weare of an extraordinary height, lying all along the strand asleepe. Brother, you must know that we weare all in feare to see Such a man and woman of a vast length. They weare by two feete taller then I, and big accordingly. They had by them two basquetts, a bow and arrows. I came nigh the place. Their arrows weare not so long as ours, but bigger, and their bows the same; each had a small stagg's skin to cover their nakednesse. They have noe winter in their country. After being gone we held a councell to consider what was to be done. We weare two boats; the one did carry 8 men, the other 5. That of 8 would goe back againe, but that of 5 would goe forward into another river. So we departed. The night being come, as precedent nights, we saw fires in severall places on the other side of the river, which made us goe there att the breake of day, to know what it was, which was men as tall as the other man and woman, and great many of them together a fishing. We stealed away without any noise and resolved not to stay longer in them parts, where every thing was so bigg. The fruits of trees are as bigg as the heart of an horiniac, which is bigger then that of an oxe.

"The day after our retourne, being in cottages covered with bushes, we heard a noise in the wood, which made us speedily take our weopens, every one hiding himselfe behind a tree the better to defend himselfe, but perceaved it was a beast like a Dutch horse, that had a long & straight horne in the forehead, & came towards us. We shott twice at him; [he] falls downe on the ground, but on a sudaine starts up againe and runs full boot att us; and as we weare behind the trees, thrusts her home very farr into the tree, & so broak it, and died. We would eat non of her flesh, because the flemings eat not their horses' flesh, but tooke off the skin, which proved heavy, so we left it there. Her horne 5 feet long, and bigger then the biggest part of an arme." [Footnote: In O'Callaghan's Documentary History of New York, Vol. IV. p. 77, 1851, is given an engraving of this animal, with the title, "Wild Animals of New Netherlands," taken from a Dutch work published in

Amsterdam in 1671. In this work it is thus described: "On the borders of Canada animals are now and again seen somewhat resembling a horse; they have cloven hoofs, shaggy manes, a horn right out of the forehead, a tail like that of the wild hog, black eyes, a stag's neck, and love the gloomiest wildernesses, are shy of each other. So that the male never feeds with the female except when they associate for the purpose of increase. Then they lay aside their ferocity. As soon as the rutting season is past, they again not only become wild but even attack their own."]

We still proceeded in our journey. In 7 dayes we overtook the boat that left us. Now whether it was an unicorne, or a fibbe made by that wild man, yet I cannot tell, but severall others tould me the same, who have seene severall times the same beast, so that I firmly believe it. So his story ended, which lasted a great while; ffor having an excellent memory, tould me all the circumstances of his rencounters.

We [went] from thence the next morning. We came to a beatifull river, wide one league and a halfe, which was not violent nor deepe, soe that we made no carriages for 15 or 20 leagues, where we had the view of eagles and other birds taking fishes, which we ourselves have done, & killed salmons with staves. One of my compagnions landed a sturgeon six fadoms deepe and brought it. Going along the woodside we came where a greate many trees weare cutt, as it weare intended for a fort. At the end of it there was a tree left standing, but the rind taken away from it. Upon it there was painted with a coale 6 men hanged, with their heads at their feete, cutt off. They weare so well drawen, that the one of them was father by the shortnesse of his haire, which lett us know that the french that was before us weare executed. A litle further an other was painted of 2 boats, one of 3 men, an other of 2, whereof one was standing with a hattchett in his hands striking on the head.

Att an other weare represented 7 boats, pursueing 3 bears, a man drawn as if he weare on land with his gune shooting a stagge. I considering these things, troubled me very much, yea, caused my heart to tremble within me; and moreover when those that weare with me certified me of what I was too sure, telling me the 6 ffrenchmen weare dead, but tould me to be cheerfull, that I should not die. After I found so much treachery in them I could but trust litle in their words or promises, yett must shew good countenance to a wors game then I had a minde, telling me the contrary of what they told me of the death of the frenchmen, to shew them that I was in no feare.

Being embarqued, the wild men tould me we should goe on the other side of that broad river. It was extreamly hott, no wind stiring. I was ready that both should be together for the better assurance of my life. I perceived well that he alone was not able to performe the voyage; there was the other sick of the other boat, that did row but very slowly. I thought to meselfe they must needs bring me into their countrey if they meet non by the way, and so I comforted meselfe with better hope. We soone came to the other side of the river. The other boat followed not, being nigh the land. My comrade perceaved an eagle on a tree, the feathers of which are in esteeme among them. He lands and takes his gunne, charges it, and goes into the wood. I was in feare, without blame, for I knewed not what he meant. I remembered how the poore Hurron was served so a litle before in his boat, and in like manner. As he went about, I could not imagine what was best, but resolved to kill [rather] then be killed. Upon this I take my gunne, which the other saw, desires me not to make any noise, shewing me the eagle, that as yett I have not seene. To obey him I stoope downe like a monkey, visiting my weapon that he should not suspect. My eyes neverthelesse followed for feare. I see at last the truth of his designe; he shoots and kills the eagle.

[We] after imbarqued ourselves, the night drawing on, and must think to goe to the other boat or he to us, which he did. I admired the weather, cleare and calme that we could scarce see him, yet that we should heare them speake, and understand, as if they weare but 20 or 30 paces from us. He being come, we sought for conveniency to make cottages, which soone was done. The others sooner landed then we. They came to receive us att our landing. One tooke my gunne, the other a litle bondle of mine. I was surprised att this. Then they asked me [for] my powder and shott, and opened my bagge, began to partage my combs & other things that I had. I thought it the consultest way to submit to the strongest party, therefore I tooke [no] notice of what they did. The woman kindled the fire. Seeing myselfe out of care of my fright, satt me selfe downe by the woman. Shee looked now and then uppon me, which made me more and more mistrust. In the meane while he that was sick calls me. I came and asked him what he pleased. "I will," sayd he, "that you imbarque your selfe by me," and throws his cappot away, bidding me also to leave my capot. He takes his hattchett, and hangs it to his wrest, goes into the boat, & I with him. I would have carryed my gunne. I tooke it from the place where they layd it. They, seeing, laughed & gave a shout, as many beasts, yett it was not in their power to make me goe to the boat without my weapon; so lett me have it, and went straight as if we weare to goe on the other side of the river. About the midle the wild man bids mee goe out, to which I would not consent. I bid him goe. After we disputed awhile, I not obeying, began to consider if he had a minde to drowne me, that he himselfe would not go in the water. Being come a litle to myselfe I perceaved that the water was not 2 foote deepe. It was so darke, yett one might perceive the bottom covered with muskles. Having so much experience, I desired him to have patience; so gott of my shirt & lep't into the watter & gathered about half a bushell of those shells or mussells. I made sure that the boat should not leave me, for I fastened my girdle to it, and held the end. Mistrust is the mother of safety. We came back againe. We found the kettle ready; they gave me meat and a dish of broth, which exercised me a while. Having done, the man comes and makes me pull of my shirt, having then nothing but my drawers to cover my nackednesse. He putts on my shirt on his back, takes a knif and cutts a medail that hung to my necke. He was a great while searching me and feeling if I was fatt. I wished him farr enough. I looked [for] an opportunity to be from him, thinking to be better sheltered by the woman. I thought every foot he was to cutt my troat. I could [not] beare [it]. I had rather dye [at] once then being so often tormented. I rose and satt me downe by the woman, in whome was all my trust. Shee perceived I was in great feare, whether by collour of my face or other, I know not. Shee putts her hands uppon my head & combs it downe with her fingers. "My son," says shee, "be chearfull. It is my husband; he will not hurt thee; he loves me and knoweth that I love thee, and have a mind to have thee to our dwelling." Then shee rose and takes my shirt from her husband and brings it me. Shee gave me one of her covers. "Sleepe," said shee. I wanted not many persuasions. So chuse rather the fatall blow sleeping then awake, for I thought never to escape.

The next morning I finding meselfe freed, which made me hope for the future. I have reason to remember that day for two contrary things; first, for my spirits being very much perplexed, and the other for that the weather was contrary though very lovely. That morning they rendered all my things againe, & filled my bagge with victualls. We left this place, which feared me most then hurt was done. Some laughed att me afterwards for my feares wherein I was, which I more & more hoped for better intertainment. The weather was fair all that day, but the next wee must make a waynage, which [was] not very hard; but my comrade drew carelessly, and the boat slipps from his hands, which turned with such force that it had me along if I had not lett my hould goe, chusing [rather] that then venter my selfe in danger. Soe that it [no] sooner gott downe then we gott it up againe; but by fortune was not hurted, yett it runn'd aground among rocks. We must goe downe the river. I was driven to swime to it, where I found it full of watter, and a hole that 2 fists might goe through it, so that I could not drive it to land without mending it. My compagnion must also in the water like a watter dogg, comes and takes hould of the foure oares. All the wild men swims like watter doggs, not as we swime. We mende the boat there neatly, not without miscalling one another. They spoake to me a word that I understood not because of the difference betweene the low Iroquoits and their speech, and in the anger and heat we layde the blame upon one another to have lett the boat flippe purposely. I tooke no heed of what he alleadged. He comes sudainly uppon me & there cuffed one another untill we weare all in bloode. Being weary, att last, out of breath, we gave over like 2 cocks over tyred with fighting. We could not fight longer, but must find strength to draw up the boat against the streame and overtake the other, which was a good way from us. It was impossible to overtake the day, nor the next. So that we must lay 3 nights by our selves.

The third day we arrived to a vast place full of Isls, which are called the Isles of Toniata, where we overtooke our compagnions, who stayd for us. There they killed a great bigg and fatt beare. We tooke some of it into our boats & went on our journey together. We came thence to a place like a bazon, made out of an Isle like a halfe moone. Here we caught eeles five fadoms or more deepe in the waiter, seeing cleerly the bottome in abundance of fishes. We finde there 9 low country Iroquoits in their cabbans that came back from the warre that was against the nation of the Catts. They had with them 2 women with a young man of 25 years & a girle of 6 years, all prisoners. They had a head with short haire of one of that nation, that uses to have their hair turned up like the prickles of an headg hogge. We cottaged ourselves by them. Some of them knewed me & made much of mee. They gave me a guirland of porcelaine & a girdle of goat's haire. They asked when should I visit my ffriends. I promissed to come there as soone as I could arrive att the upper village. I gave them my hattchett to give to my ffather, and 2 dozen of brass rings & 2 shooting-knives for my sisters, promissing to bring a cover for my mother. They inquired what was it that made me goe away, and how. I tould them through woods & arrived att the 3 rivers in 12 dayes, and that I souffred much hunger by the way. I would not tell them that I escaped by reason of the Duch. They called me often Devill to have undertaken such a task. I resolved to goe along with them. Heere I found certainty, and not till then, of the 6 ffrenchmen, whom they have seene seaven dayes before att the coming in of the great Lake D'ontario; and that undoubtedly the markes we have seene on the trees weare done by seaven other boats of their owne nation that came backe from the warres in the north, that mett 2 hurron boats of 8 men, who fought & killed 3 Iroquoits and wounded others. Of the hurrons 6 weare slained, one taken alive, and the other escaped. Those 2 boats weare going to the ffrench to live there. That news satisfied much my wild men, and much more I rejoiced at this. We stayed with them the next day, feasting one another. They cutt and burned the fingers of those miserable wretches, making them sing while they plucked out some of their nailes, which done, wee parted well satisfied for our meeting. From that place we came to lye att the mouth of a lake in an island where we have had some tokens of our frenchmen by the impression of their shooes on the sand that was in the island. In that island our wild men hid 10 caskes of Indian Corne, which did us a kindnesse, ffor there was no more veneson pye to be gotten.

The next day we make up our bundles in readinesse to wander uppon that sweet sea, as is the saying of the Iroquoits, who rekens by their daye's journey. This was above 100 leagues in length & 30 in breadth. Seeing the water so calme and faire, we ventured some 3 leagues, to gaine a point of the firme land, that by that means we should shorten 7 or 8 leagues in our way. We went on along the lake in that maner with great delight, sometimes with paine and labour. As we went along the water side, the weather very faire, it comes to my mind to put out a cover instead of a saile. My companion liked it very well, for generally wild men are given to leasinesse. We seeing that our sayle made us goe faster then the other boat, not perceiving that the wind came from the land, which carried us far into the lake, our compagnions made a signe, having more experience then wee, and judged of the weather that was to come. We would not heare them, thinking to have an advantage.

Soone after the wind began to blow harder, made us soone strike sayle, and putt our armes to worke. We feeled not the wind because it was in our backs, but turning aside we finde that we had enough to doe. We must gett ourselves to a better element then that [where] we weare. Instantly comes a shower of raine with a storme of winde that was able to perish us by reason of the great quantity of watter that came into our boat. The lake began to vapour and make a show of his neptune's sheep. Seeing we went backwards rather then forwards, we thought ourselves uterly lost. That rogue that was with me sayd, "See thy God that thou sayest he is above. Will you make me believe now that he is good, as the black-coats [the ffather Jesuits] say? They doe lie, and you see the contrary; ffor first you see that the sun burns us often, the raine wetts us, the wind makes us have shipwrake, the thundering, the lightnings burns and kills, and all come from above, and you say that it's good to be there. For my part I will not goe there. Contrary they say that the reprobats and guilty goeth downe & burne. They are mistaken; all is goode heare. Doe not you see the earth that nourishes all living creatures, the water the fishes, and the yus, and that corne and all other seasonable fruits for our foode, which things are not soe contrary to us as that from above?" As he said so he coursed vehemently after his owne maner. He tooke his instruments & shewed them to the heavens, saying, "I will not be above; here will [I] stay on earth, where all my friends are, and not with the french, that are to be burned above with torments." How should one think to escape this torments and storms, but God who through his tender mercy ceas'd the tempest and gave us strength to row till we came to the side of the water? I may call it a mighty storme by reason of the litlenesse of the boat, that are all in watter to the breadth of 5 fingers or lesse. I thought uppon it, and out of distress made a vertue to seeke the means to save ourselves. We tyed a sack full of corne in the fore end of our boat, & threw it into the watter, which hung downe some foure fathoms, and wee putt our selves in the other end, so that the end that was towards the wind was higher then the other, and by that means escaped the waves that without doubt, if we had not used that means, we had sunk'd. The other boat landed to lett that storme [pass] over. We found them in the even att their cottages, and thought impossible for us to escape.

After severall dayes' travell we came to an isle where we made cottages. We went so farre that evening that we might be so much the neerer to take a broader passage which should shorten our voyage above 20 leagues. Att night wee saw severall fires uppon the land. We all judged that it was our company that went before us. Before brake of day we did what we could to overtake them, not without hazard, by reason the winds that blewed hard, which we could not perceive before. Being come to the bay of the isle we could not turne back without greater danger, so resolved to proceede. We came to the very place where we saw the fires, & found that we weare not mistaken in our opinions. By good looke they weare there, else we had perished for all being so neere the land, for the lake swelled by reason of the great wind that blew, which stayed them there above 14 nights. Neither for this reason was there any landing, because of a great banck or heape of rocks, untill those that weare ashore came to us into the watter to their oxtars [Footnote: Oxtars, up to their armpits.] and stoped our boats. We then cast our selves and all that we had overboord, leaving our boats there, which weare immediately in thousands [of] peaces.

Being arrived, we placed our cottages by a most pleasant delicat river, where for delightfullnesse was what man's heart could wish. There weare woods, forests, meddows. There we stayed 3 dayes by reason of the weather. One night I layd neare a faire comely lasse that was with us. There they take no notice, for they live in so great liberty that they are never jealous one of another. I admired of a sudaine to heare new musick. Shee was in travell and immediately delivered. I awaked all astonished to see her drying her child by the fire side. Having done, [she] lapt the child in her bosome and went to bed as if that had ben nothing, without moan or cry, as doe our Europian women. Before we left the place that babe died. I had great mind to baptize him, but feared least they should accuse me to be the cause of his death.

Being come to the above named place, where weare the ghostly ffathers with 8 other french, 3 came to meet us from the fort, which weare but 30 leagues off, where I have receaved a censure for being so timidous, [in] not dareing to ffling watter on the head of that poore innocent to make him happy. We frenchmen began to tell our adventures, having ben out of hopes of ever to see one another, being exceeding glad that we weare deceaved in our opinions. Some leaves us & went by land to their cabbans. The rest stayes for faire weather to come to our journey's ende. We wanted not slaves from that place to carry our packs. We came into a river towards the fort which was dangerous for its swiftnesse. From that river that brought us within 30 leagues of the lake we came into a narrower river from a small lake where a french fort was built. This river was 2 leagues long & the lake 5 in compasse. About it a most pleasant country, very fruitfull. Goeing up that same river we meet 2 french that weare fishing a kind of fish called dab, which is excellent, & have done us great kindnesse, having left no more provision then what we needed much.

Having come to the landing place att the foot of the fort, we found there a most faire castle very neatly built, 2 great & 2 small ones. The bottom was built with great trees & well tyed in the topp with twiggs of ashure, strengthened with two strong walles & 2 bastions, which made the fort imppregnable of the wild men. There was also a fine fall of woods about it. The french corne grewed there exceeding well, where was as much as covered half a league of land. The country smooth like a boord, a matter of some 3 or 4 leagues about. Severall fields of all sides of Indian corne, severall of french tournaps, full of chestnutts and oakes of accorns, with thousand such like fruit in abundance. A great company of hoggs so fatt that they weare not able to goe. A plenty of all sortes of fowles. The ringdoves in such a number that in a nett 15 or 1600 att once might be taken.

So this was not a wild country to our imagination, but plentyfull in every thing.

We weare humanly receaved by the Reverend ffathers Jesuits and some other 40 frenchmen, as well domestiques as volontiers. We prepared ourselves to take the country's recreation, some to hunt, some to fish, but prevented by a feaver that seised on us all. Some continued a month, some more and some lesse, which is the tribut that one must pay for the changment of climat.

Some dayes after we had news that another company of Iroquoits weare arrived att mont Royall. As soone [as] we went from thence the father & the rest of the ffrench that did stay behind did imbark themselves with them and followed us so close that ere long would be at us. As they went up to make cottages in the island of the massacre, which was 16 dayes before our departure, one of the company goes to shute for his pleasure, finds a woman half starved for hunger, lying on a rock by a water. He brings her to the cottages & made so much by giving her some luckwarme water, which he boyled with flower & grease, that she came to herselfe entirely againe. Shee was examined. Shee told them what is above said, and when it happened. Shee hid her selfe in a rotten tree during the slaughter, where shee remained 3 dayes; after we weare gone shee came foorth for to gett some food, and found nothing, but founde onely some small grapes, of roots the 3 first dayes, & nothing else. Shee finding her selfe feeble and weake, not able to sustaine such, resolved for death. The father, knowing her to be a Christian, had a singular care for her, & brought her where I overtooke the said father with the 8 french. Being brought [she] was frightened againe for seeing a man charging his gunne to kill her, as shee said, so went away that night, & non knowes what became of her. Being weake, not thoroughly healed, shee fancied that such a thing might be done. By this, we poore, many have recovered. The father arrives, that affirmes this newes to us, being very sorry for the losse of this poore creature that God has so long preserved without any subsistance, which shews us apparently that wee ought not to despaire, & that keeps those that lives in his feare. We went to meete the father, I meane those that weare able, to bid the father welcome & his company. Being come safe & in a good disposition together, we rendered God thanks.

There weare many that waited for us, desiring to tourne back againe to Quebecq, obtaining their desier from the fathers & the governour of the fort. They weare 13 in number & one father. After 6 weeks end we recovered our health. So we went to bring them a part of the way, some to the water side, some to the laksende, where we tooke of one another farewell, with such ceremonys as are used when friends depart. Some dayes after we heare that the poore woman was in the woods; not that shee knew'd which way to tourne, but did follow her owne fancy whersoever it lead her, & so wandered 6 dayes, getting some times for her subsistance wild garlick, yong buds of trees, & roots. Shee was seene in an evening by a river, whereby shee was for 3 dayes, by 3 hurrons renegades. They tooke her, but in a sad condition. They not considering that shee was of their owne nation, stript her. It is the custom to strip whomsoever is lost in the woods. They brought her to the village, where the father was that brought her from the place of murdering to that place whence shee runned away the second time. This father, knowing her, brings her to our fort, that we might see her as a thing incredible but by the mercy of God. I was in the village with the father and with another frenchman, where we see the crudest thing in nature acted. Those Iroquoits that came along the river with us, some weare about fishing, some a hunting, they seeing this woman makes her [their] slave.

One day a man or theirs was forwearned for his insolency, for not referring to the Governor, doing all out of his owne head. [He him] selfe was to come that day, leading 2 women with their 2 children, he not intending to give an account of anything but by his owne authority. The elders, heering this, goes and meets him some 50 paces out of the village for to maintain their rights. They stayed this man. What weare those beasts? He answered they weare his; he no sooner had spoaken, but one old man spoak to him thus: "Nephew, you must know that all slaves, as well men as women, are first brought before the Councell, and we alone can dispose [of] them." So said, & turned to the other side, and gave a signe to some soldiers that they brought for that purpose, to knock those beasts in the head, who executed their office & murdered the women. One tooke the child, sett foot on his head, taking his leggs in his hands, wrought the head, by often turning, from off the body. An other souldier tooke the other child from his mother's brest, that was not yett quite dead, by the feete and knocks his head against the trunck of a tree. This [is] a daily exercise with them, nor can I tell the one half of their cruelties in like sortes. Those with many others weare executed, some for not being able to serve, and the children for hindering their mothers to worke. So they reckne a trouble to lett them live. O wicked and barbarious inhumanity! I forgott to tell that the day the woman layed in, some houres before, shee and I roasted some Indian Corn in the fire: being ready, shee pulled out the grains one by one with a stick, and as shee was so doing, shee made a horrid outcry, shewing me a toad, which was in the breadth of a dish, which was in the midle of the redd ashes striving to gett out. We wondered, for the like was never seene before. After he gott out of the fire we threwed stoanes & staves att him till it was killed. That toad lived 2 dayes in or under the fire.

Having remained in that village 6 dayes, we have seene horrible cruelties committed. Three of us resolved to turne back to our fort, which was 5 miles off. We brought above 100 women, hurron slaves & others, all loadened with corne. We weare allwayes in scarcity for pollicy, though we had enough, ffor certainty is farre better then the incertainry. Before we departed this base place we received [news] that the hurron who was saved by the consent of the rest in the Isle of Massacre, as is above said, 2 dayes after his deliverance run'd away by night towards the lower country of the Iroquoits, where he arrived safe, not without sufferings in the way, ffor such long voyages cannot be performed otherwise, having gon through vast forests, finding no inn in the way, neither having the least provision. Att his coming there he spoake whatever the reveng, wrath, and indignation could provoke or utter against the ffrench, especially against the ffathers, saying that it was they that have sold and betrayed them; and that he would bestow the same uppon them if ever he should meet with them. As for him, he gave heaven thanks that he was yett living; that he had his life saved by them to whome he would render like service, warning them not to lett the french build a fort, as the upper Iroquoits had done; that he could tell them of it by experience; that they should remember the nation of the Stagges so bigg. As soone as the french came there, nothing but death and slaughter was expected, having caused their death by sorcery, which brought a strange sicknesse amongst them. Such things can prevaile much uppon such a wild, credulous nation; their minds alltogether for the warrs in which they delight most of any thing in the world. We came our way; this news troubled us very much, knowing the litle fidelity that is [in] that wild nation, that have neither faith nor religion, neither law nor absolut government, as we shall heare the effects of it.

The autumn scarce began but we heare that the lower Iroquoits contrived a treason against the ffrench. So having contrived & discovered that they weare resolved to leavy an armie of 500 men of their owne nation, who are esteemed the best souldiers, having the Anojot to assist them; a bold, rash nation, and so thought to surprise the inhabitants of that place. As they weare contriving and consequently seased upon the fort and towne, thinking to execute their plot with ease, because of their assurance, trusting (if contrary to their contrivance) to the peace, saying that the ffrench weare as many hoggs layed up to be fatted in their country. But, O liberality, what strength hast thou! thou art the onely means wherby men know all and pierce the hearts of the most wild & barbarous people of the world. Hearing such news, we make friends by store of guifts, yea such guifts that weare able to betray their country. What is that, that interrest will not do? We discover dayly new contryvances of treason by a Councellor. There is nothing done or said but we have advice of it. Their dayly exercise is feasting, of warrs, songs, throwing of hattchetts, breaking kettles. What can we do? We are in their hands. It's hard to gett away from them. Yea, as much as a ship in full sea without pilot, as passengers without skill. We must resolve to be uppon our guard, being in the midle of our Ennemy. For this purpose we begin to make provisions for the future end. We are tould that a company of the Aniot nation volontiers was allready in their march to breake heads & so declare open warres. This company finds enough to doe att Mount Royall; ffor the ffrench being carelesse of themselves, working incomparably afarre from their fortifications without the least apprehension. They killed 2 french and brought them away in triumph, their heads sett up for a signe of warrs. We seeing no other remedy but must be gon and leave a delightful country. The onely thing that we wanted most was that wee had no boats to carry our bagage. It's sad to tend from such a place that is compassed with those great lakes that compose that Empire that can be named the greatest part of the knowne world. Att last they contrived some deale boords to make shipps with large bottoms, which was the cause of our destruction sooner then was expected.

You have heard above said how the ffathers inhabited the hurron country to instruct them in Christian doctrine. They preach the mighty power of the Almighty, who had drowned the world for to punish the wicked, saving onely our father Noe with his familie was saved in an arke. One came bringing Indian corne, named Jaluck, who escaped the shipwrake that his countrymen had gone, being slave among us. He received such instructions of those deale boords, & reflected soundly upon the structure that he thought verily they weare to make an other arke to escape their hands, and by our inventions cause all the rest to be drowned by a second deluge. They imputing so much power to us, as Noe had that grace from God, thought that God at least commanded us so to doe. All frightened [he] runns to his village. This comes back makes them all afraid. Each talkes of it. The elders gathered together to consult what was to be done. In their councell [it] was concluded that our fort should be visited, that our fathers should be examined, & according to their answers deliberation should be taken to preserve both their life and countrey. We had allwayes spyes of our side, which weare out of zele and obedience. The ffathers Jesuits and others voluntarily ventured their lives for the preservation of the common liberty. They remaine in the village of those barbars to spie what their intent should be, houlding correspondence with some of those of the councell by giving them guifts, to the end that we might know what was concluded in the Councell & give us advise with all speede. We by these means had intelligence that they weare to come & visit our forts.

To take away all suspicion of our innocency from thinking to build any shipp, which if it had come to their knowledge had don a great prejudice to our former designe, a shippe then uppon the docke almost finished. Heere we made a double floore in the hall where the shippe was abuilding, so that the wild men, being ignorant of our way of building, could not take any notice of our cuningnesse, which proved to our desire. So done, finding nothing that was reported, all began to be quiet and out of feare. By this we weare warned from thencefoorth, mistrusting all that came there, so preserved ourselves, puting nothing in fight that should give the least suspition. Both shipps weare accomplished; we kept them secretly & covered them with 12 boats of rind that we kept for fishing and hunting. The wildmen knewed of these small things, but suspected nothing, believing that the french would never suspect to venture such a voyage for the difficultie of the way and violence of the swiftnesse of the rivers and length of the way. We stayed for opportunity in some quietnesse, devising to contrive our game as soone as the spring should begin. The winter we past not without apprehensions, having had severall allarmes, false as [well] as true; for often weare we putt to our armes, in so much that one of our sentryes was once by force drawen from the doore of the fort. He, to avoid the danger, drawes his sword & wounds one of them & comes to the fort, crying, "To your armes." This was soone appeased; some guifts healed the wound.

The season drawing nigh we must think of some stratageme to escape their hands and the rest of ours that weare among them; which was a difficulty, because they would have some of us by them allwaye for the better assurance. But all their contrivances & wit weare too weake to strive against our plotts which weare already invented to their deceipt that would deceave us. We lett them understand that the time drew neere that the french uses to trait their friends in feasting and meriment, and all should be welcome, having no greater ffriends then they weare. They, to see our fashions as well as to fill their gutts, gave consent. By that means the considerablest persons are invited, the ffather & 2 ffrench. There they weare made much of 2 dayes with great joy, with sounds of trompetts, drumms, and flageoletts, with songs in french as wild. So done, they are sent away, the ffather with them. He was not a mile off but fains to gett a falle and sighed that his arme was broken. The wild men being much troubled att this accident brings the father back and makes guifts that he may be cured. A plaster was sett to his arme, which done [he is] putt into a bed. Then all the wildmen came to see him; he incouraged them that he should soone recover and see them. The french that knewed not the plott cryed for the ffather, which confirmed the belief of the wildmen. They all retyred to their village and we [sought] the meanes to embarke ourselves.

We resolved once more to make another feast when we should have everything ready for our purpose; that is, when the father should be well of his fayned sicknesse, ffor they allso doe delight in feasting, which was to be done for the safe recovery of the ffather's health. We dayly had messengers from the elders of the country to know how he did, who (after the lake was opened from the ice that was covered with ice) should be in good disposition. Many wished to have the suneshine ardently, their desire was so great to be gone. Att last our patient begins to walke with a scharfe about his armes.

When the shippes and boats weare ready, we sent them word that the father was well, & for joy would make a feast. The elders are invited. They weare sure not to faile, but to be first. Being come, there are speeches made to incourage them to sing and eat. It's folly to induce them to that, for they goe about it more bould then welcome. They are told that the morow should be the day of mirth. Heare is but play and dances, the ffrench by turns, to keepe them still in exercise, shewing them tricks to keepe them awake, as the bird-catcher doth to teach the bird to sing and not to fly away, as we then intended. Not one wildman was admitted to come into the fort that day, saying it was not our coustomes to shew the splendour of our banquetts before they should be presented att table. The wildmen have no other then ground for their table.

In the meantime we weare not idle, the impatient father exercising himselfe as the rest. The evening being come, the wildmen are brought to the place destinated, not far from our fort. Every one makes his bundle of provisions & marchandises & household stuff, gunns, &c., some hid in the ground, and the rest scattered because we could not save them. We made excellent bisquetts of the last year's corne, & forgott not the hoggs that weare a fatning. Att last the trumpetts blowes, putt yourselves in order; there is nothing but outcryes, clapping of hands, & capering, that they may have better stomach to their meat. There comes a dozen of great kettles full of beaten Indian corne dressed with mince meate. The wisest begins his speech, giving heaven thanks to have brought such generous ffrench to honnour them so. They eate as many wolves, having eyes bigger then bellies; they are rare att it without noise. The time was not yett com'd to acknowledge the happinesse we received from such incompareable hosts. Heare comes 2 great kettles full of bussards broyled & salted before the winter, with as many kettles full of ducks. As many turtles was taken in the season by the nett. Heere att this nothing but hooping to man's admiration whilst one was a eating, and other sort comes, as divers of fish, eels, salmon, and carps, which gives them a new stomach. Weare they to burst, heere they will shew their courage. The time comes on. The best is that we are sure none will forsake his place, nor man nor woman. A number of french entertaines them, keeping them from sleepe in dancing & singing, for that is the custome. Their lutrill, an instrumentall musick, is much heere in use. Yett nothing is done as yett, ffor there comes the thickened flower, the oyle of bears, venison. To this the knif is not enough; the spunes also are used. Wee see allready severall postures: the one beats his belly, the other shakes his head, others stopp their mouthes to keepe in what they have eaten. They weare in such an admiration, making strange kinds of faces, that turned their eyes up and downe. We bid them cheare up, & tould them it was an usuall custome with the ffrench to make much of themselves & of their friends. "They affect you, and yee must shew such like to them by shewing your respects to them that they so splendidly trait you. Cheere up like brave men. If your sleepe overcomes you, you must awake; come, sound [the] drumme, it is not now to beat the Gien; [Footnote: "To beat the gien," probably meaning the guitar, as Charlevoix mentions that at the feast to the Indians one of the French young men played upon that instrument for their amusement.] come, make a noise. Trumpett blow and make thy cheeks swell, to make the belly swell alsoe."

In the end nothing [is] spared that can be invented to the greater confusion. There is a strife between the french who will make the greatest noise. But there is an end to all things; the houre is come, ffor all is embarked. The wildman can hold out no longer; they must sleepe. They cry out, Skenon, enough, we can beare no more. "Lett them cry Skenon; we will cry hunnay, we are a going," sayes we.

They are told that the ffrench are weary & will sleepe alsoe awhile. They say, "Be it so." We come away; all is quiet. Nobody makes a noise after Such a hurly-burly. The fort is shutt up as if we had ben in it. We leave a hogg att the doore for sentery, with a rope tyed to his foot. He wanted no meat for the time. Here we make a proposition, being three and fifty ffrench in number, to make a slaughter without any difficulty, they being but 100 beasts not able to budge, & as many women. That done, we could goe to their village att the breake of the day, where we weare sure there weare not 20 men left, nor yong nor old. It was no great matter to deale with 5 or 600 women, & may be 1000 children; besides, the huntsmen should not be ready this 2 moneths to come home. Having done so, we might have a great hole in the skirts of that untoward & pervers nation, that it was in way of revenge, because of their disloyalty, breaking the peace & watching an opportunity to doe the like to us, that we should by that means have a better opportunity to escape; shewing by this whosoever intends to betray, betrays himselfe. The ffathers' answer was to this, that they weare sent to instruct the people in the faith of Jesus Christ and not to destroy; that the crosse must be their sword; moreover that they are told that we weare able to keepe the place, having victualls for the space of 4 yeares, with other provisions. [Footnote: The new Governor, Viscount d'Argenson, who arrived in Canada a few months after, disapproved of the evacuation of Onondaga. "The location of this fortification was probably about three quarters of a mile below Green Point, on the farm now occupied [in 1849] by Mr. Myrick Bradley, in the town of Salina, where the embankment and outlines were plain to be seen fifty years ago." History of Onondaga, by J. V. H. Clarke, Vol. I. p. 161, n., 1849.] So done, in the meanewhile some 16 french should goe downe to the french & tell the news; ffor the rest they weare able to oppose all the Iroquoits, having such a strong fort, and before the time could be expired some succour was to be expected out of ffrance, as well as with the helpe of some of the wildmen, their allies, make an assault, and so free ourselves of such a slavery & the many miseries wherin we weare dayly to undergoe, that by that means we might save the lives of many french and cleare a way from such inhumans. It was in vaine to think to convert them, but the destroying of them was to convert them. So discover nations and countryes, and that the ffrench finding some fourty resolut brothers that would have ventured themselves full liberty & assurance of their lives to preserve them from the cruelest enemy that ever was found uppon the earth. All these sayings could prevaile nothing uppon people that will avoid all slaughter.

So to be obedient to our superiours, without noise of trompet or drum, but zeal with griefe, we left that place. We are all embarked, and now must looke for the mouth of the river; and weare put to it, ffor it frized every night and the Ice of good thicknesse, and consequently dangerous to venture our boats against it. We must all the way breake the ice with great staves to make a passage. This gave us paines enough. Att the breake of day we weare in sight att the mouth of the river, where we weare free from ice. If those had but the least suspicion or had looked out, they had seene us. We soone by all diligence putt ourselves out of that apprehension, and came att the first rising of the river, where freed from ice tenne leagues from the fort, where we kept a good watch.

The day following we came to the Lake d'Ontario. The wind being boisterous, could goe no further. There we sought for a place to make cottages, which was in an Island very advantageous, where we stayed 2 dayes for the weather. We weare not without feare, thinking that the wildmen should follow us. They contrary wise stayed (as we heard) seaven nights, thinking that we weare asleepe, onely that some rose now and then, and rung the litle bell which stooke to the hogg's foot. So mystifying the businesse affaire, [they] went & brought news to the village, which made them come and looke over the pallisados, and saw in good earnest the Anomiacks weare gone.

In our journey [we had] bad weather, high winds, snow, and every day raine on our backs. We came to the river att last, where was difficulty enough by reason of the goeing out of the lake, which is hard to find, by the many isles that are about the opening of the river. We weare in a maner of sheepe scattered. After many crossings to and fro we find ourselves att the first streame; the watters high, went on without danger, but the navigation proved worse & worse because we came into a coulder country and into the most dangerousest precipices. Now the river [was] covered over with ice and snow which made the river give a terrible noise. The land also covered all over with snow, which rendered us incapable of knowledge where we weare, & consequently found ourselves in great perils. It was well that the river swelled, for not a mother's son of us could else escape; ffor where we might have made carriages we [would] innocently have gone uppon those currents. One of our greatest vessells runned on sand and soone full by reason of the running of the stream, but by tournings, with much adoe we gott it out againe, and by all dexterity brought to a harbour, which is hard to find in that place, ffor the ice and the streame continually cutts the coasts steepe downe, & so no landing thereabouts.

Heere a boat of 4 men made shipwrake. Heere every one for himselfe & God for all. Heere is no reliefe. There the 3 that could swime weare drowned, because they held not [to] the boat, but would swime to land. The other that had held it was saved with much adoe. Afterwards we came where the streame was not so swifte at all, but as dangerous for its ice. We cutt the ice with hattchetts & we found places where [it] was rotten, so we hazarded ourselves often to sinke downe to our necks. We knewed the isle of murder againe because of the woman that runn'd away was with us. Shee had reason to know it, though all covered with snow. The ffathers some dayes before our departur caused her to come to the fort to deliver her out of the hands of her ennemy, because she was a Christian. In short time after her arrivall att Quebecq [she] was marry'd, and died in childbed.

Six weeks being expired we came to the hight of St Louis, 3 leagues from mont royal, the first habitation of the ffrench. We went all that hight without making carriages, trusting to the depth of the watter, & passed it by God's providence, that have made us that passage free; ffor if we had come there the day before we could not possibly passe (by the report of the ffrench), by reason that underneath the water was mighty swift, the river was frozen and covered with ice, and could not have turned back, for the streame could bring us against our will under the ice. It was our lott to come after the ice was melted. The french inquire who is there with astonishment, thinking that it should be the charge of the Iroquoits. We thanked God for our deliverance.

Heere we had time to rest ourselves awhile att ease, which was not permitted by the way. About the last of March we ended our great paines and incredible dangers. About 14 nights after we went downe the 3 rivers, where most of us stayed. A month after my brother and I resolves to travell and see countreys. We find a good opportunity. In our voyage wee proceeded three yeares. During that time we had the happinesse to see very faire countryes.

The ende of the second voyage made in the Upper Country of the Iroquoits.

THIRD VOYAGE, MADE TO THE GREAT LAKE OF THE HURONS, UPPER SEA OF THE EAST, AND BAY OF THE NORTH

Now followeth the Auxoticiat Voyage into the Great and filthy Lake of the Hurrons, Upper Sea of the East, and Bay of the North.

Being come to the 3 rivers, where I found my brother who the yeare before came back from the lake of the Hurrons with other french, both weare upon the point of resolution to make a journey a purpose for to discover the great lakes that they heard the wild men speak off; yea, have seene before, ffor my brother made severall journeys when the ffathers lived about the lake of the hurrons, which was upon the border of the sea. So my brother seeing me back from those 2 dangerous voyages, so much by the cruelties of the barbars as for the difficulties of the wayes, for this reason he thought I was fitter & more faithfull for the discovery that he was to make. He plainly told me his minde. I knowing it, longed to see myselfe in a boat. There weare severall companies of wild men Expected from severall places, because they promised the yeare before, & [to] take the advantage of the Spring (this for to deceive the Iroquoits, who are allwayes in wait for to destroy them), and of the rivers which is by reason of the melting of the great snows, which is onely that time, ffor otherwise no possibility to come that way because for the swift streams that runs in summer, and in other places the want of watter, so that no boat can come through. We soone see the performance of those people, ffor a company came to the 3 rivers where we weare. They tould us that another company was arrived att Mont Royal, and that 2 more weare to come shortly, the one to the Three Rivers, the other to Saegne, [Footnote: Saegne, Sacgnes, Sacquenes, or the River

Saguenay.] a river of Tudousack, who arrived within 2 dayes after. They divided themselves because of the scant of provision; ffor if they weare together they could not have victualls enough. Many goes and comes to Quebecq for to know the resolution of mr. Governor, who together with the ffathers thought fitt to send a company of ffrench to bring backe, if possible, those wildmen the next yeare, or others, being that it is the best manna of the countrey by which the inhabitants doe subsist, and makes the ffrench vessells to come there and goe back loaden with merchandises for the traffique of furriers who comes from the remotest parts of the north of America.

As soone as the resolution was made, many undertakes the voyage; for where that there is lucre there are people enough to be had. The best and ablest men for that businesse weare chosen. They make them goe up the 3 rivers with the band that came with the Sacques. There take those that weare most capable for the purpose. Two ffathers weare chosen to conduct that company, and endeavoured to convert some of those foraigners of the remotest country to the Christian faith. We no sooner heard their designe, but saw the effects of the buisnesse, which effected in us much gladnesse for the pleasure we could doe to one another, & so abler to oppose an ennemy if by fortune we should meet with any that would doe us hurt or hinder us in our way.

About the midle of June we began to take leave of our company and venter our lives for the common good. We find 2 and 30 men, some inhabitants, some Gailliards that desired but doe well. What fairer bastion then a good tongue, especially when one sees his owne chimney smoak, or when we can kiss our owne wives or kisse our neighbour's wife with ease and delight? It is a strange thing when victualls are wanting, worke whole nights & dayes, lye downe on the bare ground, & not allwayes that hap, the breech in the watter, the feare in the buttocks, to have the belly empty, the wearinesse in the bones, and drowsinesse of the body by the bad weather that you are to suffer, having nothing to keepe you from such calamity.

Att last we take our journey to see the issue of a prosperous adventure in such a dangerous enterprise. We resolved not to be the first that should complaine. The ffrench weare together in order, the wildmen also, saving my brother & I that weare accustomed to such like voyages, have foreseene what happened afterwards. Before our setting forth we made some guifts, & by that means we weare sure of their good will, so that he & I went into the boats of the wild men. We weare nine and twenty french in number and 6 wildmen. We embarked our traine in the night, because our number should not be knowne to some spyes that might bee in some ambush to know our departure; ffor the Iroquoits are allwayes abroad. We weare 2 nights to gett to mont royall, where 8 Octanac stayed for us & 2 ffrench. If not for that company, we had passed the river of the meddowes, which makes an isle of Mont royall and joines itselfe to the lake of St Louis, 3 leagues further then the hight of that name.

We stayed no longer there then as the french gott themselves ready. We tooke leave without noise of Gun. We cannot avoid the ambush of that eagle, which is like the owle that sees better in the night then in the day. We weare not sooner come to the first river, but our wildmen sees 5 sorts of people of divers countrys laden with marchandise and gunns, which served them for a shew then for defence if by chance they should be sett on. So that the glorie begins to shew itsselfe, no order being observed among them. The one sings, the other before goes in that posture without bad encounter. We advanced 3 dayes. There was no need of such a silence among us. Our men composed onely of seaven score men, we had done well if we had kept together, not to goe before in the river, nor stay behind some 2 or 3 leagues. Some 3 or 4 boats now & then to land to kill a wild beast, & so putt themselves into a danger of their lives, & if there weare any precipice the rest should be impotent to helpe. We warned them to looke to themselves. They laughed att us, saying we weare women; that the Iroquoits durst not sett on them. That pride had such power that they thought themselves masters of the earth; but they will see themselves soone mistaken. How that great God that takes great care of the most wild creatures, and will that every man confesses his faults, & gives them grace to come to obedience for the preservation of their lives, sends them a remarquable power & ordnance, which should give terrour and retinue to those poore misled people from the way of assurance.

As we wandered in the afforesaid maner all a sunder, there comes a man alone out of the wood with a hattchett in his hand, with his brayer, & a cover over his shoulders, making signes aloud that we should come to him. The greatest part of that flock shewed a palish face for feare att the sight of this man, knowing him an ennemy. They approached not without feare & apprehension of some plot. By this you may see the boldnesse of those buzards, that think themselves hectors when they see but their shadowes, & tremble when they see a Iroquoit. That wild man seeing us neerer, setts him downe on the ground & throwes his hattchett away & raises againe all naked, to shew that he hath no armes, desires them to approach neerer for he is their friend, & would lose his life to save theirs. Hee shewed in deed a right captayne for saveing of men that runned to their ruine by their indiscretion & want of conduct; and what he did was out of meere piety, seeing well that they wanted wit, to goe so like a company of bucks, every one to his fancy, where his little experience leads him, nor thinking that danger wherin they weare, shewing by their march they weare no men, for not fearing. As for him, he was ready to die to render them service & prisoner into their hands freely. "For," saith he, "I might have escaped your sight, but that I would have saved you. I feare," sayth he, "not death"; so with that comes downe into the watter to his midle. There comes many boats about him, takes him into one of the boats, tying a coard fast about his body. There is he fastned. He begins to sing his fatal song that they call a nouroyall. That horrid tone being finished, makes a long, a very long speech, saying, "Brethren, the day the sunne is favourable to mee, appointed mee to tell you that yee are witlesse before I die, neither can they escape their ennemys, that are spred up and downe everywhere, that watches all moments their coming to destroy them. Take great courage, brethren, sleepe not; the ennemy is att hand. They wait for you; they are soe neare that they see you, and heare you, & are sure that you are their prey. Therefore I was willing to die to give you notice. For my part that what I have ben I am a man & commander in the warrs, and tooke severall prisoners; yet I would put meselfe in death's hands to save your lives. Believe me; keepe you altogether; spend not your powder in vaine, thinking to frighten your enemys by the noise of your guns. See if the stoanes of your arrowes be not bent or loose; bend your bowes; open your ears; keepe your hattchetts sharpe to cutt trees to make you a fort; doe not spend soe much greas to greas yourselves, but keep it for your bellies. Stay not too long in the way. It's robbery to die with conduct."

That poore wretch spake the truth & gave good instructions, but the greatest part did not understand what he said, saving the hurrons that weare with him, and I, that tould them as much as I could perceive. Every one laughs, saying he himself is afraid & tells us that story. We call him a dogg, a woman, and a henne. We will make you know that we weare men, & for his paines we should burne him when we come to our country. Here you shall see the brutishnesse of those people that think themselves valliant to the last point. No comparison is to be made with them for vallour, but quite contrary. They passe away the rest of that day with great exclamations of joy, but it will not last long.

That night wee layd in our boats and made not the ketle boyle, because we had meat ready dressed. Every boat is tyed up in the rushes, whether out of feare for what the prisoner told them, or that the prisoner should escape, I know not. They went to sleepe without any watch. The ffrench began to wish & moane for that place from whence they came from. What will it be if wee heare yeatt cryes & sorrows after all? Past the breake of day every one takes his oare to row; the formost oares have great advantage. We heard the torrent rumble, but could not come to the land that day, although not farr from us. Some twelve boats gott afore us. These weare saluted with guns & outcrys. In the meane while one boat runs one way, one another; some men lands and runs away. We are all put to it; non knowes where he is, they are put to such a confusion. All those beasts gathers together againe frighted. Seeing no way to escape, gott themselves all in a heape like unto ducks that sees the eagle come to them.

That first feare being over a litle, they resolved to land & to make a fort with all speed, which was done in lesse then two houres. The most stupidest drowsy are the nimblest for the hattchett & cutting of trees. The fort being finished, every one maketh himselfe in a readiness to sustaine the assult if any had tempted. The prisoner was brought, who soone was despatched, burned & roasted & eaten. The Iroquoits had so served them, as many as they have taken.

We mist 20 of our company, but some came safe to us, & lost 13 that weare killed & taken in that defeat. The Iroquoite finding himselfe weake would not venture, & was obliged to leave us least he should be discovered & served as the other. Neverthelesse they shewed good countenances, went & builded a fort as we have done, where they fortified themselves & feed on human flesh which they gott in the warres. They weare afraid as much as we, but far from that; ffor the night being come, every one imbarks himselfe, to the sound of a low trumpet, by the help of the darknesse. We went to the other side, leaving our marchandises for our ransome to the ennemy that used us so unkindly. We made some cariages that night with a world of paines. We mist 4 of our boats, so that we must alter our equipages. The wildmen complained much that the ffrench could not swime, for that they might be together. The ffrench seeing that they weare not able to undergo such a voyage, they consult together & for conclusion resolved to give an end to such labours & dangers; moreover, found themselves incapable to follow the wildmen who went with all the speed possible night & day for the feare that they weare in. The ffathers, seeing our weaknesse, desired the wildmen that they might have one or two to direct them, which by no means was granted, but bid us doe as the rest. We kept still our resolution, & knowing more tricks then they, would not goe back, which should be but disdainful & prejudiciall. We told them so plainly that we would finish that voyage or die by the way. Besides that the wildmen did not complaine of us att all, but incouraged us. After a long arguing, every one had the liberty to goe backwards or forwards, if any had courage to venter himselfe with us. Seeing the great difficulties, all with one consent went back againe, and we went on.

The wildmen weare not sorry for their departure, because of their ignorance in the affaire of such navigation. It's a great alteration to see one and 30 reduced to 2. We encouraged one another, both willing to live & die with one another; & that [is] the least we could doe, being brothers. Before we [went] to the lake of the hurrons we had crosses enough, but no encounter. We travelled onely in the night in these dangerous places, which could not be done without many vexations & labours. The vanity was somewhat cooler for the example we have seene the day before. The hungar was that tormented us most; for him we could not goe seeke for some wild beasts. Our chiefest food was onely some few fishes which the wildmen caught by a line, may be two dozens a whole day, no bigger then my hand.

Being come to the place of repose, some did goe along the water side on the rocks & there exposed ourselves to the rigour of the weather. Upon these rocks we find some shells, blackish without and the inner part whitish by reason of the heat of the sun & of the humidity. They are in a maner glued to the rock; so we must gett another stone to gett them off by scraping them hard. When we thought to have enough [we] went back again to the Cottages, where the rest weare getting the litle fishes ready with trips, [Footnote: Trips,—meaning "tripe des boiled resolves itself into a black glue, roche, a species of lichen, which being nauseous but not without nourishment." Discovery of the Great West, by Parkman.] gutts and all. The kittle was full with the scraping of the rocks, which soone after it boyled became like starch, black and clammie & easily to be swallowed. I think if any bird had lighted upon the excrements of the said stuff, they had stuckt to it as if it weare glue. In the fields we have gathered severall fruits, as goosberyes, blackberrys, that in an houre we gathered above a bushell of such sorte, although not as yett full ripe. We boyled it, and then every one had his share. Heere was daintinesse slighted. The belly did not permitt us to gett on neither shoos nor stockins, that the better we might goe over the rocks, which did [make] our feet smart [so] that we came backe. Our feet & thighs & leggs weare scraped with thorns, in a heape of blood. The good God looked uppon those infidels by sending them now & then a beare into the river, or if we perceived any in an Isle forced them to swime, that by that means we might the sooner kill them. But the most parts there abouts is so sterill that there is nothing to be seene but rocks & sand, & on the high wayes but deale trees that grow most miraculously, for that earth is not to be seene than can nourish the root, & most of them trees are very bigg & high. We tooke a litle refreshment in a place called the lake of Castors, which is some 30 leagues from the first great lake. Some of those wildmen hid a rest [Footnote: "Hid a rest," or cache.] as they went down to the ffrench; but the lake was so full of fishes we tooke so much that served us a long while.

We came to a place where weare abundance of Otters, in so much that I believe all gathered to hinder our passage. We killed some with our arrows, not daring to shoote because we discovered there abouts some tracks, judging to be our ennemy by the impression of their feet in the sand. All knowes there one another by their march, for each hath his proper steps, some upon their toes, some on their heele, which is natural to them, for when they are infants the mother wrapeth them to their mode. Heer I speake not of the horrid streams we passed, nor of the falls of the water, which weare of an incredible height. In some parts most faire & delicious, where people formerly lived onely by what they could gett by the bow & arrows. We weare come above 300 leagues allwayes against the streame, & made 60 carriages, besides drawing, besides the swift streams we overcame by the oares & poles to come to that litle lake of Castors which may be 30 or 40 leagues in compasse. The upper end of it is full of Islands, where there is not time lost to wander about, finding wherewithall to make the kettle boyle with venison, great bears, castors & fishes, which are plenty in that place. The river that we goe to the great lake is somewhat favorable. We goe downe with ease & runing of the watter, which empties itsselfe in that lake in which we are now coming in. This river hath but 8 high & violent streams, which is some 30 leagues in length. The place where we weare is a bay all full of rocks, small isles, & most between wind and water which an infinite [number] of fishes, which are seene in the water so cleare as christiall. That is the reason of so many otters, that lives onely uppon fish. Each of us begins to looke to his bundle & merchandizes and prepare himselfe for the bad weather that uses to be on that great extent of water. The wildmen finds what they hid among the rocks 3 months before they came up to the french. Heere we are stiring about in our boats as nimble as bees and divided ourselves into 2 companys. Seaven boats went towards west norwest and the rest to the South.

After we mourned enough for the death of our deare countrymen that weare slained coming up, we take leave of each other with promise of amitie & good correspondence one with another, as for the continuance of peace, as for the assistance of strength, if the enemy should make an assault. That they should not goe to the french without giving notice one to another & soe goe together. We that weare for the South went on severall dayes merily, & saw by the way the place where the ffathers Jesuits had heretofore lived; a delicious place, albeit we could but see it afarre off. The coast of this lake is most delightfull to the minde. The lands smooth, and woods of all sorts. In many places there are many large open fields where in, I believe, wildmen formerly lived before the destruction of the many nations which did inhabit, and tooke more place then 600 leagues about; for I can well say that from the river of Canada to the great lake of the hurrons, which is neere 200 leagues in length & 60 in breadth, as I guesse, for I have [been] round about it, plenty of fish. There are banks of sand 5 or 6 leagues from the waterside, where such an infinite deale of fish that scarcely we are able to draw out our nett. There are fishes as bigg as children of 2 years old. There is sturgeon enough & other sorte that is not knowne to us. The South part is without isles, onely in some bayes where there are some. It is delightfull to goe along the side of the watter in summer where you may pluck the ducks.

We must stay often in a place 2 or 3 dayes for the contrary winds; ffor [if] the winds weare anything high, we durst not venter the boats against the impetuosity of the waves, which is the reason that our voyages are so long and tedious. A great many large deep rivers empties themselves in that lake, and an infinit number of other small rivers, that cann beare boats, and all from lakes & pools which are in abundance in that country.

After we travelled many dayes we arrived att a large island where we found their village, their wives & children. You must know that we passed a strait some 3 leagues beyond that place. The wildmen give it a name; it is another lake, but not so bigg as that we passed before. We calle it the lake of the staring hairs, because those that live about it have their hair like a brush turned up. They all have a hole in their nose, which is done by a straw which is above a foot long. It barrs their faces. Their ears have ordinarily 5 holes, where one may putt the end of his finger. They use those holes in this sort: to make themselves gallant they passe through it a skrew of coper with much dexterity, and goe on the lake in that posture. When the winter comes they weare no capes because of their haire tourned up. They fill those skrews with swan's downe, & with it their ears covered; but I dare say that the people doe not for to hold out the cold, but rather for pride, ffor their country is not so cold as the north, and other lakes that we have seene since.

It should be difficult to describe what variety of faces our arrivement did cause, some out of joy, others out of sadnesse. Neverthelesse the numbers of joyfull exceeded that of the sorrowfull. The season began to invite the lustiest to hunting. We neither desire to be idle in any place, having learned by experience that idlenesse is the mother of all evil, for it breeds most part of all sicknesse in those parts where the aire is most delightfull. So that they who had most knowledge in these quarters had familiarity with the people that live there about the last lake.

The nation that we weare with had warrs with the Iroquoits, and must trade. Our wildmen out of feare must consent to their ennemy to live in their land. It's true that those who lived about the first lake had not for the most part the conveniency of our french merchandise, as since, which obliged most of the remotest people to make peace, considering the enemy of theirs that came as a thunder bolt upon them, so that they joyned with them & forgett what was past for their owne preservation. Att our coming there we made large guifts, to dry up the tears of the friends of the deceased. As we came there the circumjacent neighbours came to visit us, that bid us welcome, as we are so. There comes newes that there weare ennemy in the fields, that they weare seene att the great field. There is a councell called, & resolved that they should be searched & sett uppon them as [soon as] possible may be, which [was] executed speedily. I offered my service, soe went and looked for them 2 dayes; finding them the 3rd day, gave them the assault when they least thought off it. We played the game so furiously that none escaped.

The day following we returned to our village with 8 of our enemys dead and 3 alive. The dead weare eaten & the living weare burned with a small fire to the rigour of cruelties, which comforted the desolat to see them revenged of the death of their relations that was so served. We weare then possessed by the hurrons and Octanac; but our minde was not to stay in an island, but to be knowne with the remotest people. The victory that we have gotten made them consent to what we could desire, & because that we shewed willing [ness] to die for their defence. So we desired to goe with a company of theirs that was going to the nation of the stairing haires.

We weare wellcomed & much made of, saying that we weare the Gods & devils of the earth; that we should fournish them, & that they would bring us to their ennemy to destroy them. We tould them [we] were very well content. We persuaded them first to come peaceably, not to destroy them presently, and if they would not condescend, then would wee throw away the hattchett and make use of our thunders. We sent ambassadors to them with guifts. That nation called Pontonatemick without more adoe comes & meets us with the rest, & peace was concluded. Feasts were made & dames with guifts came of each side, with a great deale of mirth.

We visited them during that winter, & by that means we made acquaintance with an other nation called Escotecke, which signified fire, a faire proper nation; they are tall & bigg & very strong. We came there in the spring. When we arrived there weare extraordinary banquetts. There they never have seen men with beards, because they pull their haires as soone as it comes out; but much more astonished when they saw our armes, especially our guns, which they worshipped by blowing smoake of tobacco instead of sacrifice. I will not insist much upon their way of living, ffor of their ceremonys heere you will see a pattern.

In the last voyage that wee made I will lett you onely know what cours we runned in 3 years' time. We desired them to lett us know their neighboring nations. They gave us the names, which I hope to describe their names in the end of this most imperfect discours, at least those that I can remember. Among others they told us of a nation called Nadoneceronon, which is very strong, with whome they weare in warres with, & another wandering nation, living onely uppon what they could come by. Their dwelling was on the side of the salt watter in summer time, & in the land in the winter time, for it's cold in their country. They calle themselves Christinos, & their confederats from all times, by reason of their speech, which is the same, & often have joyned together & have had companys of souldiers to warre against that great nation. We desired not to goe to the North till we had made a discovery in the South, being desirous to know what they did. They told us if we would goe with them to the great lake of the stinkings, the time was come of their trafick, which was of as many knives as they could gett from the french nation, because of their dwellings, which was att the coming in of a lake called Superior, but since the destructions of many neighboring nations they retired themselves to the height of the lake. We knewed those people well. We went to them almost yearly, and the company that came up with us weare of the said nation, but never could tell punctually where they lived because they make the barre of the Christinos from whence they have the Castors that they bring to the french. This place is 600 leagues off, by reason of the circuit that we must doe. The hurrons & the Octanacks, from whence we came last, furnishes them also, & comes to the furthest part of the lake of the stinkings, there to have light earthen pots, and girdles made of goat's hairs, & small shells that grow art the sea side, with which they trim their cloath made of skin.

We finding this opportunity would not lett it slippe, but made guifts, telling that the other nation would stand in feare of them because of us. We flattered them, saying none would dare to give them the least wrong, in so much that many of the Octanacks that weare present to make the same voyage. I can assure you I liked noe country as I have that wherein we wintered; ffor whatever a man could desire was to be had in great plenty; viz. staggs, fishes in abundance, & all sort of meat, corne enough. Those of the 2 nations would not come with us, but turned back to their nation. We neverthelesse put ourselves in hazard, for our curiosity, of stay 2 or 3 years among that nation. We ventured, for that we understand some of their idiome & trusted to that.

We embarked ourselves on the delightfullest lake of the world. I tooke notice of their Cottages & of the journeys of our navigation, for because that the country was so pleasant, so beautifull & fruitfull that it grieved me to see that the world could not discover such inticing countrys to live in. This I say because that the Europeans fight for a rock in the sea against one another, or for a sterill land and horrid country, that the people sent heere or there by the changement of the aire ingenders sicknesse and dies thereof. Contrarywise those kingdoms are so delicious & under so temperat a climat, plentifull of all things, the earth bringing foorth its fruit twice a yeare, the people live long & lusty & wise in their way. What conquest would that bee att litle or no cost; what laborinth of pleasure should millions of people have, instead that millions complaine of misery & poverty! What should not men reape out of the love of God in converting the souls heere, is more to be gained to heaven then what is by differences of nothing there, should not be so many dangers committed under the pretence of religion! Why so many thoesoever are hid from us by our owne faults, by our negligence, covetousnesse, & unbeliefe. It's true, I confesse, that the accesse is difficult, but must say that we are like the Cockscombs of Paris, when first they begin to have wings, imagining that the larks will fall in their mouths roasted; but we ought [to remember] that vertue is not acquired without labour & taking great paines.

We meet with severall nations, all sedentary, amazed to see us, & weare very civil. The further we sejourned the delightfuller the land was to us. I can say that [in] my lifetime I never saw a more incomparable country, for all I have ben in Italy; yett Italy comes short of it, as I think, when it was inhabited, & now forsaken of the wildmen. Being about the great sea, we conversed with people that dwelleth about the salt water, [Footnote: "That dwelleth about the salt water;" namely, Hudson's Bay.] who tould us that they saw some great white thing sometimes uppon the water, & came towards the shore, & men in the top of it, and made a noise like a company of swans; which made me believe that they weare mistaken, for I could not imagine what it could be, except the Spaniard; & the reason is that we found a barill broken as they use in Spaine. Those people have their haires long. They reape twice a yeare; they are called Tatarga, that is to say, buff. They warre against Nadoneceronons, and warre also against the Christinos. These 2 doe no great harme to one another, because the lake is betweene both. They are generally stout men, that they are able to defend themselves. They come but once a year to fight. If the season of the yeare had permitted us to stay, for we intended to goe backe the yeare following, we had indeavoured to make peace betweene them. We had not as yett seene the nation Nadoneceronons. We had hurrons with us. Wee persuaded them to come along to see their owne nation that fled there, but they would not by any means. We thought to gett some castors there to bring downe to the ffrench, seeing [it] att last impossible to us to make such a circuit in a twelve month's time. We weare every where much made of; neither wanted victualls, for all the different nations that we mett conducted us & furnished us with all necessaries. Tending to those people, went towards the South & came back by the north.

The Summer passed away with admiration by the diversity of the nations that we saw, as for the beauty of the shore of that sweet sea. Heere we saw fishes of divers, some like the sturgeons & have a kind of slice att the end of their nose some 3 fingers broad in the end and 2 onely neere the nose, and some 8 thumbs long, all marbled of a blakish collor. There are birds whose bills are two and 20 thumbs long. That bird swallows a whole salmon, keeps it a long time in his bill. We saw alsoe shee-goats very bigg. There is an animal somewhat lesse then a cow whose meat is exceeding good. There is no want of Staggs nor Buffes. There are so many Tourkeys that the boys throws stoanes att them for their recreation. We found no sea-serpents as we in other laks have seene, especially in that of d'Ontario and that of the stairing haires. There are some in that of the hurrons, but scarce, for the great cold in winter. They come not neere the upper lake. In that of the stairing haires I saw yong boy [who] was bitten. He tooke immediately his stony knife & with a pointed stick & cutts off the whole wound, being no other remedy for it. They are great sorcerors & turns the wheele. I shall speake of this at large in my last voyage. Most of the shores of the lake is nothing but sand. There are mountains to be seene farre in the land. There comes not so many rivers from that lake as from others; these that flow from it are deeper and broader, the trees are very bigg, but not so thick. There is a great distance from one another, & a quantitie of all sorts of fruits, but small.

The vines grows all by the river side; the lemons are not so bigg as ours, and sowrer. The grape is very bigg, greene, is seene there att all times. It never snows nor freezes there, but mighty hot; yett for all that the country is not so unwholsom, ffor we seldome have seene infirmed people. I will speake of their manners in my last voyage, which I made in October.

We came to the strait of the 2 lakes of the stinkings and the upper lake, where there are litle isles towards Norwest, ffew towards the Southest, very small. The lake towards the North att the side of it is full of rocks & sand, yett great shipps can ride on it without danger. We being of 3 nations arrived there with booty, disputed awhile, ffor some would returne to their country. That was the nation of the fire, & would have us backe to their dwelling. We by all means would know the Christinos. To goe backe was out of our way. We contented the hurrons to our advantage with promises & others with hope, and persuaded the Octonack to keepe his resolution, because we weare but 5 small fine dayes from those of late that lived in the sault of the coming in of the said upper lake, from whence that name of salt, which is panoestigonce in the wild language, which heerafter we will call the nation of the salt.

Not many years since that they had a cruell warre against the Nadoneseronons. Although much inferiour in numbers, neverthelesse that small number of the salt was a terror unto them, since they had trade with the ffrench. They never have seene such instruments as the ffrench furnished them withall. It is a proude nation, therfore would not submitt, although they had to doe with a bigger nation 30 times then they weare, because that they weare called ennemy by all those that have the accent of the Algonquin language, that the wild men call Nadone, which is the beginning of their name. The Iroquoits have the title of bad ennemy, Maesocchy Nadone. Now seeing that the Christinos had hattchetts & knives, for that they resolved to make peace with those of the sault, that durst not have gon hundred of leagues uppon that upper lake with assurance. They would not hearken to anything because their general resolved to make peace with those of the Christinos & an other nation that gott gunns, the noise of which had frighted them more then the bulletts that weare in them. The time approached, there came about 100 of the nation of the Sault to those that lived towards the north. The christinos gott a bigger company & fought a batail. Some weare slaine of both sids. The Captayne of these of the Sault lost his eye by an arrow. The batail being over he made a speech, & said that he lost his fight of one side, & of the other he foresee what he would doe; his courage being abject by that losse, that he himselfe should be ambassador & conclud the peace.

He seeing that the Iroquoits came too often, a visit I must confesse very displeasing, being that some [of] ours looses their lives or liberty, so that we retired ourselves to the higher lake neerer the nation of the Nadoneceronons, where we weare well receaved, but weare mistrusted when many weare seene together. We arrived then where the nation of the Sault was, where we found some french men that came up with us, who thanked us kindly for to come & visit them. The wild Octanaks that came with us found some of their nations slaves, who weare also glad to see them. For all they weare slaves they had meat enough, which they have not in their owne country so plentifull, being no huntsmen, but altogether ffishers. As for those towards the north, they are most expert in hunting, & live uppon nothing else the most part of the yeare. We weare long there before we gott acquaintance with those that we desired so much, and they in lik maner had a fervent desire to know us, as we them. Heer comes a company of Christinos from the bay of the North sea, to live more at ease in the midle of woods & forests, by reason they might trade with those of the Sault & have the Conveniency to kill more beasts.

There we passed the winter & learned the particularitie that since wee saw by Experience. Heere I will not make a long discours during that time, onely made good cheere & killed staggs, Buffes, Elends, and Castors. The Christinos had skill in that game above the rest. The snow proved favourable that yeare, which caused much plenty of every thing. Most of the woods & forests are very thick, so that it was in some places as darke as in a cellar, by reason of the boughs of trees. The snow that falls, being very light, hath not the strenght to stopp the eland, [Footnote: Elend, plainly the Moose. "They appear to derive their Dutch appellation (eelanden) from elende, misery, they die of the smallest wound." Documentary History of New York, by O'Callaghan, Vol. IV. p. 77.] which is a mighty strong beast, much like a mule, having a tayle cutt off 2 or 3 or 4 thumbes long, the foot cloven like a stagge. He has a muzzle mighty bigge. I have seene some that have the nostrills so bigg that I putt into it my 2 fists att once with ease. Those that uses to be where the buffes be are not so bigg, but about the bignesse of a coach horse. The wildmen call them the litle sort. As for the Buff, it is a furious animal. One must have a care of him, for every yeare he kills some Nadoneseronons. He comes for the most part in the plaines & meddows; he feeds like an ox, and the Oriniack so but seldom he galopps. I have seene of their hornes that a man could not lift them from of the ground. They are branchy & flatt in the midle, of which the wildman makes dishes that can well hold 3 quarts. These hornes fall off every yeare, & it's a thing impossible that they will grow againe. The horns of Buffs are as those of an ox, but not so long, but bigger, & of a blackish collour; he hath a very long hairy taile; he is reddish, his haire frized &

very fine. All the parts of his body much [like] unto an ox. The biggest are bigger then any ox whatsoever. Those are to be found about the lake of the Stinkings & towards the North of the same. They come not to the upper lake but by chance. It's a pleasur to find the place of their abode, for they tourne round about compassing 2 or 3 acres of land, beating the snow with their feete, & coming to the center they lye downe & rise againe to eate the bows of trees that they can reach. They go not out of their circle that they have made untill hunger compells them.

We did what we could to have correspondence with that warlick nation & reconcile them with the Christinos. We went not there that winter. Many weare slained of both sides the summer last. The wound was yett fresh, wherfore it was hard to conclude peace between them. We could doe nothing, ffor we intended to turne back to the ffrench the summer following. Two years weare expired. We hoped to be att the 2 years end with those that gave us over for dead, having before to come back at a year's end. As we are once in those remote countreys we cannot doe as we would. Att last we declared our mind first to those of the Sault, encouraging those of the North that we are their brethren, & that we would come back & force their enemy to peace or that we would help against them. We made guifts one to another, and thwarted a land of allmost 50 leagues before the snow was melted. In the morning it was a pleasur to walke, for we could goe without racketts. The snow was hard enough, because it freezed every night. When the sun began to shine we payed for the time past. The snow sticks so to our racketts that I believe our shoes weighed 30 pounds, which was a paine, having a burden uppon our backs besides.

We arrived, some 150 of us, men & women, to a river side, where we stayed 3 weeks making boats. Here we wanted not fish. During that time we made feasts att a high rate. So we refreshed ourselves from our labours. In that time we tooke notice that the budds of trees began to spring, which made us to make more hast & be gone. We went up that river 8 dayes till we came to a nation called Pontonatenick & Matonenock; that is, the scrattchers. There we gott some Indian meale & corne from those 2 nations, which lasted us till we came to the first landing Isle. There we weare well received againe. We made guifts to the Elders to encourage the yong people to bring us downe to the ffrench. But mightily mistaken; ffor they would reply, "Should you bring us to be killed? The Iroquoits are every where about the river & undoubtedly will destroy us if we goe downe, & afterwards our wives & those that stayed behinde. Be wise, brethren, & offer not to goe downe this yeare to the ffrench. Lett us keepe our lives." We made many private suits, but all in vaine. That vexed us most that we had given away most of our merchandises & swapped a great deale for Castors. Moreover they made no great harvest, being but newly there. Beside, they weare no great huntsmen. Our journey was broaken till the next yeare, & must per force.

That summer I went a hunting, & my brother stayed where he was welcome & putt up a great deale of Indian corne that was given him. He intended to furnish the wildmen that weare to goe downe to the ffrench if they had not enough. The wild men did not perceive this; ffor if they wanted any, we could hardly kept it for our use. The winter passes away in good correspondence one with another, & sent ambassadors to the nations that uses to goe downe to the french, which rejoyced them the more & made us passe that yeare with a greater pleasur, saving that my brother sell into the falling sicknesse, & many weare sorry for it. That proceeded onely of a long stay in a new discovered country, & the idlenesse contributs much to it. There is nothing comparable to exercise. It is the onely remedy of such diseases. After he languished awhile God gave him his health againe.

The desire that every one had to goe downe to the ffrench made them earnestly looke out for castors. They have not so many there as in the north part, so in the beginning of spring many came to our Isle. There weare no lesse, I believe, then 500 men that weare willing to venter themselves. The corne that my brother kept did us a world of service. The wildmen brought a quantity of flesh salted in a vesell. When we weare ready to depart, heere comes strang news of the defeat of the hurrons, which news, I thought, would putt off the voyage. There was a councell held, & most of them weare against the goeing downe to the ffrench, saying that the Iroquoits weare to barre this yeare, & the best way was to stay till the following yeare. And now the ennemy, seeing himselfe frustrated of his expectation, would not stay longer, thinking thereby that we weare resolved never more to go downe, and that next yeare there should be a bigger company, & better able to oppose an ennemy. My brother & I, feeing ourselves all out of hopes of our voyage, without our corne, which was allready bestowed, & without any merchandise, or scarce having one knife betwixt us both, so we weare in a great apprehension least that the hurrons should, as they have done often, when the ffathers weare in their country, kill a frenchman.

Seeing the equipage ready & many more that thought long to depart thence for marchandise, we upon this resolved to call a publique councell in the place; which the Elders hearing, came and advised us not to undertake it, giving many faire words, saying, "Brethren, why are you such ennemys to yourselves to putt yourselves in the hands of those that wait for you? They will destroy you and carry you away captives. Will you have your brethren destroyed that loves you, being slained? Who then will come up and baptize our children? Stay till the next yeare, & then you are like to have the number of 600 men in company with you. Then you may freely goe without intermission. Yee shall take the church along with you, & the ffathers & mothers will send their children to be taught in the way of truth of the Lord." Our answer was that we would speake in publique, which granted, the day appointed is come. There gathered above 800 men to see who should have the glorie in a round. They satt downe on the ground. We desired silence. The elders being in the midle & we in their midle, my brother began to Speake. "Who am I? am I a foe or a friend? If I am a foe, why did you suffer me to live so long among you? If I am friend, & if you take so to be, hearken to what I shall say. You know, my uncles & brethren, that I hazarded my life goeing up with you; if I have no courage, why did you not tell me att my first coming here? & if you have more witt then we, why did not you use it by preserving your knives, your hattchetts, & your gunns, that you had from the ffrench? You will see if the ennemy will sett upon you that you will be attraped like castors in a trape; how will you defend yourselves like men that is not courageous to lett yourselves be catched like beasts? How will you defend villages? with castors' skins? how will you defend your wives & children from the ennemy's hands?"

Then my brother made me stand up, saying, "Shew them the way to make warrs if they are able to uphold it." I tooke a gowne of castors' skins that one of them had uppon his shoulder & did beat him with it. I asked the others if I was a souldier. "Those are the armes that kill, & not your robes. What will your ennemy say when you perish without defending yourselves? Doe not you know the ffrench way? We are used to fight with armes & not with robes. You say that the Iroquoits waits for you because some of your men weare killed. It is onely to make you stay untill you are quite out of stocke, that they dispatch you with ease. Doe you think that the ffrench will come up here when the greatest part of you is slained by your owne fault? You know that they cannot come up without you. Shall they come to baptize your dead? Shall your children learne to be slaves among the Iroquoits for their ffathers' cowardnesse? You call me Iroquoit. Have not you seene me disposing my life with you? Who has given you your life if not the ffrench? Now you will not venter because many of your confederates are come to visit you & venter their lives with you. If you will deceave them you must not think that they will come an other time for shy words nor desire. You have spoaken of it first, doe what you will. For myne owne part, I will venter choosing to die like a man then live like a beggar. Having not wherewithal to defend myselfe, farewell; I have my sack of corne ready. Take all my castors. I shall live without you." & then departed that company.

They weare amazed of our proceeding; they stayed long before they spoake one to another. Att last sent us some considerable persons who bid us cheare up. "We see that you are in the right; the voyage is not broaken. The yong people tooke very ill that you have beaten them with the skin. All avowed to die like men & undertake the journey. You shall heare what the councell will ordaine the morrow. They are to meet privatly & you shall be called to it. Cheare up & speake as you have done; that is my councell to you. For this you will remember me when you will see me in your country; ffor I will venter meselfe with you." Now we are more satisfied then the day before. We weare to use all rhetorique to persuade them to goe downe, ffor we saw the country languish very much, ffor they could not subsist, & moreover they weare afraid of us. The councell is called, but we had no need to make a speech, finding them disposed to make the voyage & to submitt. "Yee women gett your husbands' bundles ready. They goe to gett wherwithall to defend themselves & you alive."

Our equipage was ready in 6 dayes. We embarked ourselves. We weare in number about 500, all stout men. We had with us a great store of castors' skins. We came to the South. We now goe back to the north, because to overtake a band of men that went before to give notice to others. We passed the lake without dangers. We wanted nothing, having good store of corne & netts to catch fish, which is plentyfull in the rivers. We came to a place where 8 Iroquoits wintered. That was the company that made a slaughter before our departure from home. Our men repented now they did not goe sooner, ffor it might be they should have surprised them.

Att last we are out of those lakes. One hides a caske of meale, the other his campiron, & all that could be cumbersome. After many paines & labours wee arrived to the Sault of Columest, so called because of the Stones that are there very convenient to make tobacco pipes. We are now within 100 leagues of the french habitation, & hitherto no bad encounter. We still found tracks of men which made us still to have the more care and guard of ourselves. Some 30 leagues from this place we killed wild cowes & then gott ourselves into cottages, where we heard some guns goe off, which made us putt out our fires & imbark ourselves with all speed. We navigated all that night. About the breake of day we made a stay, that not to goe through the violent streames for feare the Ennemy should be there to dispute the passage. We landed & instantly sent 2 men to know whether the passage was free. They weare not halfe a mile off when we see a boat of the ennemy thwarting the river, which they had not done without discovering our boats, having nothing to cover our boats nor hide them. Our lightest boats shewed themselves by pursueing the ennemy.

They did shoot, but to no effect, which made our two men come back in all hast. We seeing ourselves but merchandmen, so we would not long follow a man of warre, because he runned swifter then ours.

We proceeded in our way with great diligence till we came to the carriage place, where the one halfe of our men weare in readinesse, whilst the other halfe carried the baggage & the boats. We had a great alarum, but no hurt done. We saw but one boat, but have seene foure more going up the river. Methinks they thought themselves some what weake for us, which persuaded us [of] 2 things: 1st, that they weare afraid; andly, that they went to warne their company, which thing warned us the more to make hast.

The 2nd day att evening after we landed & boyled an horiniack which we killed. We then see 16 boats of our ennemy coming. They no sooner perceived us but they went on the other side of the river. It was a good looke for us to have seene them. Our wildmen did not say what they thought, ffor they esteemed themselves already lost. We encouraged them & desired them to have courage & not [be] afraid, & so farr as I think we weare strong enough for them, that we must stoutly goe & meet them, and they should stand still. We should be alltogether, & put our castors' skins upon pearches, which could keepe us from the shott, which we did. We had foure & 20 gunns ready, and gave them to the hurrons, who knewed how to handle them better then the others. The Iroquoits seeing us come, & that we weare 5 to 1, could not imagine what to doe. Neverthelesse they would shew their courage; being that they must passe, they putt themselves in array to fight. If we had not ben with some hurrons that knewed the Iroquoits' tricks, I believe that our wild men had runned away, leaving their fusiques behind. We being neere one another, we commanded that they should row with all their strength towards them. We kept close one to another to persecut what was our intent. We begin to make outcryes & sing. The hurrons in one side, the Algonquins att the other side, the Ottanak, the panoestigons, the Amickkoick, the Nadonicenago, the ticacon, and we both encouraged them all, crying out with a loud noise. The Iroquoits begin to shoot, but we made ours to goe one forwards without any shooting, and that it was the onely way of fighting. They indeed turned their backs & we followed them awhile. Then was it that we weare called devils, with great thanks & incouragements that they gave us, attributing to us the masters of warre and the only Captaynes. We desired them to keepe good watch and sentry, and if we weare not surprized we should come safe and sound without hurt to the ffrench. The Iroquoite seeing us goe on our way, made as if they would leave us.

We made 3 carriages that day, where the ennemy could doe us mischief if they had ben there. The cunning knaves followed us neverthelesse pritty close. We left 5 boats behind that weare not loaden. We did so to see what invention our enemy could invent, knowing very well that his mind was to surprize us. It is enough that we are warned that they follow us. Att last we perceived that he was before us, which putt us in some feare; but seeing us resolut, did what he could to augment his number. But we weare mighty vigilent & sent some to make a discovery att every carriage through the woods. We weare told that they weare in an ambush, & there built a fort below the long Sault, where we weare to passe. Our wildmen said doubtlesse they have gott an other company of their nation, so that some minded to throw their castors away & returne home. We told them that we weare almost att the gates of the ffrench habitation, & bid [them] therefore have courage, & that our lives weare in as great danger as theirs, & if we weare taken we should never escape because they knewed us, & I because I runned away from their country having slained some of their brethren, & my brother that long since was the man that furnished their enemy with arms.

They att last weare persuaded, & landed within a mile of the landing place, & sent 300 men before armed. We made them great bucklers that the shot could not pearce in some places. They weare to be carried if there had ben occasion for it. Being come neere the torrent, we finding the Iroquoits lying in ambush, who began to shoot. The rest of our company went about cutting of trees & making a fort, whilst some brought the boats; which being come, we left as few means possible might bee. The rest helped to carry wood. We had about 200 men that weare gallant souldiers. The most weare hurrons, Pasnoestigons, & Amickkoick frequented the ffrench for a time. The rest weare skillfull in their bows & arrows. The Iroquoits perceiving our device, resolved to fight by forceing them to lett us passe with our arms. They did not know best what to doe, being not so munished nor so many men above a hundred and fifty. They forsooke the place & retired into the fort, which was underneath the rapide. We in the meane while have slained 5 of theirs, & not one of ours hurted, which encouraged our wildmen. We bid them still to have good courage, that we should have the victory. Wee went & made another fort neere theirs, where 2 of our men weare wounded but lightly.

It is a horrid thing to heare [of] the enormity of outcryes of those different nations. The Iroquoits sung like devils, & often made salleys to make us decline. They gott nothing by that but some arrows that did incommodat them to some purpose. We foresee that such a batail could not hold out long for want of powder, of shott & arrows; so by the consent of my brother & the rest, made a speech in the Iroquoit language, inducing meselfe with armours that I might not be wounded with every bullett or arrow that the ennemy sent perpetually. Then I spoake. "Brethren, we came from your country & bring you to ours, not to see you perish unlesse we perish with you. You know that the ffrench are men, & maks forts that cannot be taken so soone therefore cheare upp, ffor we love you & will die with you." This being ended, nothing but howling & crying. We brought our castors & tyed them 8 by 8, and rowled them before us. The Iroquoits finding that they must come out of their fort to the watterside, where they left their boats, to make use of them in case of neede, where indeed made an escape, leaving all their baggage behind, which was not much, neither had we enough to fill our bellyes with the meat that was left; there weare kettles, broaken gunns, & rusty hattchetts.

They being gone, our passage was free, so we made hast & endeavoured to come to our journey's end; and to make the more hast, some boats went downe that swift streame without making any carriage, hoping to follow the ennemy; but the bad lacke was that where my brother was the boat turned in the torrent, being seaven of them together, weare in great danger, ffor God was mercifull to give them strength to save themselves, to the great admiration, for few can speed so well in such precipices. When they came to lande they cutt rocks. My brother lost his booke of annotations of the last yeare of our being in these foraigne nations. We lost never a castor, but may be some better thing. It's better [that one] loose all then lose his life.

We weare 4 moneths in our voyage without doeing any thing but goe from river to river. We mett severall sorts of people. We conversed with them, being long time in alliance with them. By the persuasion of som of them we went into the great river that divides itselfe in 2, where the hurrons with some Ottanake & the wild men that had warrs with them had retired. There is not great difference in their language, as we weare told. This nation have warrs against those of [the] forked river. It is so called because it has 2 branches, the one towards the west, the other towards the South, which we believe runns towards Mexico, by the tokens they gave us. Being among these people, they told us the prisoners they take tells them that they have warrs against a nation, against men that build great cabbans & have great beards & had such knives as we have had. Moreover they shewed a Decad of beads & guilded pearls that they have had from that people, which made us believe they weare Europeans. They shewed one of that nation that was taken the yeare before. We understood him not; he was much more tawny then they with whome we weare. His armes & leggs weare turned outside; that was the punishment inflicted uppon him. So they doe with them that they take, & kill them with clubbs & doe often eat them. They doe not burne their prisoners as those of the northern parts.

We weare informed of that nation that live in the other river. These weare men of extraordinary height & biggnesse, that made us believe they had no communication with them. They live onely uppon Corne & Citrulles, [Footnote: Citrulles, pumpkins.] which are mighty bigg. They have fish in plenty throughout the yeare. They have fruit as big as the heart of an Oriniak, which grows on vast trees which in compasse are three armefull in compasse. When they see litle men they are affraid & cry out, which makes many come help them. Their arrows are not of stones as ours are, but of fish boans & other boans that they worke greatly, as all other things. Their dishes are made of wood. I having seene them, could not but admire the curiosity of their worke. They have great calumetts of great stones, red & greene. They make a store of tobacco.

They have a kind of drink that makes them mad for a whole day. This I have not seene, therefore you may believe as you please.

When I came backe I found my brother sick, as I said before. God gave him his health, more by his courage then by any good medicine, ffor our bodyes are not like those of the wildmen. To our purpose; we came backe to our carriage, whilst wee endeavoured to ayde our compagnions in their extremity. The Iroquoits gott a great way before, not well satisfied to have stayed for us, having lost 7 of their men; 2 of them weare not nimble enough, ffor our bulletts & arrows made them stay for good & all. Seaven of our men weare sick, they have ben like to be drowned, & the other two weare wounded by the Iroquoits.

The next day we went on without any delay or encounter. I give you leave if those of mont Royall weare not overjoyed to see us arrived where they affirme us the pitifull conditions that the country was by the cruelty of these cruell barbars, that perpetually killed & slaughtered to the very gate of the ffrench fort. All this hindered not our goeing to the ffrench att the 3 rivers after we refreshed ourselves 3 dayes, but like to pay dearly for our bold attempt. 20 inhabitants came downe with us in a shawlopp. As we doubled the point of the river of the meddows we weare sett uppon by severall of the Iroquoits, but durst not come neare us, because of two small brasse pieces that the shalop carryed. We tyed our boats together & made a fort about us of castors' skins, which kept us from all danger. We went downe the streame in that posture. The ennemy left us, & did well; for our wildmen weare disposed to fight, & our shaloupp could not come neare them because for want of watter. We came to Quebecq, where we are saluted with the thundring of the guns & batteryes of the fort, and of the 3 shipps that weare then att anchor, which had gon back to france without castors if we had not come. We weare well traited for 5 dayes. The Governor made guifts & sent 2 Brigantins to bring us to the 3 rivers, where we arrived the 2nd day of, & the 4th day they went away.

That is the end of our 3 years' voyage & few months. After so much paine & danger God was so mercifull [as] to bring us back saf to our dwelling, where the one was made much off by his wife, the other by his friends & kindred. The ennemy that had discovered us in our goeing downe gott more company, with as many as they could to come to the passages, & there to waite for the retourne of those people, knowinge well that they could not stay there long because the season of the yeare was almost spent; but we made them by our persuasions goe downe to Quebecq, which proved well, ffor the Iroquoits thought they weare gone another way. So came the next day after our arrivall to make a discovery to the 3 rivers, where being perceived, there is care taken to receive them.

The ffrench cannot goe as the wildmen through the woods, but imbarks themselves in small boats & went along the river side, knowing that if the ennemy was repulsed, he would make his retreat to the river side. Some Algonquins weare then att the habitation, who for to shew their vallour disposed themselves to be the first in the poursuit of the enemy. Some of the strongest and nimblest ffrench kept them company, with an other great number of men called Ottanacks, so that we weare soone together by the ears. There weare some 300 men of the enemy that came in the space of a fourteen night together; but when they saw us they made use of their heels. We weare about 500; but the better to play their game, after they runned half a mile in the wood they turned againe, where then the batail began most furiously by shooting att one another.

That uppermost nation, being not used to shooting nor heare such noise, began to shake off their armours, and tooke their bows and arrows, which indeed made [more] execution then all the guns that they had brought. So seeing 50 Algonquins & 15 ffrench keep to it, they resolved to stick to it also, which had not long lasted; ffor seeing that their arrows weare almost spent & they must close together, and that the enemy had an advantage by keeping themselves behind the trees, and we to fall uppon we must be without bucklers, which diminished much our company that was foremost, we gave them in spight us place to retire themselves, which they did with all speed. Having come to the watter side, where their boats weare, saw the ffrench all in a row, who layd in an ambush to receive them, which they had done if God had not ben for us; ffor they, thinking that the enemy was att hand, mistrusted nothing to the contrary. The ffrench that weare in the wood, seeing the evident danger where their countrymen layd, encouraged the Ottanaks, who tooke their armes againe and followed the enemy, who not feared that way arrived before the ffrench weare apprehended, by good looke.

One of the Iroquoits, thinking his boat would be seene, goes quickly and putts it out of sight, & discovers himselfe, which warned the ffrench to hinder them to goe further uppon that score. Our wildmen made a stand and fell uppon them stoutly. The combat begins a new; they see the ffrench that weare uppon the watter come neere, which renforced them to take their boats with all hast, and leave their booty behind. The few boats that the french had brought made that could enter but the 60 ffrench, who weare enough. The wildmen neverthelesse did not goe without their prey, which was of three men's heads that they killed att the first fight; but they left Eleven of theirs in the place, besides many more that weare wounded. They went straight to their countrey, which did a great service to the retourne of our wildmen, and mett with non all their journey, as we heard afterwards.

They went away the next day, and we stayed att home att rest that yeare. My brother and I considered whether we should discover what we have seene or no; and because we had not a full and whole discovery, which was that we have not ben in the bay of the north, not knowing anything but by report of the wild Christinos, we would make no mention of it for feare that those wild men should tell us a fibbe. We would have made a discovery of it ourselves and have an assurance, before we should discover anything of it.
The ende of the Auxotacicac voyage, which is the third voyage.

FOURTH VOYAGE OF PETER ESPRIT RADISSON

The spring following we weare in hopes to meet with some company, having ben so fortunat the yeare before. Now during the winter, whether it was that my brother revealed to his wife what we had seene in our voyage and what we further intended, or how it came to passe, it was knowne; so much that the ffather Jesuits weare desirous to find out a way how they might gett downe the castors from the bay of the north by the Sacgnes, and so make themselves masters of that trade. They resolved to make a tryall as soone as the ice would permitt them. So to discover our intentions they weare very earnest with me to ingage myselfe in that voyage, to the end that my brother would give over his, which I uterly denied them, knowing that they could never bring it about, because I heard the wild men say that although the way be easy, the wildmen that are feed att their doors would have hindred them, because they make a livelyhood of that trade.

In my last voyage I tooke notice of that that goes to three lands, which is first from the people of the north to another nation, that the ffrench call Squerells, and another nation that they call porquepicque, and from them to the Montignes & Algonquins that live in or about Quebucque; but the greatest hinderance is the scant of watter and the horrid torrents and want of victuals, being no way to carry more then can serve 14 dayes' or 3 weeks' navigation on that river. Neverthelesse the ffathers are gone with the Governor's son of the three rivers and 6 other ffrench and 12 wildmen.

During that time we made our proposition to the governor of Quebuc that we weare willing to venture our lives for the good of the countrey, and goe to travell to the remotest countreys with 2 hurrons that made their escape from the Iroquoits. They wished nothing more then to bee in those parts where their wives and families weare, about the Lake of the stairing haire; to that intent would stay untill august to see if any body would come from thence. My brother and I weare of one minde; and for more assurance my brother went to Mont royall to bring those two men along. He came backe, being in danger. The Governor gives him leave, conditionaly that he must carry two of his servants along with him and give them the moitie of the profit. My brother was vexed att such an unreasonable a demand, to take inexperted men to their ruine. All our knowledge and desir depended onely of this last voyage, besides that the governor should compare 2 of his servants to us, that have ventured our lives so many years and maintained the countrey with our generosity in the presence of all; neither was there one that had the courage to undertake what wee have done. We made the governor a slight answer, and tould him for our part we knewed what we weare, Discoverers before governors. If the wild men came downe, the way for them as for us, and that we should be glad to have the honnour of his company, but not of that of his servants, and that we weare both masters and servants. The Governor was much displeased att this, & commanded us not to go without his leave. We desired the ffathers to Speake to him about it. Our addresses were slight because of the shame was putt uppon them the yeare before of their retourne, besids, they stayed for an opportunity to goe there themselves; ffor their designe is to further the Christian faith to the greatest glory of God, and indeed are charitable to all those that are in distresse and needy, especially to those that are worthy or industrious in their way of honesty. This is the truth, lett who he will speak otherwise, ffor this realy I know meselfe by experience. I hope I offend non to tell the truth. We are forced to goe back without doeing any thing.

The month of August that brings a company of the Sault, who weare come by the river of the three rivers with incredible paines, as they said. It was a company of seaven boats. We wrote the news of their arrivement to Quebuc. They send us word that they will stay untill the 2 fathers be turned from Sacquenes, that we should goe with them. An answer without reason. Necessity obliged us to goe. Those people are not to be inticed, ffor as soone as they have done their affaire they goe. The governor of that place defends us to goe. We tould him that the offense was pardonable because it was every one's interest; neverthelesse we knewed what we weare to doe, and that he should not be blamed for us. We made guifts to the wildmen, that wished with all their hearts that we might goe along with them. We told them that the governor minded to send servants with them, and forbids us to goe along with them. The wild men would not accept of their company, but tould us that they would stay for us two dayes in the Lake of St Peter in the grasse some 6 leagues from the 3 rivers; but we did not lett them stay so long, for that very night, my brother having the keys of the Brough as being Captayne of the place, we embarqued ourselves.

We made ready in the morning, so that we went, 3 of us, about midnight. Being come opposit to the fort, they aske who is there. My brother tells his name. Every one knows what good services we had done to the countrey, and loved us, the inhabitants as well as the souldiers. The sentrey answers him, "God give you a good voyage." We went on the rest of that night. Att 6 in the morning we are arrived to the appointed place, but found no body. We weare well armed, & had a good boat. We resolved to goe day and night to the river of the meddows to overtake them. The wildmen did feare that it was somewhat else, but 3 leagues beyond that of the fort of Richlieu we saw them coming to us. We putt ourselves uppon our guards, thinking they weare ennemy; but weare friends, and received us with joy, and said that if we had not come in 3 dayes' time, they would have sent their boats to know the reason of our delay. There we are in that river waiting for the night. Being come to the river of the medows, we did separat ourselves, 3 into 3 boats. The man that we have taken with us was putt into a boat of 3 men and a woman, but not of the same nation as the rest, but of one that we call sorcerors. They weare going downe to see some friends that lived with the nation of the fire, that now liveth with the Ponoestigonce or the Sault. It is to be understood that this river is divided much into streams very swift & small before you goe to the river of Canada; [on account] of the great game that there is in it, the ennemy is to be feared, which made us go through these torrents. This could make any one afraid who is inexperted in such voyages.

We suffered much for 3 dayes and 3 nights without rest. As we went we heard the noise of guns, which made us believe firmly they weare ennemyes. We saw 5 boats goe by, and heard others, which daunted our hearts for feare, although wee had 8 boats in number; but weare a great distance one from another, as is said in my former voyage, before we could gaine the height of the river. The boat of the sorcerors where was one of us, albeit made a voyage into the hurrons' country before with the ffathers, it was not usefull, soe we made him embark another, but stayed not there long. The night following, he that was in the boat dreamed that the Iroquoits had taken him with the rest. In his dreame he cryes out aloud; those that weare att rest awakes of the noise. We are in alarum, and ready to be gone. Those that weare with the man resolved to goe back againe, explicating that an evill presage. The wildmen councelled to send back the ffrenchman, saying he should die before he could come to their countrey. It's usually spoken among the wildmen when a man is sick or not able to doe anything to discourage him in such sayings.

Here I will give a relation of that ffrenchman before I goe farther, and what a thing it is to have an intrigue. The next day they see a boat of their ennemys, as we heard since. They presently landed. The wild men runned away; the ffrenchman alsoe, as he went along the watter side for fear of loosing himselfe. He finds there an harbour very thick, layes himselfe downe and falls asleepe. The night being come, the wildmen being come to know whether the ennemy had perceived them, but non pursued them, and found their boat in the same place, and imbarques themselves and comes in good time to mount royall. They left the poore ffrenchman there, thinking he had wit enough to come along the watter side, being not above tenne leagues from thence. Those wild men, after their arrivement, for feare spoak not one word of him, but went downe to the 3 rivers, where their habitation was. Fourteen days after some boats ventured to goe looke for some Oriniaks, came to the same place, where they made cottages, and that within a quarter of mille where this wrech was. One of the ffrench finds him on his back and almost quite spent; had his gunne by him. He was very weake, and desirous that he should be discovered by some or other. He fed as long as he could on grappes, and at last became so weake that he was not able any further, untill those ffrench found him. After awhile, being come to himselfe, he tends downe the three rivers, where being arrived the governor emprisons him. He stayed not there long. The inhabitants seeing that the ennemy, the hunger, and all other miseries tormented this poore man, and that it was by a divine providence he was alive, they would not have souffred such inhumanity, but gott him out.

Three dayes after wee found the tracks of seaven boats, and fire yett burning. We found out by their characters they weare no ennemys, but imagined that they weare Octanaks that went up into their countrey, which made us make hast to overtake them. We tooke no rest till we overtooke them. They came from Mount royall and weare gone to the great river and gone by the great river. So that we weare now 14 boats together, which weare to goe the same way to the height of the upper lake.

The day following wee weare sett uppon by a Company of Iroquoits that fortified themselves in the passage, where they waited of Octanack, for they knewed of their going downe. Our wildmen, seeing that there was no way to avoid them, resolved to be together, being the best way for them to make a quick Expedition, ffor the season of the yeare pressed us to make expedition. We resolved to give a combat. We prepared ourselves with targetts. Now the businesse was to make a discovery. I doubt not but the ennemy was much surprised to see us so in number. The councell was held and resolution taken. I and a wildman weare appointed to goe and see their fort. I offered myselfe with a free will, to lett them see how willing I was to defend them; that is the onely way to gaine the hearts of those wildmen. We saw that their fort was environed with great rocks that there was no way to mine it, because there weare no trees neere it. The mine was nothing else but to cutt the nearest tree, and so by his fall make a bracke, and so goe and give an assault. Their fort was nothing but trees one against another in a round or square without sides.

The ennemy seeing us come neere, shott att us, but in vaine, ffor we have fforewarned ourselves before we came there. It was a pleasur to see our wildmen with their guns and arrows, which agreed not together. Neverthelesse we told them when they received a breake their guns would be to no purpose; therefore to putt them by and make use of their bows and arrows. The Iroquoits saw themselves putt to it, and the evident danger that they weare in, but to late except they would runne away. Yett our wildmen weare better wild footemen then they. These weare ffrenchmen that should give them good directions to overthrow them, resolved to speake for peace, and throw necklaces of porcelaine over the stakes of their fort. Our wildmen weare dazelled att such guifts, because that the porcelaine is very rare and costly in their countrey, and then seeing themselves flattered with faire words, to which they gave eare. We trust them by force to putt their first designe in Execution, but feared their lives and loved the porcelaine, seeing they had it without danger of any life. They weare persuaded to stay till the next day, because now it was almost night. The Iroquoits make their escape. This occasion lost, our consolation was that we had that passage free, but vexed for having lost that opportunity, & contrarywise weare contented of our side, for doubtlesse some of us had ben killed in the bataill.

The day following we embarqued ourselves quietly, being uppon our guard for feare of any surprize, ffor that ennemy's danger scarcely begane, who with his furour made himselfe so redoubted, having ben there up and downe to make a new slaughter. This morning, in assurance enough; in the afternoone the two boats that had orders to land some 200 paces from the landing place, one tooke onely a small bundle very light, tends to the other side of the carriage, imagining there to make the kettle boyle, having killed 2 staggs two houres agoe, and was scarce halfe way when he meets the Iroquoits, without doubt for that same businesse. I think both weare much surprized. The Iroquoits had a bundle of Castor that he left behind without much adoe. Our wild men did the same; they both runne away to their partners to give them notice. By chance

164

my brother meets them in the way. The wild men seeing that they all weare frightned and out of breath, they asked the matter, and was told, nadonnee, and so soone said, he letts fall his bundle that he had uppon his back into a bush, and comes backe where he finds all the wildmen dispaired. He desired me to encourage them, which I performed with all earnestnesse. We runned to the height of the carriage. As we weare agoing they tooke their armes with all speed. In the way we found the bundle of castors that the ennemy had left. By this means we found out that they weare in a fright as wee, and that they came from the warrs of the upper country, which we told the wildmen, so encouraged them to gaine the watter side to discover their forces, where wee no sooner came but 2 boats weare landed & charged their guns, either to defend themselves or to sett uppon us. We prevented this affair by our diligence, and shott att them with our bows & arrows, as with our gunns.

They finding such an assault immediately forsooke the place. They would have gone into their boats, but we gave them not so much time. They threwed themselves into the river to gaine the other side. This river was very narrow, so that it was very violent. We had killed and taken them all, if 2 boats of theirs had not come to their succour, which made us gave over to follow them, & looke to ourselves, ffor we knewed not the number of their men. Three of their men neverthelesse weare killed; the rest is on the other side of the river, where there was a fort which was made long before. There they retired themselves with all speed. We passe our boats to augment our victory, seeing that they weare many in number. They did what they could to hinder our passage, butt all in vaine, ffor we made use of the bundle of Castors that they left, which weare to us instead of Gabbions, for we putt them att the heads of our boats, and by that means gott ground in spight of their noses. They killed one of our men as we landed. Their number was not to resist ours. They retired themselves into the fort and brought the rest of their [men] in hopes to save it. In this they were far mistaken, for we furiously gave an assault, not sparing time to make us bucklers, and made use of nothing else but of castors tyed together. So without any more adoe we gathered together. The Iroquoits spared not their powder, but made more noise then hurt. The darknesse covered the earth, which was somewhat favorable for us; but to overcome them the sooner, we filled a barill full of gun powder, and having stoped the whole of it well and tyed it to the end of a long pole, being att the foote of the fort. Heere we lost 3 of our men; our machine did play with an execution. I may well say that the ennemy never had seen the like. Moreover I tooke 3 or 4 pounds of powder; this I put into a rind of a tree, then a fusy to have the time to throw the rind, warning the wildmen as soone as the rind made his execution that they should enter in and breake the fort upside down, with the hattchett and the sword in their hands.

In the meane time the Iroquoits did sing, expecting death, or to their heels, att the noise of such a smoake & noise that our machines made, with the slaughter of many of them. Seeing themselves soe betrayed, they lett us goe free into their fort, that thereby they might save themselves; but having environed the fort, we are mingled pell mell, so that we could not know one another in that skirmish of blowes. There was such an noise that should terrifie the stoutest men. Now there falls a showre of raine and a terrible storme, that to my thinking there was somthing extraordinary, that the devill himselfe made that storme to give those men leave to escape from our hands, to destroy another time more of these innocents. In that darknesse every one looked about for shelter, not thinking of those braves, that layd downe halfe dead, to pursue them. It was a thing impossible, yett doe believe that the ennemy was not far. As the storme was over, we came together, making a noise, and I am persuaded that many thought themselves prisoners that weare att Liberty. Some sang their fatall song, albeit without any wounds. So that those that had the confidence to come neare the others weare comforted by assuring them the victory, and that the ennemy was routed. We presently make a great fire, and with all hast make upp the fort againe for feare of any surprize. We searched for those that weare missing. Those that weare dead and wounded weare visited. We found 11 of our ennemy slain'd and 2 onely of ours, besides seaven weare wounded, who in a short time passed all danger of life. While some weare busie in tying 5 of the enemy that could not escape, the others visited the wounds of their compagnions, who for to shew their courage sung'd lowder then those that weare well. The sleepe that we tooke that night did not make our heads guidy, although we had need of reposeing. Many liked the occupation, for they filled their bellyes with the flesh of their ennemyes. We broiled some of it and kettles full of the rest. We bourned our comrades, being their custome to reduce such into ashes being stained in bataill. It is an honnour to give them such a buriall.

Att the brake of day we cooked what could accommodate us, and flung the rest away. The greatest marke of our victory was that we had 10 heads & foure prisoners, whom we embarqued in hopes to bring them into our countrey, and there to burne them att our owne leasures for the more satisfaction of our wives. We left that place of masacre with horrid cryes. Forgetting the death of our parents, we plagued those infortunate. We plucked out their nailes one after another. The next morning, after we slept a litle in our boats, we made a signe to begone. They prayed to lett off my peece, which made greate noise. To fullfill their desire, I lett it of. I noe sooner shott, butt perceived seaven boats of the Iroquoits going from a point towards the land. We were surprised of such an incounter, seeing death before us, being not strong enough to resist such a company, ffor there weare 10 or 12 in every boat. They perceiving us thought that we weare more in number, began in all hast to make a fort, as we received from two discoverers that wee sent to know their postures. It was with much adoe that those two went. Dureing we perswaded our wildmen to send seaven of our boats to an isle neare hand, and turne often againe to frighten our adversaryes by our shew of our forces. They had a minde to fortifie themselves in that island, but we would not suffer it, because there was time enough in case of necessity, which we represent unto them, making them to gather together all the broaken trees to make them a kind of barricado, prohibiting them to cutt trees, that thereby the ennemy might not suspect our feare & our small number, which they had knowne by the stroaks of their hattchetts. Those wildmen, thinking to be lost, obeyed us in every thing, telling us every foot, "Be chearfull, and dispose of us as you will, for we are men lost." We killed our foure prisoners because they embarassed us. They sent, as soone as we weare together, some fourty, that perpetually went to and againe to find out our pollicy and weaknesse.

In the meane time we told the people that they weare men, & if they must, die altogether, and for us to make a fort in the lande was to destroy ourselves, because we should put ourselves in prison; to take courage, if in case we should be forced to take a retreat the Isle was a fort for us, from whence we might well escape in the night. That we weare strangers and they, if I must say so, in their countrey, & shooting ourselves in a fort all passages would be open uppon us for to save ourselves through the woods, was a miserable comfort. In the mean time the Iroquoits worked lustily, think att every step we weare to give them an assault, but farr deceived, ffor if ever blind wished the

Light, we wished them the obscurity of the night, which no sooner approached but we embarqued ourselves without any noise, and went along. It's strang to me that the ennemy did not encounter us. Without question he had store of prisoners and booty. We left the Iroquoits in his fort and the feare in our breeches, for without apprehension we rowed from friday to tuesday without intermission. We had scarce to eat a bitt of sault meat. It was pitty to see our feete & leggs in blood by drawing our boats through the swift streames, where the rocks have such sharp points that there is nothing but death could make men doe what we did. On the third day the paines & labour we tooke forced us to an intermission, ffor we weare quite spent. After this we went on without any encounter whatsoever, having escaped very narrowly. We passed a sault that falls from a vast height. Some of our wildmen went underneath it, which I have seene, & I myselfe had the curiosity, but that quiver makes a man the surer. The watter runs over the heads with such impetuosity & violence that it's incredible. Wee went under this torrent a quarter of a mille, that falls from the toppe above fourty foot downwards.

Having come to the lake of the Castors, we went about the lake of the castors for some victuals, being in great want, and suffered much hunger. So every one constituts himselfe; some went a hunting, some a fishing. This done, we went downe the river of the sorcerers, which brought us to the first great lake. What joy had we to see ourselves out of that river so dangerous, after we wrought two and twenty dayes and as many nights, having not slept one houre on land all that while. Now being out of danger, as safe from our enemy, perhaps we must enter into another, which perhaps may give practice & trouble consequently. Our equipage and we weare ready to wander uppon that sweet sea; but most of that coast is void of wild beasts, so there was great famine amongst us for want. Yett the coast afforded us some small fruits. There I found the kindnesse & charity of the wildmen, ffor when they found any place of any quantity of it they called me and my brother to eat & replenish our bellys, shewing themselves far gratfuller then many Christians even to their owne relations.

I cannot forgett here the subtilty of one of these wildmen that was in the same boat with me. We see a castor along the watter side, that puts his head out of the watter. That wildman no sooner saw him but throwes himself out into the watter and downe to the bottom, without so much time as to give notice to any, and before many knewed of anything, he brings up the castor in his armes as a child, without fearing to be bitten. By this we see that hunger can doe much.

Afterwardes we entered into a straight which had 10 leagues in length, full of islands, where we wanted not fish. We came after to a rapid that makes the separation of the lake of the hurrons, that we calle Superior, or upper, for that the wildmen hold it to be longer & broader, besids a great many islands, which maks appeare in a bigger extent. This rapid was formerly the dwelling of those with whome wee weare, and consequently we must not aske them if they knew where they have layed. Wee made cottages att our advantages, and found the truth of what those men had often [said], that if once we could come to that place we should make good cheare of a fish that they call Assickmack, which signifieth a white fish. The beare, the castors, and the Oriniack shewed themselves often, but to their cost; indeed it was to us like a terrestriall paradise. After so long fastning, after so great paines that we had taken, finde ourselves so well by chossing our dyet, and resting when we had a minde to it, 'tis here that we must tast with pleasur a sweet bitt. We doe not aske for a good sauce; it's better to have it naturally; it is the way to distinguish the sweet from the bitter.

But the season was far spent, and use diligence and leave that place so wished, which wee shall bewaile, to the coursed Iroquoits. What hath that poore nation done to thee, and being so far from thy country? Yett if they had the same liberty that in former dayes they have had, we poore ffrench should not goe further with our heads except we had a strong army. Those great lakes had not so soone comed to our knowledge if it had not ben for those brutish people; two men had not found out the truth of these seas so cheape; the interest and the glorie could not doe what terror doth att the end. We are a litle better come to ourselves and furnished. We left that inn without reckoning with our host. It is cheape when wee are not to put the hand to the purse; nevertheless we must pay out of civility: the one gives thanks to the woods, the other to the river, the third to the earth, the other to the rocks that stayes the ffish; in a word, there is nothing but kinekoiur of all sorts; the encens of our Encens (?) is not spared. The weather was agreable when we began to navigat upon that great extent of watter, finding it so calme and the aire so cleare. We thwarted in a pretty broad place, came to an isle most delightfull for the diversity of its fruits. We called it the isle of the foure beggars. We arrived about 5 of the clocke in the afternone that we came there. We sudainly put the kettle to the fire. We reside there a while, and seeing all this while the faire weather and calme. We went from thence att tenne of the clocke the same night to gaine the firme lande, which was 6 leagues from us, where we arrived before day. Here we found a small river. I was so curious that I inquired my dearest friends the name of this streame. They named me it pauabickkomesibs, which signifieth a small river of copper. I asked him the reason. He told me, "Come, and I shall shew thee the reason why." I was in a place which was not 200 paces in the wood, where many peeces of copper weare uncovered. Further he told me that the mountaine I saw was of nothing else. Seeing it so faire & pure, I had a minde to take a peece of it, but they hindred me, telling my brother there was more where we weare to goe. In this great Lake of myne owne eyes have seene which are admirable, and cane maintaine of a hundred pounds teem will not be decayed. [Footnote: "Of a hundred pounds teem." This sentence seems somewhat obscure. The writer perhaps meant to say that he had seen masses of copper not less than a hundred pounds weight.]

From this place we went along the coasts, which are most delightfull and wounderous, for it's nature that made it so pleasant to the eye, the sperit, and the belly. As we went along we saw banckes of sand so high that one of our wildmen went upp for curiositie; being there, did shew no more then a crow. That place is most dangerous when that there is any storme, being no landing place so long as the sandy bancks are under watter; and when the wind blowes, that sand doth rise by a strang kind of whirling that are able to choake the passengers. One day you will see 50 small mountaines att one side, and the next day, if the wind changes, on the other side. This putts me in mind of the great and vast wildernesses of Turkey land, as the Turques makes their pylgrimages.

Some dayes after we observed that there weare some boats before us, but knewed not certainely what they weare. We made all the hast to overtake them, fearing the ennemy no more. Indeed the faster we could goe the better for us, because of the season of the yeare, that began to be cold & freeze. They weare a nation that lived in a land towards the South. This nation is very small, being not 100 in all, men & women together. As we came neerer them they weare surprized of our safe retourne, and astonied to see us, admiring the rich marchandises that their confederates brought from the ffrench, that weare hattchetts and knives and other utensils very commodious, rare, precious, and necessary in those countreys. They told the news one to another whilst we made good cheere and great fires. They mourned for the death of [one] of their comrades; the heads of their ennemy weare danced. Some dayes [after] we separated ourselves, and presented guiftes to those that weare going an other way, for which we received great store of meate, which was putt up in barrills, and grease of bears & Oriniacke.

After this we came to a remarquable place. It's a banke of Rocks that the wild men made a sacrifice to; they calls it Nanitoucksinagoit, which signifies the likenesse of the devill. They fling much tobacco and other things in its veneration. It is a thing most incredible that that lake should be so boisterous, that the waves of it should have the strength to doe what I have to say by this my discours: first, that it's so high and soe deepe that it's impossible to claime up to the point. There comes many sorte of birds that makes there nest here, the goilants, which is a white sea-bird of the bignesse of pigeon, which makes me believe what the wildmen told me concerning the sea to be neare directly to the point. It's like a great Portail, by reason of the beating of the waves. The lower part of that oppening is as bigg as a tower, and grows bigger in the going up. There is, I believe, 6 acres of land. Above it a shipp of 500 tuns could passe by, soe bigg is the arch. I gave it the name of the portail of St Peter, because my name is so called, and that I was the first Christian [Footnote: "The first Christian that ever saw it." French Jesuits and fur-traders pushed deeper and deeper into the wilderness of the northern lakes. In 1641 Jacques and Raynbault preached the Faith to a concourse of Indians at the outlet of Lake Superior. Then came the havoc and desolation of the Iroquois war, and for years further exploration was arrested. At length, in 1658, two daring traders penetrated to Lake Superior, wintered there, and brought back the tales they had heard of the ferocious Sioux, and of a great western river on which they dwelt. Two years later the aged Jesuit Mesnard attempted to plant a mission on the southern shore of the lake, but perished in the forest by famine or the tomahawk. Allouez succeeded him, explored a part of Lake Superior, and heard in his turn of the Sioux and their great river, the "Messipi."—Introduction to Parkman's Discovery of the Great West. There can be no doubt but that the "two daring traders who in 1658 penetrated to Lake Superior," and dwelt on the great river, were Radisson and Des Groseilliers, who repeated their journey a few years after, described in this narrative. The "Pictured Rocks" and the "Doric Rock" were so named in Governor Cass's and Schoolcraft's Travels in 1820.] that ever saw it. There is in that place caves very deepe, caused by the same violence. We must looke to ourselves, and take time with our small boats. The coast of rocks is 5 or 6 leagues, and there scarce a place to putt a boat in assurance from the waves. When the lake is agitated the waves goeth in these concavities with force and make a most horrible noise, most like the shooting of great guns.

Some dayes afterwards we arrived to a very beautifull point of sand where there are 3 beautifull islands, [Footnote: "Three beautiful islands." In Cass's and Schoolcraft's Travels (1820) through the chain of American lakes these islands are called Huron Islands, and the bay beyond is marked on their map "Keweena Bay."] that we called of the Trinity; there be 3 in triangle. From this place we discovered a bay very deepe, where a river empties its selfe with a noise for the quantitie & dept of the water. We must stay there 3 dayes to wait for faire weather to make the Trainage, which was about 6 leagues wide. Soe done, we came to the mouth of a small river, where we killed some Oriniacks. We found meddows that weare squared, and 10 leagues as smooth as a boord. We went up some 5 leagues further, where we found some pools made by the castors. We must breake them that we might passe. The sluce being broaken, what a wounderfull thing to see the industrie of that animal, which had drowned more then 20 leagues in the grounds, and cutt all the trees, having left non to make a fire if the countrey should be dried up. Being come to the height, we must drague our boats over a trembling ground for the space of an houre. The ground became trembling by this means: the castor drowning great soyles with dead water, herein growes mosse which is 2 foot thick or there abouts, and when you think to goe safe and dry, if you take not great care you sink downe to your head or to the middle of your body. When you are out of one hole you find yourselfe in another. This I speake by experience, for I meselfe have bin catched often. But the wildmen warned me, which saved me; that is, that when the mosse should breake under I should cast my whole body into the watter on sudaine. I must with my hands hold the mosse, and goe soe like a frogg, then to draw my boat after me. There was no danger.

Having passed that place, we made a carriage through the land for 2 leagues. The way was well beaten because of the commers and goers, who by making that passage shortens their passage by 8 dayes by tourning about the point that goes very farr in that great lake; that is to say, 5 to come to the point, and 3 for to come to the landing of that place of cariage. In the end of that point, that goeth very farre, there is an isle, as I was told, all of copper. This I have not seene. They say that from the isle of copper, which is a league in the lake when they are minded to thwart it in a faire and calme wether, beginning from sun rising to sun sett, they come to a great island, from whence they come the next

175

morning to firme lande att the other side; so by reason of 20 leagues a day that lake should be broad of 6 score and 10 leagues. The wildmen doe not much lesse when the weather is faire.

Five dayes after we came to a place where there was a company of Christinos that weare in their Cottages. They weare transported for joy to see us come backe. They made much of us, and called us men indeed, to perform our promise to come and see them againe. We gave them great guifts, which caused some suspicion, for it is a very jealous nation. But the short stay that we made tooke away that jealousy. We went on and came to a hollow river which was a quarter of a mile in bredth. Many of our wildmen went to win the shortest way to their nation, and weare then 3 and 20 boats, for we mett with some in that lake that joyned with us, and came to keepe us company, in hopes to gett knives from us, which they love better then we serve God, which should make us blush for shame. Seaven boats stayed of the nation of the Sault. We went on half a day before we could come to the landing place, and wear forced to make another carriage a point of 2 leagues long and some 60 paces broad. As we came to the other sid we weare in a bay of 10 leagues about, if we had gone in. By goeing about that same point we passed a straight, for that point was very nigh the other side, which is a cape very much elevated like piramides. That point should be very fitt to build & advantgeous for the building of a fort, as we did the spring following. In that bay there is a chanell where we take great store of fishes, sturgeons of a vast biggnesse, and Pycks of seaven foot long. Att the end of this bay we landed. The wildmen gave thanks to that which they worship, we to God of Gods, to see ourselves in a place where we must leave our navigation and forsake our boats to undertake a harder peece of worke in hand, to which we are forced. The men told us that wee had 5 great dayes' journeys before we should arrive where their wives weare. We foresee the hard task that we weare to undergoe by carrying our bundles uppon our backs. They weare used to it. Here every one for himselfe & God for all.

We finding ourselves not able to performe such a taske, & they could not well tell where to finde their wives, fearing least the Nadoneceronons had warrs against their nation and forced them from their appointed place, my brother and I we consulted what was best to doe, and declared our will to them, which was thus: "Brethren, we resolve to stay here, being not accustomed to make any cariage on our backs as yee are wont. Goe yee and looke for your wives. We will build us a fort here. And seeing that you are not able to carry all your marchandizes att once, we will keepe them for you, and will stay for you 14 dayes. Before the time expired you will send to us if your wives be alive, and if you find them they will fetch what you leave here & what we have; ffor their paines they shall receive guifts of us. Soe you will see us in your countrey. If they be dead, we will spend all to be revenged, and will gather up the whole countrey for the next spring, for that purpose to destroy those that weare the causers of their death, and you shall see our strenght and vallour. Although there are seaven thousand fighting men in one village, you'll see we will make them runne away, & you shall kill them to your best liking by the very noise of our armes and our presence, who are the Gods of the earth among those people."

They woundered very much att our resolution. The next day they went their way and we stay for our assurance in the midst of many nations, being but two almost starved for want of food. We went about to make a fort of stakes, which was in this manner. Suppose that the watter side had ben in one end; att the same end there should be murtherers, and att need we made a bastion in a triangle to defend us from an assault. The doore was neare the watter side, our fire was in the midle, and our bed on the right hand, covered. There weare boughs of trees all about our fort layed a crosse, one uppon an other. Besides these boughs we had a long cord tyed with some small bells, which weare senteryes. Finally, we made an ende of that fort in 2 dayes' time. We made an end of some fish that we putt by for neede. But as soone as we are lodged we went to fish for more whilst the other kept the house. I was the fittest to goe out, being yongest. I tooke my gunne and goes where I never was before, so I choosed not one way before another. I went to the wood some 3 or 4 miles. I find a small brooke, where I walked by the sid awhile, which brought me into meddowes. There was a poole where weare a good store of bustards. I began to creepe though I might come neare. Thought to be in Canada, where the fowle is scared away; but the poore creatures, seeing me flatt uppon the ground, thought I was a beast as well as they, so they come neare me, whisling like gosslings, thinking to frighten me. The whistling that I made them heare was another musick then theirs. There I killed 3 and the rest scared, which neverthelesse came to that place againe to see what sudaine sicknesse befeled their comrads. I shott againe; two payed for their curiosity. I think the Spaniards had no more to fullfill then as kill those birds, that thought not of such a thunder bolt. There are yett more countreys as fruitfull and as beautifull as the Spaniards to conquer, which may be done with as much ease & facility, and prove as rich, if not richer, for bread & wine; and all other things are as plentifull as in any part of Europ. This I have seene, which am sure the Spaniards have not in such plenty. Now I come backe with my victory, which was to us more then tenne thousand pistoles. We lived by it 5 dayes. I tooke good notice of the place, in hopes to come there more frequent, but this place is not onely so.

There we stayed still full 12 dayes without any news, but we had the company of other wild men of other countreys that came to us admiring our fort and the workmanshipp. We suffered non to goe in but one person, and liked it so much the better, & often durst not goe in, so much they stood in feare of our armes, that weare in good order, which weare 5 guns, two musquetons, 3 fowling-peeces, 3 paire of great pistoletts, and 2 paire of pockett ons, and every one his sword and daggar. So that we might say that a Coward was not well enough armed. Mistrust neverthelesse is the mother of safety, and the occasion makes the thief. During that time we had severall alarums in the night. The squerels and other small beasts, as well as foxes, came in and assaulted us. One night I forgott my bracer, which was wett; being up and downe in those pooles to fetch my fowles, one of these beasts carried it away, which did us a great deal of wrong, and caused the life to great many of those against whom I declared myselfe an ennemy. We imagined that some wildmen might have surprized us; but I may say they weare far more afrayd then we. Some dayes after we found it one half a mile from the fort in a hole of a tree, the most part torne. Then I killed an Oriniack. I could have killed more, but we liked the fowles better. If we had both libertie to goe from our fort, we should have procured in a month that should serve us a whole winter. The wildmen brought us more meate then we would, and as much fish as we might eate.

The 12th day we perceived afarr off some 50 yong men coming towards us, with some of our formest compagnions. We gave them leave to come into our fort, but they are astonied, calling us every foot devills to have made such a machine. They brought us victualls, thinking we weare halfe starved, but weare mightily mistaken, for we had more for them then they weare able to eate, having 3 score bussards and many sticks where was meate hanged plentifully. They offred to carry our baggage, being come a purpose; but we had not so much marchandize as when they went from us, because we hid some of them, that they might not have suspicion of us. We told them that for feare of the dayly multitud of people that came to see us, for to have our goods would kill us. We therefore tooke a boat and putt into it our marchandises; this we brought farre into the bay, where we sunke them, biding our devill not to lett them to be wett nor rusted, nor suffer them to be taken away, which he promised faithlesse that we should retourne and take them out of his hands; att which they weare astonished, believing it to be true as the Christians the Gospell. We hid them in the ground on the other sid of the river in a peece of ground. We told them that lye that they should not have suspicion of us. We made good cheere. They stayed there three dayes, during which time many of their wives came thither, and we traited them well, for they eat not fowle att all, scarce, because they know not how to catch them except with their arrowes. We putt a great many rind about our fort, and broake all the boats that we could have, for the frost would have broaken them or wild men had stolen them away. That rind was tyed all in length to putt the fire in it, to frighten the more these people, for they could not approach it without being discovered. If they ventured att the going out we putt the fire to all the torches, shewing them how we would have defended ourselves. We weare Cesars, being nobody to contradict us. We went away free from any burden, whilst those poore miserable thought themselves happy to carry our Equipage, for the hope that they had that we should give them a brasse ring, or an awle, or an needle.

There came above foure hundred persons to see us goe away from that place, which admired more our actions [than] the fools of Paris to see enter their King and the Infanta of Spaine, his spouse; for they cry out, "God save the King and Queene!" Those made horrid noise, and called Gods and Devills of the Earth and heavens. We marched foure dayes through the woods. The countrey is beautifull, with very few mountaines, the woods cleare. Att last we came within a league of the Cabbans, where we layed that the next day might be for our entrey. We 2 poore adventurers for the honneur of our countrey, or of those that shall deserve it from that day; the nimblest and stoutest went before to warne before the people that we should make our entry to-morow. Every one prepares to see what they never before have seene. We weare in cottages which weare neare a litle lake some 8 leagues in circuit. Att the watterside there weare abundance of litle boats made of trees that they have hollowed, and of rind.

The next day we weare to embarque in them, and arrived att the village by watter, which was composed of a hundred cabans without pallasados. There is nothing but cryes. The women throw themselves backwards uppon the ground, thinking to give us tokens of friendship and of wellcome. We destinated 3 presents, one for the men, one for the women, and the other for the children, to the end that they should remember that journey; that we should be spoaken of a hundred years after, if other Europeans should not come in those quarters and be liberal to them, which will hardly come to passe. The first was a kettle, two hattchetts, and 6 knives, and a blade for a sword. The kettle was to call all nations that weare their friends to the feast which is made for the remembrance of the death; that is, they make it once in seaven years; it's a renewing of ffriendshippe. I will talke further of it in the following discours. The hattchetts weare to encourage the yong people to strengthen themselves in all places, to preserve their wives, and shew themselves men by knocking the heads of their ennemyes with the said hattchetts. The knives weare to shew that the ffrench weare great and mighty, and their confederats and ffriends. The sword was to signifie that we would be masters both of peace and warrs, being willing to healpe and relieve them, & to destroy our Ennemyes with our armes. The second guift was of 2 and 20 awles, 50 needles, 2 gratters of castors, 2 ivory combs and 2 wooden ones, with red painte, 6 looking-glasses of tin. The awles signifieth to take good courage, that we should keepe their lives, and that they with their hushands should come downe to the ffrench when time and season should permitt. The needles for to make them robes of castor, because the ffrench loved them. The 2 gratters weare to dresse the skins; the combes, the paint, to make themselves beautifull; the looking-glasses to admire themselves. The 3rd guift was of brasse rings, of small bells, and rasades of divers couleurs, and given in this maner. We sent a man to make all the children come together. When they weare there we throw these things over their heads. You would admire what a beat was among them, every one striving to have the best. This was done uppon this consideration, that they should be allwayes under our protection, giving them wherewithall to make them merry & remember us when they should be men.

This done, we are called to the Councell of welcome and to the feast of ffriendshipp, afterwards to the dancing of the heads; but before the dancing we must mourne for the deceased, and then, for to forgett all sorrow, to the dance. We gave them foure small guifts that they should continue such ceremonyes, which they tooke willingly and did us good, that gave us authority among the whole nation. We knewed their councels, and made them doe whatsoever we thought best. This was a great advantage for us, you must think. Amongst such a rowish kind of people a guift is much, and well bestowed, and liberality much esteemed; but not prodigalitie is not in esteeme, for they abuse it, being brutish. Wee have ben useing such ceremonyes 3 whole dayes, & weare lodged in the cabban of the chiefest captayne, who came with us from the ffrench. We liked not the company of that blind, therefore left him. He wondred at this, but durst not speake, because we weare demi-gods. We came to a cottage of an ancient witty man, that had had a great familie and many children, his wife old, neverthelesse handsome. They weare of a nation called Malhonmines; that is, the nation of Oats, graine that is much in that countrey. Of this afterwards more att large. I tooke this man for my ffather and the woman for my mother, soe the children consequently brothers and sisters. They adopted me. I gave every one a guift, and they to mee.

Having so disposed of our buissinesse, the winter comes on, that warns us; the snow begins to fall, soe we must retire from the place to seeke our living in the woods. Every one getts his equipage ready. So away we goe, but not all to the same place; two, three att the most, went one way, and so of an other. They have so done because victuals weare scant for all in a place. But lett us where we will, we cannot escape the myghty hand of God, that disposes as he pleases, and who chastes us as a good & a common loving ffather, and not as our sins doe deserve. Finaly wee depart one from an other. As many as we weare in number, we are reduced to a small company. We appointed a rendezvous after two months and a half, to take a new road & an advice what we should doe. During the said terme we sent messengers everywhere, to give speciall notice to all manner of persons and nation that within 5 moons the feast of death was to be celebrated, and that we should apeare together and explain what the devill should command us to say, and then present them presents of peace and union. Now we must live on what God sends, and warre against the bears in the meane time, for we could aime att nothing else, which was the cause that we had no great cheare. I can say that we with our comrades, who weare about 60, killed in the space of 2 moons and a halfe, a thousand moons [Footnote: The writer no doubt meant that they killed so many that they had bear's grease enough to last for a thousand moons.] we wanted not bear's grease to annoint ourselves, to runne the better. We beated downe the woods dayly for to discover novellties. We killed severall other beasts, as Oriniacks, staggs, wild cows, Carriboucks, fallow does and bucks, Catts of mountains, child of the Devill; in a word, we lead a good life. The snow increases dayly. There we make raketts, not to play att ball, but to exercise ourselves in a game harder and more necessary. They are broad, made like racketts, that they may goe in the snow and not sinke when they runne after the eland or other beast.

We are come to the small lake, the place of rendezvous, where we found some company that weare there before us. We cottage ourselves, staying for the rest, that came every day. We stayed 14 dayes in this place most miserable, like to a churchyard; ffor there did fall such a quantity of snow and frost, and with such a thick mist, that all the snow stoocke to those trees that are there so ruffe, being deal trees, prusse cedars, and thorns, that caused the darknesse uppon the earth that it is to be believed that the sun was eclipsed them 2 months; ffor after the trees weare so laden with snow that fel'd afterwards, was as if it had been sifted, so by that means very light and not able to beare us, albeit we made racketts of 6 foot long and a foot and a halfe broad; so often thinking to tourne ourselves we felld over and over againe in the snow, and if we weare alone we should have difficultie enough to rise againe. By the noyse we made, the Beasts heard us a great way off; so the famine was among great many that had not provided before hand, and live upon what they gett that day, never thinking for the next. It grows wors and wors dayly.

To augment our misery we receive news of the Octanaks, who weare about a hundred and fifty, with their families. They had a quarell with the hurrons in the Isle where we had come from some years before in the lake of the stairing hairs, and came purposely to make warres against them the next summer. But lett us see if they brought us anything to subsist withall. But are worst provided then we; having no huntsmen, they are reduced to famine. But, O cursed covetousnesse, what art thou going to doe? It should be farr better to see a company of Rogues perish, then see ourselves in danger to perish by that scourg so cruell. Hearing that they have had knives and hattchetts, the victualls of their poore children is taken away from them; yea, what ever they have, those doggs must have their share. They are the coursedest, unablest, the unfamous & cowarliest people that I have seene amongst fower score nations that I have frequented. O yee poore people, you shall have their booty, but you shall pay dearly for it! Every one cryes out for hungar; the women become baren, and drie like wood. You men must eate the cord, being you have no more strength to make use of the bow. Children, you must die. ffrench, you called yourselves Gods of the earth, that you should be feared, for your interest; notwithstanding you shall tast of the bitternesse, and too happy if you escape. Where is the time past? Where is the plentynesse that yee had in all places and countreys? Here comes a new family of these poore people dayly to us, halfe dead, for they have but the skin & boans. How shall we have strength to make a hole in the snow to lay us downe, seeing we have it not to hale our racketts after us, nor to cutt a litle woad to make a fire to keepe us from the rigour of the cold, which is extreame in those Countreyes in its season. Oh! if the musick that we heare could give us recreation, we wanted not any lamentable musick nor sad spectacle. In the morning the husband looks uppon his wife, the Brother his sister, the cozen the cozen, the Oncle the nevew, that weare for the most part found deade. They languish with cryes & hideous noise that it was able to make the haire starre on the heads that have any apprehension. Good God, have mercy on so many poore innocent people, and of us that acknowledge thee, that having offended thee punishes us. But wee are not free of that cruell Executioner. Those that have any life seeketh out for roots, which could not be done without great difficultie, the earth being frozen 2 or 3 foote deepe, and the snow 5 or 6 above it. The greatest susibstance that we can have is of rind tree which growes like ivie about the trees; but to swallow it, we cutt the stick some 2 foot long, tying it in faggott, and boyle it, and when it boyles one houre or two the rind or skinne comes off with ease, which we take and drie it in the smoake and then reduce it into powder betwixt two graine-stoans, and putting the kettle with the same watter uppon the fire, we make it a kind of broath, which nourished us, but becam thirstier and drier then the woode we eate.

The 2 first weeke we did eate our doggs. As we went backe uppon our stepps for to gett any thing to fill our bellyes, we weare glad to gett the boans and carcasses of the beasts that we killed. And happy was he that could gett what the other did throw away after it had ben boyled 3 or foure times to gett the substance out of it. We contrived an other plott, to reduce to powder those boanes, the rest of crows and doggs. So putt all that together halfe foot within grounde, and so makes a fire uppon it, We covered all that very well with earth, soe seeling the heat, and boyled them againe and gave more froth then before; in the next place, the skins that weare reserved to make us shoose, cloath, and stokins, yea, most of the skins of our cottages, the castors' skins, where the children beshit them above a hundred times. We burned the haire on the coals; the rest goes downe throats, eating heartily these things most abhorred. We went so eagerly to it that our gumms did bleede like one newly wounded. The wood was our food the rest of sorrowfull time. Finaly we became the very Image of death. We mistook ourselves very often, taking the living for the dead and the dead for the living. We wanted strength to draw the living out of the cabans, or if we did when we could, it was to putt them four paces in the snow. Att the end the wrath of God begins to appease itselfe, and pityes his poore creatures. If I should expresse all that befell us in that strange accidents, a great volume would not centaine it. Here are above 500 dead, men, women, and children. It's time to come out of such miseryes. Our bodyes are not able to hold out any further.

After the storme, calme comes. But stormes favoured us, being that calme kills us. Here comes a wind and raine that putts a new life in us. The snow sails, the forest cleers itselfe, att which sight those that had strings left in their bowes takes courage to use it. The weather continued so 3 dayes that we needed no racketts more, for the snow hardned much. The small staggs are [as] if they weare stakes in it after they made 7 or 8 capers. It's an easy matter for us to take them and cutt their throats with our knives. Now we see ourselves a litle fournished, but yett have not payed, ffor it cost many their lives. Our gutts became very straight by our long fasting, that they could not centaine the quantity that some putt in them. I cannot omitt the pleasant thoughts of some of them wildmen. Seeing my brother allwayes in the same condition, they said that some Devill brought him wherewithall to eate; but if they had seene his body they should be of another oppinion. The beard that covered his face made as if he had not altered his face. For me that had no beard, they said I loved them, because I lived as well as they. From the second day we began to walke.

There came 2 men from a strange countrey who had a dogg; the buissinesse was how to catch him cunningly, knowing well those people love their beasts. Neverthelesse wee offred guifts, but they would not, which made me stubborne. That dogge was very leane, and as hungry as we weare, but the masters have not suffered so much. I went one night neere that same cottage to doe what discretion permitts me not to speake. Those men weare Nadoneseronons. They weare much respected that no body durst not offend them, being that we weare uppon their land with their leave. The dogg comes out, not by any smell, but by good like. I take him and bring him a litle way. I stabbed him with my dagger. I brought him to the cottage, where [he] was broyled like a pigge and cutt in peeces, gutts and all, soe every one of the family had his share. The snow where he was killed was not lost, ffor one of our company went and gott it to season the kettles. We began to looke better dayly. We gave the rendezvous to the convenientest place to celebrat that great feast.

Some 2 moons after there came 8 ambassadors from the nation of Nadoneseronons, that we will call now the Nation of the beefe. Those men each had 2 wives, loadened of Oats, corne that growes in that countrey, of a small quantity of Indian Corne, with other grains, & it was to present to us, which we received as a great favour & token of friendshippe; but it had been welcome if they had brought it a month or two before. They made great ceremonys in greasing our feete and leggs, and we painted them with red. They stript us naked and putt uppon us cloath of buffe and of white castors. After this they weeped uppon our heads untill we weare wetted by their tears, and made us smoake in their pipes after they kindled them. It was not in common pipes, but in pipes of peace and of the warrs, that they pull out but very seldom, when there is occasion for heaven and earth. This done, they perfumed our cloaths and armour one after an other, and to conclude did throw a great quantity of tobbacco into the fire. We told them that they prevented us, for letting us know that all persons of their nation came to visit us, that we might dispose of them.

The next morning they weare called by our Interpretor. We understood not a word of their language, being quit contrary to those that we weare with. They are arrived, they satt downe. We made a place for us more elevated, to be more att our ease & to appeare in more state. We borrowed their Calumet, saying that we are in their countrey, and that it was not lawfull for us to carry anything out of our countrey. That pipe is of a red stone, as bigge as a fist and as long as a hand. The small reede as long as five foot, in breadth, and of the thicknesse of a thumb. There is tyed to it the tayle of an eagle all painted over with severall couleurs and open like a fan, or like that makes a kind of a wheele when he shuts; below the toppe of the steeke is covered with feathers of ducks and other birds that are of a fine collour. We tooke the tayle of the eagle, and instead of it we hung 12 Iron bows in the same manner as the feathers weare, and a blade about it along the staffe, a hattchett planted in the ground, and that calumet over it, and all our armours about it uppon forks. Every one smoaked his pipe of tobacco, nor they never goe without it. During that while there was a great silence. We prepared some powder that was litle wetted, and the good powder was precious to us. Our Interpreter told them in our name, "Brethren, we have accepted of your guifts. Yee are called here to know our will and pleasur that is such: first, we take you for our brethren by taking you into our protection, and for to shew you, we, instead of the eagles' tayle, have putt some of our armours, to the end that no ennemy shall approach it to breake the affinitie that we make now with you." Then we tooke the 12 Iron off the bowes and lift them up, telling them those points shall passe over the whole world to defend and destroy your ennemyes, that are ours. Then we putt the Irons in the same place againe. Then we tooke the sword and bad them have good courage, that by our means they should vanquish their Ennemy. After we tooke the hattchett that was planted in the ground, we tourned round about, telling them that we should kill those that would warre against them, and that we would make forts that they should come with more assurance to the feast of the dead. That done, we throw powder in the fire, that had more strenght then we thought; it made the brands fly from one side to the other. We intended to make them believe that it was some of our Tobacco, and make them smoake as they made us smoake. But hearing such a noise, and they seeing that fire fled of every side, without any further delay or looke for so much time as looke for the dore of the cottage, one runne one way, another an other way, ffor they never saw a sacrifice of tobacco so violent. They went all away, and we onely stayed in the place. We followed them to reassure them of their faintings. We visited them in their appartments, where they received [us] all trembling for feare, believing realy by that same meanes that we weare the Devils of the earth. There was nothing but feasting for 8 dayes.

The time now was nigh that we must goe to the rendezvous; this was betwixt a small lake and a medow. Being arrived, most of ours weare allready in their cottages. In 3 dayes' time there arrived eighten severall nations, and came privatly, to have done the sooner. As we became to the number of 500, we held a councell. Then the shouts and cryes and the encouragments weare proclaimed, that a fort should be builded. They went about the worke and made a large fort. It was about 603 score paces in lenght and 600 in breadth, so that it was a square. There we had a brooke that came from the lake and emptied itselfe in those medows, which had more then foure leagues in lenght. Our fort might be seene afar off, and on that side most delightfull, for the great many stagges that took the boldnesse to be carried by quarters where att other times they made good cheare.

In two dayes this was finished. Soone 30 yong men of the nation of the beefe arrived there, having nothing but bows and arrows, with very short garments, to be the nimbler in chasing the stagges. The Iron of their arrows weare made of staggs' pointed horens very neatly. They weare all proper men, and dressed with paint. They weare the discoverers and the foreguard. We kept a round place in the midle of our Cabban and covered it with long poles with skins over them, that we might have a shelter to keepe us from the snow. The cottages weare all in good order; in each 10, twelve companies or families. That company was brought to that place where there was wood layd for the fires. The snow was taken away, and the earth covered with deale tree bows. Severall kettles weare brought there full of meate. They rested and eat above 5 houres without speaking one to another. The considerablest of our companyes went and made speeches to them. After one takes his bow and shoots an arrow, and then cryes aloud, there speaks some few words, saying that they weare to lett them know the Elders of their village weare to come the morrow to renew the friendship and to make it with the ffrench, and that a great many of their yong people came and brought them some part of their wayes to take their advice, ffor they had a minde to goe against the Christinos, who weare ready for them, and they in like manner to save their wives & children. They weare scattered in many Cabbans that night, expecting those that weare to come. To that purpose there was a vast large place prepared some hundred paces from the fort, where everything was ready for the receiving of those persons. They weare to sett their tents, that they bring uppon their backs. The pearches weare putt out and planted as we received the news; the snow putt aside, and the boughs of trees covered the ground.

The day following they arrived with an incredible pomp. This made me thinke of the Intrance that the Polanders did in Paris, saving that they had not so many Jewells, but instead of them they had so many feathers. The ffirst weare yong people with their bows and arrows and Buckler on their shoulders, uppon which weare represented all manner of figures, according to their knowledge, as of the sun and moone, of terrestriall beasts, about its feathers very artificialy painted. Most of the men their faces weare all over dabbed with severall collours. Their hair turned up like a Crowne, and weare cutt very even, but rather so burned, for the fire is their cicers. They leave a tuff of haire upon their Crowne of their heads, tye it, and putt att the end of it some small pearles or some Turkey stones, to bind their heads. They have a role commonly made of a snake's skin, where they tye severall bears' paws, or give a forme to some bitts of buff's horns, and put it about the said role. They grease themselves with very thick grease, & mingle it in reddish earth, which they bourne, as we our breeks. With this stuffe they gett their haire to stand up. They cutt some downe of Swan or other fowle that hath a white feather, and cover with it the crowne of their heads. Their ears are pierced in 5 places; the holes are so bigg that your little finger might passe through. They have yallow waire that they make with copper, made like a starr or a half moone, & there hang it. Many have Turkeys. They are cloathed with Oriniack & staggs' skins, but very light. Every one had the skin of a crow hanging att their guirdles. Their stokens all inbrodered with pearles and with their own porke-pick worke. They have very handsome shoose laced very thick all over with a peece sowen att the side of the heele, which was of a haire of Buff, which trailed above halfe a foot upon the earth, or rather on the snow. They had swords and knives of a foot and a halfe long, and hattchetts very ingeniously done, and clubbs of wood made like backswords; some made of a round head that I admired it. When they kille their ennemy they cutt off the tuffe of haire and tye it about their armes. After all, they have a white robe made of Castors' skins painted. Those having passed through the midle of ours, that weare ranged att every side of the way. The Elders came with great gravitie and modestie, covered with buff coats which hung downe to the grounde. Every one had in his hand a pipe of Councell sett with precious jewells. They had a sack on their shoulders, and that that holds it grows in the midle of their stomacks and on their shoulders. In this sacke all the world is inclosed. Their face is not painted, but their heads dressed as the foremost. Then the women laden like unto so many mules, their burdens made a greater sheu then they themselves; but I supose the weight was not equivolent to its bignesse. They weare conducted to the appointed place, where the women unfolded their bundles, and slang their skins whereof their tents are made, so that they had houses [in] less then half an hour.

After they rested they came to the biggest cabbane constituted for that purpose. There were fires kindled. Our Captayne made a speech of thanksgiving, which should be long to writ it. We are called to the councell of new come chiefe, where we came in great pompe, as you shall heare. First they come to make a sacrifice to the french, being Gods and masters of all things, as of peace, as warrs; making the knives, the hattchetts, and the kettles rattle, etc. That they came purposely to putt themselves under their protection. Moreover, that they came to bring them back againe to their countrey, having by their means destroyed their Ennemyes abroad & neere. So Said, they present us with guifts of Castors' Skins, assuring us that the mountains weare elevated, the valleys risen, the ways very smooth, the bows of trees cutt downe to goe with more ease, and bridges erected over rivers, for not to wett our feete; that the dores of their villages, cottages of their wives and daughters, weare open at any time to receive us, being wee kept them alive by our marchandises. The Second guift was, yet they would die in their alliance, and that to certifie to all nations by continuing the peace, & weare willing to receive and assist them in their countrey, being well satisfied they weare come to celebrat the feast of the dead. The 3rd guift was for to have one of the doors of the fort opened, if neede required, to receive and keepe them from the Christinos that come to destroy them; being allwayes men, and the heavens made them so, that they weare obliged to goe before to defend their country and their wives, which is the dearest thing they had in the world, & in all times they weare esteemed stout & true soldiers, & that yett they would make it appeare by going to meet them; and that they would not degenerat, but shew by their actions that they weare as valiant as their fore ffathers. The 4th guift was presented to us, which [was] of Buff Skins, to desire our assistance ffor being the masters of their lives, and could dispose of them as we would, as well of the peace as of the warrs, and that we might very well see that they did well to goe defend their owne countrey; that the true means to gett the victory was to have a thunder. They meant a gune, calling it miniskoick.

The speech being finished, they intreated us to be att the feast. We goe presently back againe to fournish us with woaden bowls. We made foure men to carry our guns afore us, that we charged of powder alone, because of their unskillfullnesse that they might have killed their ffathers. We each of us had a paire of pistoletts and Sword, a dagger. We had a role of porkepick about our heads, which was as a crowne, and two litle boyes that carryed the vessells that we had most need of; this was our dishes and our spoons.

They made a place higher & most elevate, knowing our customs, in the midle for us to sitt, where we had the men lay our armes. Presently comes foure elders, with the calumet kindled in their hands. They present the candles to us to smoake, and foure beautifull maids that went before us carrying bears' skins to putt under us. When we weare together, an old man rifes & throws our calumet att our feet, and bids them take the kettles from of the sire, and spoake that he thanked the sun that never was a day to him so happy as when he saw those terrible men whose words makes the earth quacke, and sang a while. Having ended, came and covers us with his vestment, and all naked except his feet and leggs, he saith, "Yee are masters over us; dead or alive you have the power over us, and may dispose of us as your pleasur." So done, takes the callumet of the feast, and brings it, So a maiden brings us a coale of fire to kindle it. So done, we rose, and one of us begins to sing. We bad the interpreter to tell them we should save & keepe their lives, taking them for our brethren, and to testify that we short of all our artillery, which was of twelve gunns. We draw our Swords and long knives to our defence, if need should require, which putt the men in Such a terror that they knewed not what was best to run or stay. We throw a handfull of powder in the fire to make a greater noise and smoake.

Our songs being finished, we began our teeth to worke. We had there a kinde of rice, much like oats. It growes in the watter in 3 or 4 foote deepe. There is a God that shews himselfe in every countrey, almighty, full of goodnesse, and the preservation of those poore people who knoweth him not They have a particular way to gather up that graine. Two takes a boat and two sticks, by which they gett the eare downe and gett the corne out of it. Their boat being full, they bring it to a fitt place to dry it, and that is their food for the most part of the winter, and doe dresse it thus:

ffor each man a handfull of that they putt in the pott, that swells so much that it can suffice a man. After the feast was over there comes two maidens bringing wherewithall to smoake, the one the pipes, the other the fire. They offered ffirst to one of the elders, that satt downe by us. When he had smoaked, he bids them give it us. This being done, we went backe to our fort as we came.

The day following we made the principall Persons come together to answer to their guifts. Being come with great solemnity, there we made our Interpreter tell them that we weare come from the other side of the great salted lake, not to kill them but to make them live; acknowledging you for our brethren and children, whom we will love henceforth as our owne; then we gave them a kettle. The second guift was to encourage them in all their undertakings, telling them that we liked men that generously defended themselves against all their ennemyes; and as we weare masters of peace and warrs, we are to dispose the affairs that we would see an universall peace all over the earth; and that this time we could not goe and force the nations that weare yett further to condescend & submitt to our will, but that we would see the neighbouring countreys in peace and union; that the Christinos weare our brethren, and have frequented them many winters; that we adopted them for our children, and tooke them under our protection; that we should send them ambassadors; that I myself should make them come, and conclude a generall peace; that we weare sure of their obedience to us; that the ffirst that should breake the peace we would be their ennemy, and would reduce them to powder with our heavenly fire; that we had the word of the Christinos as well as theirs, and our thunders should serve us to make warrs against those that would not submitt to our will and desire, which was to see them good ffriends, to goe and make warrs against the upper nations, that doth not know us as yett. The guift was of 6 hattchetts. The 3rd was to oblige them to receive our propositions, likewise the Christinos, to lead them to the dance of Union, which was to be celebrated at the death's feast and banquett of kindred. If they would continue the warrs, that was not the meanes to see us againe in their Countrey. The 4th was that we thanked them ffor making us a free passage through their countreys. The guift was of 2 dozen of knives. The last was of smaller trifles,—6 gratters, 2 dozen of awles, 2 dozen of needles, 6 dozens of looking-glasses made of tine, a dozen of litle bells, 6 Ivory combs, with a litle vermillion. Butt ffor to make a recompence to the good old man that spake so favorably, we gave him a hattchett, and to the Elders each a blade for a Sword, and to the 2 maidens that served us 2 necklaces, which putt about their necks, and 2 braceletts for their armes. The last guift was in generall for all the women to love us and give us to eat when we should come to their cottages. The company gave us great Ho! ho! ho! that is, thanks. Our wildmen made others for their interest.

A company of about 50 weare dispatched to warne the Christinos of what we had done. I went myself, where we arrived the 3rd day, early in the morning. I was received with great demonstration of ffriendshippe. All that day we feasted, danced, and sing. I compared that place before to the Buttery of Paris, ffor the great quantity of meat that they use to have there; but now will compare it to that of London. There I received guifts of all sorts of meate, of grease more then 20 men could carry. The custome is not to deface anything that they present. There weare above 600 men in a fort, with a great deale of baggage on their shoulders, and did draw it upon light slids made very neatly. I have not seen them att their entrance, ffor the snow blinded mee. Coming back, we passed a lake hardly frozen, and the sun [shone upon it] for the most part, ffor I looked a while steadfastly on it, so I was troubled with this seaven or eight dayes.

The meane while that we are there, arrived above a thousand that had not ben there but for those two redoubted nations that weare to see them doe what they never before had, a difference which was executed with a great deale of mirth. I ffor feare of being inuied I will obmitt onely that there weare playes, mirths, and bataills for sport, goeing and coming with cryes; each plaid his part. In the publick place the women danced with melody. The yong men that indeavoured to gett a pryse, indeavoured to clime up a great post, very smooth, and greased with oyle of beare & oriniack grease. The stake was att least of 15 foot high. The price was a knife or other thing. We layd the stake there, but whoso could catch it should have it. The feast was made to eate all up. To honnour the feast many men and women did burst. Those of that place coming backe, came in sight of those of the village or fort, made postures in similitud of warrs. This was to discover the ennemy by signs; any that should doe soe we gave orders to take him, or kill him and take his head off. The prisoner to be tyed [and] to fight in retreating. To pull an arrow out of the body; to exercise and strike with a clubbe, a buckler to theire feete, and take it if neede requireth, and defende himselfe, if neede requirs, from the ennemy; being in sentery to heark the ennemy that comes neere, and to heare the better lay him downe on the side. These postures are playd while the drums beate. This was a serious thing, without speaking except by nodding or gesture. Their drums weare earthen potts full of watter, covered with staggs-skin. The sticks like hammers for the purpose. The elders have bomkins to the end of their staves full of small stones, which makes a ratle, to which yong men and women goe in a cadance. The elders are about these potts, beating them and singing. The women also by, having a nosegay in their hands, and dance very modestly, not lifting much their feete from the ground, keeping their heads downewards, makeing a sweet harmony. We made guifts for that while 14 days' time. Every one brings the most exquisite things, to shew what his country affoards. The renewing of their alliances, the mariages according to their countrey coustoms, are made; also the visit of the boans of their deceased ffriends, ffor they keepe them and bestow them uppon one another. We sang in our language as they in theirs, to which they gave greate attention. We gave them severall guifts, and received many. They bestowed upon us above 300 robs of castors, out of which we brought not five to the ffrench, being far in the countrey.

This feast ended, every one retourns to his countrey well satisfied. To be as good as our words, we came to the nation of the beefe, which was seaven small Journeys from that place. We promised in like maner to the Christinos the next spring we should come to their side of the upper lake, and there they should meete us, to come into their countrey. We being arrived among the nation of the beefe, we wondred to finde ourselves in a towne where weare great cabbans most covered with skins and other close matts. They tould us that there weare 7,000 men. This we believed. Those have as many wives as they can keepe. If any one did trespasse upon the other, his nose was cutt off, and often the crowne of his head. The maidens have all maner of freedome, but are forced to mary when they come to the age. The more they beare children the more they are respected. I have seene a man having 14 wives. There they have no wood, and make provision of mosse for their firing. This their place is environed with pearches which are a good distance one from an other, that they gett in the valleys where the Buffe use to repaire, uppon which they do live. They sow corne, but their harvest is small. The soyle is good, but the cold hinders it, and the graine very small. In their countrey are mines of copper, of pewter, and of ledd. There are mountains covered with a kind of Stone that is transparent and tender, and like to that of Venice. The people stay not there all the yeare; they retire in winter towards the woods of the North, where they kill a quantity of Castors, and I say that there are not so good in the whole world, but not in such a store as the Christinos, but far better.

Wee stayed there 6 weeks, and came back with a company of people of the nation of the Sault, that came along with us loaden with booty. We weare 12 days before we could overtake our company that went to the lake. The spring approaches, which [is] the fitest time to kill the Oriniack. A wildman and I with my brother killed that time above 600, besides other beasts. We came to the lake side with much paines, ffor we sent our wildmen before, and we two weare forced to make cariages 5 dayes through the woods. After we mett with a company that did us a great deale of service, ffor they carryed what we had, and arrived att the appointed place before 3 dayes ended. Here we made a fort. Att our arrivall we found att least 20 cottages full.

One very faire evening we went to finde what we hide before, which we finde in a good condition. We went about to execut our resolution, fforseeing that we must stay that yeare there, ffor which wee weare not very sorry, being resolved to know what we heard before. We waited untill the Ice should vanish, but received [news] that the Octanaks built a fort on the point that formes that Bay, which resembles a small lake. We went towards it with all speede. We had a great store of booty which we would not trust to the wildmen, ffor the occasion makes the thiefe. We overloaded our slide on that rotten Ice, and the further we went the Sun was stronger, which made our Trainage have more difficultie. I seeing my brother so strained, I tooke the slide, which was heavier then mine, and he mine. Being in that extent above foure leagues from the ground, we sunke downe above the one halfe of the legge in the Ice, and must advance in spight of our teeth. To leave our booty was to undoe us. We strived so that I hurted myselfe in so much that I could not stand up right, nor any further. This putt us in great trouble. Uppon this I advised my brother to leave me with his slide. We putt the two sleds one by another. I tooke some cloathes to cover mee. After I stripped myselfe from my wett cloathes, I layed myselfe downe on the slide; my brother leaves me to the keeping of that good God. We had not above two leagues more to goe. He makes hast and came there in time and sends wildmen for me and the slids. There we found the perfidiousnesse of the Octanaks. Seeing us in Extremitie, would prescribe us laws. We promised them whatever they asked. They came to fetch me.

For eight dayes I was so tormented I thought never to recover. I rested neither day nor night; at last by means that God and my brother did use, which was by rubbing my leggs with hott oyle of bears and keeping my thigh and leggs well tyed, it came to its former strenght. After a while I came to me selfe. There comes a great company of new wildmen to seeke a nation in that land for a weighty buissinesse. They desired me to goe a long, so I prepare myselfe to goe with them. I marched well 2 dayes, the 3rd day the sore begins to breake out againe, in so much that I could goe no further. Those left me, albeit I came for their sake. You will see the cruelties of those beasts, and I may think that those that liveth on fish uses more inhumanities then those that feed upon flesh; neverthelesse I proceeded forwards the best I could, but knewed [not] where for the most part, the sun being my onely guide.

There was some snow as yett on the ground, which was so hard in the mornings that I could not percave any tracks. The worst was that I had not a hattchett nor other arme, and not above the weight of ten pounds of victualls, without any drink. I was obliged to proceed five dayes for my good fortune. I indured much in the morning, but a litle warmed, I went with more ease. I looked betimes for som old cabbans where I found wood to make fire wherwith. I melted the snow in my cappe that was so greasy. One night I finding a cottage covered it with boughs of trees that I found ready cutt. The fire came to it as I began to slumber, which soone awaked me in hast, lame as I was, to save meselfe from the fire. My racketts, shoos, and stokens kept me my life; I must needs save them. I tooke them and flung them as farr as I could in the snow. The fire being out, I was forced to looke for them, as dark as it was, in the said snow, all naked & very lame, and almost starved both for hungar and cold. But what is it that a man cannot doe when he seeth that it concerns his life, that one day he must loose? Yett we are to prolong it as much as we cane, & the very feare maketh us to invent new wayes.

The fifth day I heard a noyse and thought it of a wolfe. I stood still, and soone perceived that it was of a man. Many wild men weare up and downe looking for me, fearing least the Bears should have devoured me. That man came neere and saluts me, and demands whether it was I. We both satt downe; he looks in my sacke to see if I had victualls, where he finds a peece as bigg as my fist. He eats this without participation, being their usuall way. He inquireth if I was a hungary. I tould him no, to shew meselfe stout and resolute. He takes a pipe of tobacco, and then above 20 pounds of victualls he takes out of his sack, and greased, and gives it me to eate. I eat what I could, and gave him the rest. He bids me have courage, that the village was not far off. He demands if I knewed the way, but I was not such as should say no. The village was att hand. The other wildmen arrived but the day before, and after a while came by boats to the lake. The boats weare made of Oriniacks' skins. I find my brother with a company of Christinos that weare arrived in my absence. We resolved to cover our buissinesse better, and close our designe as if we weare going a hunting, and send them before; that we would follow them the next night, which we did, & succeeded, but not without much labor and danger; for not knowing the right way to thwart the other side of the lake, we weare in danger to perish a thousand times because of the crums of Ice. We thwarted a place of 15 leagues. We arrived on the other side att night. When we came there, we knewed not where to goe, on the right or left hand, ffor we saw no body. Att last, as we with full sayle came from a deepe Bay, we perceived smoake and tents. Then many boats from thence came to meete us. We are received with much Joy by those poore Christinos. They suffered not that we trod on ground; they leade us into the midle of their cottages in our own boats, like a couple of cocks in a Basquett. There weare some wildmen that followed us but late. We went away with all hast possible to arrive the sooner att the great river. We came to the seaside, where we finde an old howse all demollished and battered with boulletts. We weare told that those that came there weare of two nations, one of the wolf, the other of the long-horned beast. All those nations are distinguished by the representation of the beasts or animals. They tell us particularities of the Europians. We know ourselves, and what Europ is, therefore in vaine they tell us as for that.

We went from Isle to Isle all that summer. We pluckt abundance of Ducks, as of all other sort of fowles; we wanted nor fish nor fresh meate. We weare well beloved, and weare overjoyed that we promised them to come with such shipps as we invented. This place hath a great store of cows. The wildmen kill them not except for necessary use. We went further in the bay to see the place that they weare to passe that summer. That river comes from the lake and empties itselfe in the river of Sagnes, called Tadousack, which is a hundred leagues in the great river of Canada, as where we weare in the Bay of the north. We left in this place our marks and rendezvous. The wildmen that brought us defended us above all things, if we would come directly to them, that we should by no means land, and so goe to the river to the other sid, that is, to the north, towards the sea, telling us that those people weare very treacherous. Now, whether they tould us this out of pollicy, least we should not come to them ffirst, & so be deprived of what they thought to gett from us [I know not]. In that you may see that the envy and envy raigns every where amongst poore barbarous wild people as att Courts. They made us a mapp of what we could not see, because the time was nigh to reape among the bustards and Ducks. As we came to the place where these oats growes (they grow in many places), you would think it strang to see the great number of ffowles, that are so fatt by eating of this graine that heardly they will move from it. I have seene a wildman killing 3 ducks at once with one arrow. It is an ordinary thing to see five [or] six hundred swans together. I must professe I wondred that the winter there was so cold, when the sand boyles att the watter side for the extreame heate of the Sun. I putt some eggs in that sand, and leave them halfe an houre; the eggs weare as hard as stones. We passed that summer quietly, coasting the seaside, and as the cold began, we prevented the Ice. We have the commoditie of the river to carry our things in our boats to the best place, where weare most bests.

This is a wandring nation, and containeth a vaste countrey. In winter they live in the land for the hunting sake, and in summer by the watter for fishing. They never are many together, ffor feare of wronging one another. They are of a good nature, & not great whore masters, having but one wife, and are [more] satisfied then any others that I knewed. They cloath themselves all over with castors' skins in winter, in summer of staggs' skins. They are the best huntsmen of all America, and scorns to catch a castor in a trappe. The circumjacent nations goe all naked when the season permitts it. But this have more modestie, ffor they putt a piece of copper made like a finger of a glove, which they use before their nature. They have the same tenents as the nation of the beefe, and their apparell from topp to toe. The women are tender and delicat, and takes as much paines as slaves. They are of more acute wits then the men, ffor the men are fools, but diligent about their worke. They kill not the yong castors, but leave them in the watter, being that they are sure that they will take him againe, which no other nation doth. They burne not their prisoners, but knock them in the head, or slain them with arrows, saying it's not decent for men to be so cruell. They have a stone of Turquois from the nation of the buff and beefe, with whome they had warrs. They pollish them, and give them the forme of pearle, long, flatt, round, and [hang] them att their nose. They [find] greene stones, very fine, att the side of the same bay of the sea to the norwest. There is a nation called among themselves neuter. They speake the beefe and Christinos' speech, being friends to both. Those poore people could not tell us what to give us. They weare overjoyed when we sayd we should bring them commodities. We went up on another river, to the upper lake. The nation of the beefe sent us guifts, and we to them, by [the] ambassadors. In the midle of winter we joyned with a Company of the fort, who gladly received us. They weare resolved to goe to the ffrench the next spring, because they weare quite out of stocke. The feast of the dead consumed a great deale of it. They blamed us, saying we should not trust any that we did not know. They upon this asked if we are where the trumpetts are blowne. We sayd yea, and tould that they weare a nation not to be trusted, and if we came to that sea we should warre against them, becaus they weare bad nation, and did their indeavour to tak us to make us their slaves.

In the beginning of Spring there came a company of men that came to see us from the elders, and brought us furrs to intice us to see them againe. I cannot omitt [a] pleasant encounter that happened to my brother as we weare both in a cottag. Two of the nation of the beefe came to see us; in that time my brother had some trade in his hands. The wildmen satt neere us. My brother shews unto them the Image which [re]presented the flight of Joseph and holy mary with the child Jesus, to avoid the anger of herod, and the Virgin and child weare riding the asse, and Joseph carrying a long cloake. My brother shewing that animal, naming it tatanga, which is a buffe, the wildmen, seeing the representation of a woman, weare astonished and weeps, pulls their haire, and tumbles up and downe to the fire, so continued half an houre, till he was in a sweat, and wetted with his tears the rest of the wildmen that weare there. One of them went out of the cottage. My brother and I weare surprized; thought they might have seene a vision, ffor instantly the man putt his hands on his face, as if he should make the signe of the crosse. Now as he came to himselfe, he made us understand, ffor I began to know much of their speech, that first we weare Devills, knowing all what is and what was done; moreover, that he had his desire, that was his wif and child, whome weare taken by the nation of the beefe foure years agoe. So he tooke the asse for the nation of the beefe, the Virgin mary for the picture of his wife, and Jesus for his son, and Joseph for himselfe, saying, "There am I with my long robe, seeking for my wife and child."

By our ambassadors I came to know an other Lake which is northerly of their countrey. They say that it's bigger then all the rest. The upper end is allways frozen. Their ffish comes from those parts. There are people that lives there and dare not trade in it towards the south. There is a river so deepe and blacke that there is no bottome. They say that fish goes neither out nor in to that river. It is very warme, and if they durst navigate in it, they should not come to the end in 40 dayes. That river comes from the lake, and the inhabitants makes warrs against the birds, that defends & offends with theire bills that are as sharpe as sword. This I cannot tell for truth, but told me. All the circumjacent neighbours do incourage us, saying that they would venter their lives with us, for which we weare much overjoyed to see them so freely disposed to goe along with us. Here nothing but courage. "Brother, doe not lye, ffor the ffrench will not believe thee." All men of courage and vallour, lett them fetch commodities, and not stand lazing and be a beggar in the cabbane. It is the way to be beloved of women, to goe and bring them wherewithall to be joyfull. We present guifts to one and to another for to warne them to that end that we should make the earth quake, and give terror to the Iroquoits if they weare so bold as to shew themselves. The Christinos made guifts that they might come with us. This was graunted unto them, to send 2 boats, to testifie that they weare retained slaves among the other nations, although they furnish them with castors. The boats ready, we embarque ourselves. We weare 700. There was not seene such a company to goe downe to the ffrench. There weare above 400 Christinos' boats that brought us their castors, in hopes that the people should give some marchandises for them. Att their retourne the biggest boats could carry onely the man and his wife, and could scarce carry with them 3 castors, so little weare their boats. In summer time I have seene 300 men goe to warrs, and each man his boat, ffor they are that makes the least boats. The company that we had filled above 360 boats. There weare boats that caryed seaven men, and the least two. It was a pleasur to see that imbarquing, ffor all the yong women went in stark naked, their hairs hanging down, yett it is not their coustoms to doe soe. I thought it their shame, but contrary they thinke it excellent & old custome good. They sing a loud and sweetly. They stood in their boats, and remained in that posture halfe a day, to encourage us to come and lodge with them againe. Therefore they are not alltogether ashamed to shew us all, to intice us, and inanimate the men to defend themselves valliantly and come and injoy them.

In two dayes we arrived att the River of the sturgeon, so called because of the great quantity of sturgeons that we tooke there. Here we weare to make our provissions to passe the lake some 14 dayes. In the said tearme wee dryed up above a million of sturgeons. [Footnote: He no doubt meant to say, above "un mille," or "above a thousand."] The women followed us close; after our abode there two dayes they overtooke us. We had severall fals allarums, which putt us in severall troubles. They woundred to have found an Oryanck dead uppon the place, with a boullet in his body. There thousand lyes weare forged. Therefore we goe from thence, but before we come to the Longpoint whereof we spoak before, the wildmen called it okinotoname, we perceive smoake. We goe to discover what it was, and by ill looke we found it was a Iroquoits boat of seaven men, who doubtlesse stayed that winter in the lake of the hurrons, and came there to discover somewhat. I cannot say that they weare the first that came there. God graunt that they may be the last. As they saw us, away they, as swift as their heels could drive. They left their boat and all. They to the woods, and weare pursued, but in vaine, ffor they weare gone before three houres. The pursuers came backe; the one brings a gun, the one a hattchett, the other a kettle, and so forth. The councell was called, where it was decreed to go backe and shooke off to goe downe to the ffrench till the next yeare. This vexed us sore to see such a fleete and such an opportunity come to nothing, foreseeing that such an other may be not in tenne years. We weare to persuade them to the contrary, but checked soundly, saying we weare worse then Ennemyes by perswading them to goe and be slained. In this we must lett theire feare passe over, and we back to the river of the sturgeons, where we found our wives, very buissie in killing those creatures that comes there to multiplie. We dayly heare some newe reporte. All every where ennemy by fancy.

We in the meane time buissie ourselves in the good of our country, which will recompence us badly ffor such toyle and labour. Twelve dayes are passed, in which time we gained some hopes of faire words. We called a councell before the company was disbanded, where we represented, if they weare discouvers, they had not vallued the losse of their kettle, knowing well they weare to gett another where their army layed, and if there should be an army it should appear and we in such an number, they could be well afraid and turne backe. Our reasons weare hard and put in execution. The next day we embarqued, saving the Christinos, that weare afraid of a sight of a boat made of another stuff then theirs, that they went back as we came where the Iroquoits' boat was. Our words proved true and so proceeded in our way.

Being come nigh the Sault, we found a place where 2 of these men sweated, & for want of covers buried themselves in the sand by the watter side to keepe their bodyes from the flyes called maringoines, which otherwise had killed them with their stings. We thwarted those 2 great lakes with great pleasur, having the wind faire with us. It was a great satisfaction to see so many boats, and so many that never had before commerce with the ffrench. So my brother and I thought wee should be wellcomed. But, O covetousnesse, thou art the cause of many evils! We made a small sayle to every boate; every one strived to be not the last. The wind was double wayes favourable to us. The one gave us rest, the other advanced us very much, which wee wanted much because of the above said delay. We now are comed to the cariages and swift streames to gett the lake of the Castors. We made them with a courage, promptitud, and hungar which made goe with hast as well as the wind. We goe downe all the great river without any encounter, till we came to the long Sault, where my brother some years before made a shipwrake. Being in that place we had worke enough. The first thing wee saw was severall boats that the Ennemy had left att the riverside. This putt great feare in the hearts of our people. Nor they nor we could tell what to doe; and seeing no body appeared we sent to discover what they weare. The discovers calls us, and bids us come, that those who weare there could doe us no harme.

You must know that 17 ffrench made a plott with foure Algonquins to make a league with three score hurrons for to goe and wait for the Iroquoits in the passage att their retourne with their castors on their ground, hoping to beat and destroy them with ease, being destitut of necessary things. If one hath his gun he wants his powder, and so the rest. Att the other side without doubt had notice that the travelers weare abroad, and would not faile to come downe with a company, and to make a valiant deede and heroick action was to destroy them all, and consequently make the ffrench tremble as well as the wildmen, ffor the one could not live without the other; the one for his commodities, the other ffor his castors; so that the Iroqits pretending to wait for us at the passage came thither fflocking. The ffrench and wild company, to putt the Iroquoit in some feare, and hinder his coming there so often with such confidence, weare resolved to lay a snare against him. That company of souldiers being come to the farthest place of that long sault without being discovered, thought allready to be conquerors making cariage, having abroad 15 men to make discoveries, but mett as many ennemyes. They assaulted each other, and the Iroquoits found themselves weake, left there their lives and bodyes, saving 2 that made their escape, went to give notice to 200 of theirs that made ready as they heard the gunns, to help their foreguard. The ffrench seeing such great odds made a retreat, and warned by foure Algonquins that a fort was built not afar off, built by his nation the last yeare, they fled into it in an ill houre. In the meane while the Iroquoits consulted what they should doe; they sent to 550 Iroquoits of the lower nation and 50 Orijonot that weare not afar off. Now they would asault the ffrench in their ffort, the ffort not holding but 20 men. The hurrons could not come in and could not avoid the shott of the ennemy. Then the ffrench pulled downe the fort, and closed together they stoutly began to worke. Those that the ffrench had killed, cutt their heads off & put them uppon long poles of their fort. This skermish dured two dayes & two nights. The Iroquoits finds themselves plagued, ffor the ffrench had a kind of bucklers and shelters. Now arrives 600 men that they did not think of in the least. Here is nothing but cryes, fire, and flame day & night. Here is not to be doubted, the one to take the other, the one to defend himselfe till death. The hurrons seeing such a company submitted to the ennemyes, but are like to pay for their cowardise, being in their hands weare tyed, abused, smitten, and burned as if they weare taken by force, ffor those barbarous weare revenged on their boanes as any was wounded or killed in the battaille.

In this great extremity our small company of one and twenty did resist 5 days against 800 men, and the two foremost dayes against 200 which weare seaven dayes together without intermission, & the worst was that they had no watter, as we saw, ffor they made a hole in the ground out of which they gott but litle because they weare on a hill. It was to be pitied. There was not a tree but was shot with buletts. The Iroquoits come with bucklers to make a breach. The ffrench putt fire to a barill of powder, thinking to shoake the Iroquoits or make him goe back; but did to their great prejudice, for it fell againe in their fort, which made an end of their combat. Uppon this the Ennemy enters, kills and slains all that he finds, so one did not make an escape, saveing one that was found alive; but he stayed not long, for in a short time after his fortune was as the rest; for as he was brought to one of the Forts of the Irokoits, as he was bid to sit down he finds a Pistolet by him, and takes it at adventure, not knowing whether it was charged or no. He puts the end to the breast of him that tyed him, and killd him in the presence of all his camerades; but without any more adoe he was burnt very cruelly. All the French though dead were tyed to posts along the River side, and the 4 Algonquins. As for the hurons they were burnt at their discretion. Some neverthelesse escaped to bring the certain newes how all passed. [Footnote: Frenchmen massacred at Long Sault. See Introduction.] It was a terrible spectacle to us, for wee came there 8 dayes after that defeat, which saved us without doubt. I beleeve for certain that the Iroqoits lost many men, having to doe with such brave and valiant souldiers as that company was. Wee visited that place and there was a fine Fort; three were about the other two.

Wee went down the river without making any carriage, and wee adventured very much. As Soon as wee were at the lower end many of our wildmen had a mind to goe back and not to goe any further, thinking really that all the French were killed. As for my Brother and I, wee did fear very much that after such a thing the pride of the enemy would make them attempt anything upon the habitations of mount Royall, which is but 30 leagues from thence. Wee did advise them to make a ffort, or to put us in one of the enemies', and to send immediately two very light boats, that could not be overtaken if the enemy should discover them; and that being arrived at the habitation, they should make them shoot the peeces of Ordnance, and that as soon as the night should come wee would embarque our selves and should hear the noise, or else wee should take councell of what wee should doe, and stay for them at the height of the Isle of mount Royall; which was done accordingly without any hazard, for all the enemies were gone dispairing of our comeing down, and for what they had done and for what they had lost, which by the report of some Hurons was more then four score men; and if the French had had a Fort flanke & some water they had resisted the enemy miraculously and forced them to leave them for want of powder and shott and also of other provisions. They were furnished for the whole summer. Our two boats did goe, but the rest were soe impatient that they resolved to follow them, being willing to run the same hazard; and wee arrived the next morning and were in sight when the peeces were shott off, with a great deale of Joy to see so great a number of boats that did almost cover the whole River.

Wee stayd 3 dayes at mont-Royall, and then wee went down to the three Rivers. The wildmen did aske our advice whether it was best for them to goe down further. We told them no, because of the dangers that they may meet with at their returne, for the Irokoits could have notice of their comeing down, and so come and lay in ambush for them, and it was in the latter season, being about the end of August. Well, as soon as their businesse was done, they went back again very well satisfyed and wee very ill satisfied for our reception, which was very bad considering the service wee had done to the countrey, which will at another time discourage those that by our example would be willing to venture their lives for the benefit of the countrey, seeing a Governor that would grow rich by the labours and hazards of others.

Before I goe further I have a mind to let you know the fabulous beleafe of those poore People, that you may see their ignorance concerning the soul's immortality, being separated from the body. The kindred and the friends of the deceased give notice to the others, who gather together and cry for the dead, which gives warning to the young men to take the armes to give some assistance and consolation to the deceased. Presently the corps is covered with white skins very well tyed. Afterwards all the kindred come to the cottage of the deceased and begin to mourn and lament. After they are weary of making such musick the husbands or Friends of the deceased send their wives for gifts to pacifie a little the Widdow and to dry her tears. Those guifts are of skins and of what they can get, for at such a ceremony they are very liberall. As soon as that is done and the night comes, all the young men are desired to come and doe what they will to have done to them. So that when darknesse has covered the whole face of the Earth they come all singing with staves in their hands for their armes, and after they are set round the cabbin, begin to knock and make such a noise that one would thinke they have a mind to tear all in peeces, and that they are possessed of some Devills. All this is done to expell and frighten the soule out of that poor and miserable body that she might not trouble his carcase nor his bones, and to make it depart the sooner to goe and see their Ancestors, and to take possession of their immortall glory, which cannot be obtained but a fortnight towards the setting of the sun. The first step that she makes is of seven dayes, to begin her course, but there are many difficulties, ffor it is through a very thick wood full of thorns, of stones and flints, which [brings] great trouble to that poor soule. At last having overcome all those dangers and toyles she comes to a River of about a Quarter of a mile broad where there is a bridge made onely of one planke, being supported by a beame pointed at one end, which is the reason that planke rises and falls perpetually, having not any rest nor stay, and when the soule comes near the side of that river, she meets with a man of extraordinary stature, who is very leane and holds a dagger of very hard wood and very keen in his hands, and speakes these words when he sees the petitioning soule come near: Pale, pale, which signifies, Goe, goe; and at every word the bridge ballances, and rises his knife, and the traveller offering himselfe, receives a blow by which he is cut in two, and each halfe is found upon that moving, and according as he had lived they stay upon it; that is, if his body was valiant the passage was soon made free to him, for the two halfes come together and joyn themselves again. So passe to the other side where she finds a bladder of bear's grease to grease herselfe and refresh herselfe for that which she is to do, which being done she finds a wood somewhat cleerer and a straight road that she must goe, and for 5 dayes neither goe to the right nor to the left hand, where at last being arrived she finds a very great and cleer fire, through which she must resolve to passe. That fire is kindled by the young men that dyed since the beginning of the world to know whether those that come have loved the women or have been good huntsmen; and if that soule has not had any of those rare Vertues she burnes and broiles the sole of her feet by going through the fire; but quite contrary if she has had them qualityes, she passes through without burning her selfe in the least, and from that so hot place she finds grease and paint of all sorts of colour with which she daubs and makes herselfe beautifull, to come to that place so wished for. But she has not yet all done, nor made an end of her voyage; being so dress'd she continues her course still towards the same pole for the space of two dayes in a very cleer wood, and where there is very high and tall trees of which most be oakes, which is the reason that there is great store of bears. All along that way they do nothing else but see their enemies layd all along upon the ground, that sing their fatall song for having been vanquished in this world and also in the other, not daring to be so bold as to kill one of those animalls, and feed onely upon the down of these beasts. Being arrived, if I may say, at the doore of that imaginarie paradise, they find a company of their ancestors long since deceased, by whom they are received with a great deale of ceremony, and are brought by so venerable a company within halfe a daye's journey of the place of the meeting, and all along the rest of the way they discourse of things of this world that are passd; for you must know they travell halfe a day without speaking one word, but keepe a very deep silence, for, said they, it is like the Goslings to confound one another with words. As soon as they are arrived they must have a time to come to themselves, to think well upon what they are to speak without any precipitation, but with Judgement, so that they are come where all manner of company with drumms & dryd bumpkins, full of stones and other such instruments. The elders that have brought her there cover her with a very large white skin, and colour her leggs with vermillion and her feet likewise, and so she is received amongst the Predestinates. There is a deep silence made as soon as she is come in, and then one of the elders makes a long speech to encourage the young people to go a hunting to kill some meat to make a feast for entertainment of the soul of their countryman, which is put in execution with a great deal of diligence and hast; and while the meat is boyling or roasting, and that there is great preparations made for the feast, the young maidens set out themselves with the richest Jewells and present the beesome to the new-comer. A little while after the kettles are filled, there is feasting every where, comedies acted, and whatsoever is rare is there to be seene; there is dancing every where. Now remaines nothing but to provide that poor soule of a companion, which she does presently, for she has the choice of very beautifull women, and may take as many as she pleases, which makes her felicity immortall.

By this you may see the silly beleefe of these poor People. I have seen right-minded Jesuites weep bitterly hearing me speake of so many Nations that perish for want of Instruction; but most of them are like the wildmen, that thinke they offend if they reserve any thing for the next day. I have seen also some of the same company say, "Alas, what pity 'tis to loose so many Castors. Is there no way to goe there? The fish and the sauce invite us to it; is there no meanes to catch it? Oh, how happy should I be to go in those countreys as an Envoye, being it is so good a countrey." That is the relation that was made me severall times by those wildmen, for I thought they would never have done. But let us come to our arrivall againe.

The Governour, seeing us come back with a considerable summe for our own particular, and seeing that his time was expired and that he was to goe away, made use of that excuse to doe us wrong & to enrich himselfe with the goods that wee had so dearly bought, and by our meanes wee made the country to subsist, that without us had beene, I beleeve, oftentimes quite undone and ruined, and the better to say at his last beeding, no castors, no ship, & what to doe without necessary commodities. He made also my brother prisoner for not having observed his orders, and to be gone without his leave, although one of his letters made him blush for shame, not knowing what to say, but that he would have some of them at what price soever, that he might the better maintain his coach & horses at Paris. He fines us four thousand pounds to make a Fort at the three

Rivers, telling us for all manner of satisfaction that he would give us leave to put our coat of armes upon it, and moreover 6,000 pounds for the country, saying that wee should not take it so strangely and so bad, being wee were inhabitants and did intend to finish our days in the same country with our Relations and Friends. But the Bougre did grease his chopps with it, and more, made us pay a custome which was the 4th part, which came to 14,000 pounds, so that wee had left but 46,000 pounds, and took away L. 24,000. Was not he a Tyrant to deal so with us, after wee had so hazarded our lives, & having brought in lesse then 2 years by that voyage, as the Factors of the said country said, between 40 and 50,000 pistolls? For they spoke to me in this manner: "In which country have you been? From whence doe you come? For wee never saw the like. From whence did come such excellent castors? Since your arrivall is come into our magazin very near 600,000 pounds Tournois of that filthy merchandise, which will be prized like gold in France." And them were the very words that they said to me.

Seeing ourselves so wronged, my brother did resolve to goe and demand Justice in France. It had been better for him to have been contented with his losses without going and spend the rest in halfe a year's time in France, having L. 10,000 that he left with his wife, that was as good a Houswife as he. There he is in France; he is paid with fair words and with promise to make him goe back from whence he came; but he feeing no assurance of it, did engage himselfe with a merchant of Rochell, who was to send him a Ship the next spring. In that hope he comes away in a fisher boat to the pierced Island, some 20 leagues off from the Isle d'eluticosty, [Footnote: Eluticosty, Anticosti, an island at the mouth of the river St. Lawrence.] the place where the ship was to come; that was to come whilst he was going in a shallop to Quebucq, where I was to goe away with him to the rendezvous, being he could not do anything without me; but with a great deel of difficulty it proved, so that I thought it possible to goe tast of the pleasures of France, and by a small vessell that I might not be idle during his absence. He presently told me what he had done, and what wee should doe. Wee embarked, being nine of us. In a few dayes wee came to the pierced Island, where wee found severall shipps newly arrived; & in one of them wee found a father Jesuit that told us that wee should not find what wee thought to find, and that he had put a good order, and that it was not well done to distroy in that manner a Country, and to wrong so many Inhabitants. He advised me to leave my Brother, telling me that his designs were pernicious. Wee see ourselves frustrated of our hopes. My Brother told me that wee had store of merchandize that would bring much profit to the french habitations that are in the Cadis. I, who was desirous of nothing but new things, made no scruple.

Wee arrived at St. Peter, in the Isle of Cape Breton, at the habitation of Monsr. Denier, where wee delivered some merchandizes for some Originack skins; from thence to Camseau where every day wee were threatned to be burned by the french; but God be thanked, wee escaped from their hands by avoiding a surprize. And in that place my Brother told me of his designe to come and see new England, which our servants heard, and grumbled and laboured underhand against us, for which our lives were in very great danger. Wee sent some of them away, and at last with much labour & danger wee came to Port Royall, which is inhabited by the french under the English Government, where some few dayes after came some English shipps that brought about our designes, where being come wee did declare our designes. Wee were entertained, and wee had a ship promised us, and the Articles drawn, and wee did put to sea the next spring for our discovery, and wee went to the entry of Hudson's streight by the 61 degree. Wee had knowledge and conversation with the people of those parts, but wee did see and know that there was nothing to be done unlesse wee went further, and the season of the yeare was far spent by the indiscretion of our master, that onely were accustomed to see some Barbadoes Sugers, and not mountaines of Suger candy, which did frighten him, that he would goe no further, complaining that he was furnished but for 4 months, & that he had neither Sailes, nor Cord, nor Pitch, nor Towe, to stay out a winter. Seeing well that it was too late, he would goe no further, so brought us back to the place from whence wee came, where wee were welcome, although with great losse of goods & hope, but the last was not quite lost. Wee were promised 2 shipps for a second voyage. They were made fit and ready, and being the season of the yeare was not yet come to be gone, one of them 2 shipps was sent to the Isle of Sand, there to fish for the Basse [Footnote: This fishing expedition was to the well-known Sable Island. In 1676 "The King granted Medard Chouart, Sieur des Grozelliers, and Pierre Esprit, Sieur des Radision, the privilege of establishing fisheries for white porpoises and seal in the river St. Lawrence in New France."] to make Oyle of it, where wee came in very bad weather, and the ship was lost in that Island, but the men were saved. The expectation of that ship made us loose our 2nd voyage, which did very much discourage the merchants with whom wee had to doe. They went to law with us to make us recant the bargaine that wee had made with them. After wee had disputed a long time it was found that the right was on our side, and wee innocent of what they did accuse us. So they endeavoured to come to an agreement, but wee were betrayed by our own Party. In the meantime the Commissioners of the King of Great Brittain arrived in that place, and one of them would have us goe with him to New Yorke, and the other advised us to come to England and offer our selves to the King, which wee did.

Those of new England in generall made profers unto us of what ship wee would if wee would goe on in our Designes; but wee answered them that a scalded cat fears the water though it be cold.

Wee are now in the passage, and he that brought us, which was one of the Commissioners called Collonell George Carteret, was taken by the Hollanders, and wee arrived in England in a very bad time for the Plague and the warrs. Being at Oxford, wee went to Sir George Carteret, who spoke to his Majestie, who gave us good hopes that wee should have a ship ready for the next spring, and that the king did allow us 40 shillings a week for our maintenance, and wee had chambers in the Town by his order, where wee stayed 3 months. Afterwards the King came to London and sent us to Windsor, where wee stayed the rest of the winter. Wee are sent for from that place, the season growing neare, and put into the hands of Sir Peter Colleton. The ship was got ready something too late, and our master was not fit for such a Designe. But the Hollanders being come to the River of Thames had stopp'd the passage, soe wee lost that opportunity. So wee were put off till the next yeare, & a little while after that same ship was sent to Virginia and other places to know some news of the Barbadoes, and to be informed if that Island was not in danger; which if it had been lost, had taken from the English Ladyes the meanes or the pleasure of drinking french wine. Those of Burdeaux & of Rochell were great loosers in the expectation of the ship, that was not gone to the Isle of Sand, but to Holland. Wee lost our second voyage, for the order was given to late for the fitting another ship, which cost a great deale of money to noe purpose. The third yeare wee went out with a new company in 2 small vessels, my Brother in one & I in another, & wee went together 400 leagues from the North of Ireland, where a sudden great storme did rise & put us asunder. The sea was soe furious 6 or 7 houres after that it did almost overturne our ship, so that wee were forced to cut our masts rather then cutt our lives; but wee came back safe, God be thanked, and the other, I hope, is gone on his voyage, God be with him. I hope to embarke myselfe by the helpe of God this fourth yeare, & I beseech him to grant me better successe then I have had hitherto, & beseech him to give me Grace & to make me partaker of that everlasting happinesse which is the onely thing a man ought to look after.

I have here put the names of severall Nations amongst which I have been for the most part, which I think may extend to some 900 leagues by the reckoning of my Travells.

The names of the Nations that live in the South:—

Avieronons. Khionontateronons. Oscovarahronoms. Aviottronons. Ohcrokonanechronons. Huattochronoms. Anontackeronons. Ahondironons. Skinchiohronoms. Sonontueronons. Ougmarahronoms. Attitachronoms. Oyongoironons. Akrahkuaeronoms. Ontorahronons. Audastoueronons. Oneronoms. Aoveatsiovaenhronons. Konkhaderichonons. Eressaronoms. Attochingochronoms. Andonanchronons. Attionendarouks. Maingonis. Kionontateronons. Ehriehronoms. Socoquis. Ouendack. Tontataratonhronoms. Pacoiquis.
          Ariotachronoms.

All these Nations are sedentaries, and live upon corn and other grains, by hunting and fishing, which is plentifull, and by the ragouts of roots. There were many destroyed by the Iroquoits, and I have seen most of those that are left.

The names of the Nations that live in the North:—

Chisedeck. Nipifiriniens. Piffings.
Bersiamites. Tivifeimi. Malhonniners.
Sagfeggons. Outimaganii. Afinipour.
Attikamegues. Ouachegami. Trinivoick.
Ovaouchkairing or Mitchitamon. Nafaonakouetons.
  Algonquins. Orturbi. Pontonatemick.
Kischeripirini. Ovasovarin. Escouteck.
Minifigons. Atcheligonens. Panoestigons.
Kotakoaveteny. Annikouay. Nadoucenako.
Kinoncheripirini. Otanack. Titascons.
Matouchkarini. Ouncisagay. Christinos.
Ountchatarounongha. Abaouicktigonions. Nadouceronons.
Sagahigavirini. Roquay. Quinipigousek.
Sagnitaovigama. Mantonech. Tatanga.

The two last are sedentary and doe reap, and all the rest are wandering people, that live by their hunting and Fishing, and some few of Rice that they doe labour for, and a great many of them have been destroyed by the Iroquoites. Besides all the above-named Nations I have seen eight or nine more since my voyages.

A VOYAGE TO THE NORTH PARTS OF AMERICA IN THE YEARS 1682 AND 1683

In the first place, I think myself oblidg'd to vindicat myself from the imputation of inconstancy for acting in this voyage against the English Intrest, and in the yeare 1683 against the French Intrest, for which, if I could not give a very good account, I might justly lye under the sentenc of capritiousness & inconstancy. But severall Persons of probity and good repute, being sensible what my brother-in-Law, Mr Chouard Des Groisiliers, and myself performed in severall voyadges for the Gentlemen conserned in the Hudson's Bay Trade, relating to the Comers of Bever skins, and the just cause of dissattisfaction which both of us had, to make us retire into France. I have no cause to believe that I in the least deserve to bee taxed with lightness or inconstancy for the Imployments wherein I since ingaged, although they were against the Interests of the said Company, for it is suffitiently known that my Brother nor myself omitted nothing that lay in our power, having both of us severall times adventur'd our lives, and did all that was possible for Persons of courage and Honour to perform for the advantage and profit of the said Company, ever since the yeare 1665 unto the yeare 1674. But finding that all our advise was slighted and rejected, and the Councill of other persons imbrac'd and made use of, which manifestly tended to the ruin of the setlement of the Beaver Trade, & that on all occasions wee were look'd upon as useless persons, that deserved neither reward nor incouragement, this unkinde usage made us at last take a resolution, though with very great reluctancy, to return back into France; for in the maine it is well knowne that I have a greater inclination for the Interest of England than for that of ffrance, being marry'd at London unto an Honorable familly, [Footnote: He married, between 1666 and 1673, for his second wife, the daughter of Sir John Kirke. He was one of the original founders of the Hudson's Bay Company, having subscribed L. 300 to the common stock in 1670. He was one of the seven members on the Committee of management for the Company, and was no doubt instrumental in securing to Radisson a permanent pension of 1,200 livres a year, after he left the service of France. In all probability, Radisson emigrated to Canada with his family in 1694, for in that year his son's name thus appears as holding a land patent: "1695. Another patent of confirmation to 'Sieur Etienne Volant Radisson' of the concession made to him the 19th of October, 1694, of the isles, islets, and 'baitures' not granted, that are to be found across Lake St Peter, above the islands granted to the 'Sieur Sorel,' from the edge of the north channel, as far as the great middle channel, called the channel of Platte Island," etc., etc. As Peter Radisson's will can nowhere be found at Somerset House, London, he probably died in Canada.] whos alliance had also the deeper ingadged me in the Intrest of the Nation. Morover, all my friends know the tender love I had for my wife, and that I declared unto them how much I was troubled in being reduced to the necessity of leaving her. I hope thes considerations will vindicate my proceedings touching the severall Interests which I espous'd, and what I shall relate in this ensuing Narrative touching my proceedings in regard of the English in this voyadge in the River, and also in Nelson's harbour in the year 1683, and will justify me against what has ben reported to my prejudice to render me Odious unto the nation. For it will appear that having had the good fortune to defend my setlment against those which at that time I look'd upon as my Ennemy's, & defeated them by frustrating their designes, I improv'd the advantage I had over them the best I could; yet would they do me right, they must own that they had more just cause to give me thanks than to complaine of me, having ever used them kindly as long as they pleas'd to live with me. I freely confess I used all the skill I could to compass my designes, & knowing very well what these Gentlemen intended against me, I thought it better to surprise them than that they should me; knowing that if they had ben afore hand with me, I should have passed my time wors with them than they did with me. I come now to discours of my voyadge, not thinking it materiall heere to mention the campaign I made in the french fleet, since I left England, in the Expeditions for Guinea, Tobaga, [Footnote: This expedition was commanded by Jean, Count d'Estrees. He reduced the Island of Tobaga. He was made a Marshal of France, and sent out, 1 August, 1687, as Viceroy over America.] and other occasions wherein I was concern'd before I ingadged in this voyadge.

At the time my Brother-in-Law and I were dissattisfy'd with the Hudson's Bay Company, wee were severall times invited by the late Monsieur Colbert to return back for france, with large promises that wee should bee very kindly entertain'd. Wee refused a great while all the offers that were made us; but seeing our businesse went wors and wors with the company, without any likelyhood of finding any better usage, at last wee accepted the offer that was made unto us, of paying us 400 Lewi-Dors redy money, of discharging all our Debts, and to give us good Employments. These conditions being agreed upon, wee passed over into france in Xber, 1674.

As soon as wee got to Paris wee waited upon monsieur Colbert. Hee reproached us for preferring the English Interest before that of ffrance; but having heard our defence, and observ'd by what wee said unto him of our discoverys in the Northern parts of America, and of the acquaintance wee had with the Natives, how fit wee might bee for his purpos, hee soon assur'd us of his favor & protection, & also of the King's pardon for what was past, with an intire restoration unto the same state wee were in before wee left france, upon condition that wee should employ our care & industry for the advancement & increas of the comers of the Beaver Trade in the french Collonies in Canada. Hee also confirmed the promis had ben made us at London, of the gratuity of 400 french Pistolls, that all our Debts should bee discharg'd, & that wee should bee put into Employments. Our Letters Pattents of pardon & restoration were forthwith dispatch't, & monsieur Colbert would have it expressly mention'd in them, for what caus the King granted them, viz., to employ the greatest of our skill & industry with the Natives, for the utillity & advancement of the Beaver Trade in the french Collonies. The 400 peeces of Gould was pay'd us, & all things else promised was perform'd, excepting only the Employment, for the which wee were made to attend a great while, and all to no purpos.

But at last I perceaved the cause of this delay, & that my marrying in England made me bee suspected, because my wife remained there. Monsr. Colbert having delayed us a long time with sundry Excuses, one day hee explained himself, saying I should bring my wife over into france if I expected that a full confidence should bee put in mee. I represented unto him that it was nott a thing fully in my power to doe, my wife's father refusing to give me the Liberty of bringing her over into france; but I promiss'd him to use my best endeavors to that effect. In the meantime Monsr. Colbert intimated that hee would have my Brother-in-Law & myself make a voyadge unto Canada, to advise with the Governour what was best ther to bee done, assuring us that hee would write unto him in our behalf.

Wee undertook the voyadge, but being arriv'd at Quebeck, wee found that jelosy & interest which some Persons had over those that had the absolute command, at that time, of the Trade in Canada, & whos Creatures were Imploy'd for new Discoverys, ordered things so that the Count De Frontinac, the Governor, took no care to perform what wee had ben promis'd hee should have don for us; so that finding myself slighted, I left my Brother-in-Law with his familly in Canada, & returned back again for France, intending to serve at sea in the fleet. Accordingly I there passed the Campaigns above mention'd untill wee suffer'd shippwreck at the Isle D'ane, from which being escaped, I returned with the rest of the Army unto Brest, in the moneth of July, having lost all my Equipage in this disaster. The Vice Admirall & the Intendant wrote to Court in my favour, & upon the good character they were pleas'd to give of me, I receav'd a gratuity of 100 Louis D'ors upon the King's account, to renew my Equipage; & these Gentlemen also were pleased to tell me I should ere long have the command of a Man of Warr; but thinking that could not so easily bee, I desired leave to make a turn over into England under pretext of visitting my wife & to make a farther Tryall of bringing her over into france, whereupon I had my pass granted, with a farther gratuity of 100 Louis D'ors towards the charges of my voyage. I was comanded to make what dispatch possible might bee, & espetially to mind the business of bringing my wife along with me, & then I shold not doubt of having good Imployments.

I set forwards, & arrived in London the 4th of July, & amongst other discours told my father-in-Law, Sir John Kirk, of what great importance it was unto me of making my fortune in france to take my wife along with me thither; notwithstanding, hee would by no means give his consent thereunto, but desired me to write to my friends in France concerning some pretention hee had against the Inhabitants of Canada, [Footnote: John Kirke and his elder brothers, Sir David, Sir Lewis, and others, held a large claim against Canada, or rather France, dating back to 1633, which amounted in 1654, including principal and interest, to over—L. 34.000.] which I did. I endeavor'd also, during my stay at London, both by myself & by Friends, to try if the Gentlemen of the Company might conceave any better thoughts of me, & whether I might not by some means or other be restor'd unto their good liking; but all my endevors proved in vaine. I found no likelyhood of effecting what I so much desir'd, therefore I return'd into France & arrived at Brest the 12th of 8ber, 1679.... Having inform'd the Vice Admirall & the Intendant of the litle Successe I had in my voyadge, & that it was not through any neglect of myne, they order'd me to goe give an Account of it unto the Marquis De Signelay, which I did; & telling him I could not prevaile to bring my wife over along with me, hee revil'd me, & told me hee knew very well what an Inclination I had still for the English Intrest, saying with all that I must not expect any confidence should bee put in me, nor that I shold not have the least Imployment, whilst my wife stay'd in England.

Neverthelesse, hee promis'd to speak to his Father, Monsieur Colbert, touching my affaires, which hee also performed; & afterwards waiting upon him, hee spake unto me much after the same rate his sonn, the Marquis De Signelay had don before, as to what concerned my wife, & order'd me to goe unto monsieur Bellinzany, his chief agent for the businesse of Trade, who would farther inform me of his intentions. Meeting with Monsieur Belinzany, hee told me that monsieur Colbert thought it necessary that I should conferr with monsieur De La Chesnay, [Footnote: M. Du Chesneau was appointed 30 May, 1675, Intendant of Justice, Police, and Finance of Canada, Acadia, and Isles of Newfoundland.] a Canada Merchant who mannadg'd all the

Trade of thos parts, & who was then at Paris, that with him some mesures should bee taken to make the best advantage of our Discoveries & intreagues in the Northern parts of Canada, to advance the Beaver Trade, & as much as possible might bee to hinder all strangers from driving that trade to the prejudice of the French Collonies. The said monsr. Belinzany also told me I could not more oblige monsr. Colbert, nor take any better cours to obtain his friendship by any servis whatsoever, than by using all my skill & industry in drawing all the natives of thos Northern parts of America to traffick with & to favor the French, & to hinder & disswade them from trading with strangers, assuring me of a great reward for the servis I should render the state upon this account, & that Mr. De La Chesiiay would furnish me in Cannada with all things necessary for executing what dessignes wee should conclude upon together to this intent.

According to these Instructions I went unto Mr. De La Chesnay. Wee discours'd a long time together, & after severall inquiry's of the state of the countrys that I had most frequented, having communicated unto him my observations, hee propos'd unto me to undertake to establish a treaty for the Beaver trade in the Great Bay where I had ben some years before upon the account of the English. Wee spent two Dayes in adjusting the means of selling this business; at last it was agreed that I should make a voyadge into England to endevor to perswade my wife to come away, & also at the same time to inform myself what shipps the Hudson Bay Company intended to fit out for those parts. I performed this second voyage for England with some remainder of hopes to find the Gentlemen of the Company something better inclin'd towards me than they had ben formerly; but whether they then looked upon me as wholy unneccessary for their purpos, or as one that was altogether unable to doe them any harm, I was sufferr'd to come away without receaving the least token of kindnesse. All the satisfaction I had in the voyadge was that Prince Rupert was pleas'd to tell me that hee was very sorry my offers of servis was so much slighted.

I resolv'd with myself not to bee dejected at this coldnesse, & returned into france, thinking there to have found Monsieur De La Chesnay; but being come to Paris, I heard hee was gon, & I presently resolved to follow him to Canada, to execute what wee had concluded upon at Paris. I went to take my leave of monsieur Colbert, acquainting him of my dessigne, whereof hee approved very well. Hee wished me a good voyadge, advising me to be carefull. I went to visit the Society of the Jesuits at Paris, as being also concern'd with La Chesnay in the Beaver Trade. They gave mee some money for my voyadge. I went & took shipp at Rochell, & arrived at Quebeck the 25th of 7ber, 1682. As soon as I went ashore I spake with monsieur La Chesnay, who seem'd to bee very glad to see me, and after some discours of what wee had concluded upon at Paris, hee said the businesse must bee presently set about; & being privy unto the Court Intrigues, & fully acquainted with the mesures wee were to use in this enterprize, hee took me along with him unto the Governor's house, & ingadg'd me to demand his assistance & such orders as wee should stand in need of from him for the carrying on our Dessigne. But the Governor spake unto us in a way as if hee approved not of the businesse; whereupon La Chesnay demanded a Pass for me to return back unto Europ by the way of New England, in a vessel belonging to the Governor of Accadia, which was at that instant at Quebeck, & redy to saile in som short time.
These formalitys being over, Monsieur La Chesnay & I spake home to the businesse. Wee agreed upon the voyage, & of all things that were to bee setled relative unto our

concerns & Intrest. Hee undertook to buy the Goods, & to furnish all things that concern'd the Treaty; to furnish me with a vessell well fitted & stored with good provisions. It was agreed that I should have one fourth part of the Beaver for my care and paines, & the danger I expos'd myself unto in making the setlment. My Brother-in-Law, Desgroisilliers, who was then at Quebeck, made a contract with De La Chesnay for the same voyage allmost on the same terms as I had don. All things being thus concluded, the Governor was desired that I might have leave to take three men along with me. Hee knew very well to what intent, but hee pretended to bee ignorant of it, for 'tis unlikely that hee could think I would return back to france without doing something about what La Chesnay & I had mention'd unto him, seeing I demanded these three men to goe along with me. One was my kinsman, John Baptista Des Grosiliers, of whom I made great account, having frequented the country all his life, & had contracted great familliarity & acquaintance with the natives about trade. Hee laid out L. 500 Tournais of his own money in the voyadge & charge, disbursed by monsieur De La Chesnay in the Enterprize. The second was Peter Allmand, whom I took for my Pilot, & the 3d was John Baptista Godfry, who understood perfectly well the Languadge of the natives, & one that I knew was capable of Treating. I set saile from Quebeck the 4th of 9ber, 1682, with my 3 men, in the Governor of Accady's vessell, having my orders to bee redy the Spring following, at the L'isle perse, hallow Isle, at the entrance of the River Saint Lawrence, unto which place La Chesnay was to send me a vessell well Equipp'd & fitted according to agreement for Executing the dessigne. Hee also promisd to send mee fuller Instructions in writing, for my directions when I should bee on the place.

Wee arrived at Accadia the 26th of november, 1682, and there winter'd. In the Spring I repair'd unto hallow Island. The vessell I expected arrived, but proved not so good as was promised, for it was only an old Barque of about 50 Tunns with an Equippage but of 12 men, thos with me being comprised in the number. There was goods enough on board to have carry'd on the Treaty, but Provisions were scant, so that had I not ben so deeply ingadg'd as I was in the businesse, such a kind of a vessell would have quite discouradg'd me. But the arrivall of my Brother-in-Law, Desgrosiliers, in a vessell of about 30 Tunns, with a crew of 15 men, incouradg'd me, so that wee joyntly resolved not to quit our Enterprize; but wee had much adoe to perswade our men to it, being unwilling to expose themselves to the danger of a voyadge of 900 Leagues in such small, ordinary vessells, & in such boisterous seas, where ther was also danger of Ice. However, they seeing us willing to run the same fortune as they did, they at length consented, & it was agree'd upon betwixt my Brother-in-Law & myself to steere the same cours, & to keep as neere each other as wee could, the better to assist one another as occasion required. Wee sailed from the Island the 11th July, 1682 [1683.] After the space of 19 dayes' sailing, being past the Straights of new found Land, the seamen on board my Brother-in-Law's vessell mutin'd against him, refusing to proceed any farther, pretending they feared being split with the Ice, also of ingadging in unknown countreys where they might be reduced to want Provisions in the Winter. Wee pacify'd the mutineers by threatnings & by promises, & the sight of a saile in 57 deg. 30 minutes, North Lat., upon the Coast of Brador, somwhat contributed thereunto, every one desiring to shun this sail. Wee were twixt him & the shoar, & they bore directly towards us, desirous to speak with us; but wee not being in a condition of making any resistance, I thought it the best not to stand towards him, but steering the same cours as hee did, wee recover'd under the shoar, & so out of Danger; they tackt about & stood off 2 hours before night, & wee lost sight of them. There was much ice in those seas, which drive to the Southwards. Wee put into Harbour to avoide the Danger of it, as also to take in fresh Water & some other Provisions at the Coast of the Indians called Esquimos, the most cruell of all the salvages when they meet an advantage to surprize Persons. Neverthelesse, they came to our shipp side, & traded with us for some hundred of Woolf Skins. Wee stay'd there 2 dayes, during which time there happned a nother mutiny, our men refusing to proceed any farther; but I pacify'd the seditious, & having put to sea I order'd our men to preserve the Wood & Water wee had taken on board the best they could, for my Brother-in-Law & I had resolved not to goe a shoare untill wee had gain'd our Port, unless wee were chased. The winds proving favorable, wee entred Hudson's Straight and sailed along on the Northern shoare; there was much Ice. Some of my Seamen kill'd a white Beare of Extraordinary biggness. They eat of it to such excess that they all fell Extremely sick with head akes & loosnesse, that I thought they would have dyed out. I was forc'd to give my Brother notice of this accident, & to desire his assistance, so that by takeing Orvietan & sweating they escaped that Danger, but all their skin pell'd off. Wee were inform'd by the Indians that those white Bears have a Poison in the Liver, that diffuses itself through the whole mass of the body, which occasions these distempers unto thos that eat of them.

I observ'd during this Disorder, neer Mile Island, at the western point, wee drove N. W. by the compass about 8 leagues in 6 hours, towards Cape Henry. Wee had much adoe to recover out of the Ice, & had like divers times to have perrish'd, but God was pleas'd to preserve us. My brother-in-Law, fearing to bear too much saile, stay'd behind. I arrived before him, the 26th of August, on the western coast of Hudson's Bay, & we met the 2nd of 7ber, at the entrance of the River called Kakivvakiona by the Indians, which significies "Let him that comes, goe." Being enter'd into this River, our first care was to finde a convenient place where to secure our vessels, & to build us a House. Wee sailed up the River about 15 miles, & wee stop't at a litle Canall, whrein wee lay our vessells, finding the place convenient to reside at. I left my brother-in-Law busy about building a house, & the next day after our arrivall I went up into the Country, to seek for Indians. To this purpos I went in a Canoo, with my nephew & another of my crew, being all 3 armed with firelocks & Pistolls, & in 8 dayes wee went about 40 leagues up the River, & through woods, without meeting one Indian or seeing any signe where any had lately ben; & finding severall Trees gnawed by Beavors, wee judged there was but few Inhabitants in those parts. In our travelling wee kill'd some Deere. But the 8th day after our departure, our canoo being drawn ashore & overturn'd neer the water side, reposing ourselves in a small Island, about evening an Indian pursuing a Deere espyed our Canoo. Thinking there were some of his own Nation, hee whistled to give notice of the Beast, that pass'd by to the litle Island not farr off from us. My nephew having first spyed the Indian, told me of it, not mynding the Deere. I presently went to the water side & called the Indian, who was a good while before hee spake, & then said hee understood me not, & presently run away into the woods.

I was glad of meeting this Indian, & it gave me some hopes of seeing more ere long. Wee stood upon our gard all night. Next morning I caus'd our canoo to bee carry'd the other side of the Island, to have it in readyness to use in case of danger. I caused a fier to bee made a 100 paces off. In the morning wee discovered nyne canoos at the point of the Island coming towards us, & being within hearing, I demanded who they were; they return'd a friendly answer. I told them the cause of my coming into their country, & who I was. One of the eldest of them, armed with his lance, Bow & arrows, etc., etc., rose up & took an arrow from his

Quiver, making a signe from East to West & from North to South, broke it in 2 peeces, & flung it into the River, addressing himself to his companions, saying to this purpos: "Young men, bee not afraid; the Sun is favorable unto us. Our ennemys shall feare us, for this is the man that we have wished for ever since the dayes of our fathers." After which they all swimed a shore unto me, & coming out of their canoos I invited them unto my Fier. My nephew & the other man that was with him came also within 10 paces of us without any feare, although they see the Indian well armed. I asked them who was their Chief Commander, speaking unto him unknownst to me. Hee bowed the head, & another told me it was hee that I talked unto. Then I took him by the hand, and making him sit downe, I spoke unto him according to the genius of the Indians, unto whom, if one will bee esteemed, it is necessary to bragg of one's vallour, of one's strength and ablnesse to succour & protect them from their Ennemyes. They must also bee made believe that one is wholy for their Intrest & have a great complesance for them, espetially in making them presents. This amongst them is the greatest band of friendshipp. I would at this first enterview make myself known. The chief of these salvages sitting by me, I said to him in his Languadge, "I know all the Earth; your friends shall bee my friends; & I am come hether to bring you arms to destroy your Ennemys. You nor your wife nor children shall not dye of hunger, for I have brought Merchandize. Bee of good cheere; I will bee thy sonn, & I have brought thee a father; hee is yonder below building a fort, where I have 2 great shipps. You must give me 2 or 3 of your Canoos that your people may go visit your father."

Hee made a long speech to thank me & to assure me that both himself & all his nation would venture their Lifes in my servis. I gave them some Tobacco & Pipes, & seeing one of them used a peece of flat Iron to cut his Tobacco, I desired to see that peece of Iron & flung it into the fier, wherat they all wonder'd, for at the same time I seemed to weep; & drying up my tears, I told them I was very much grieved to see my Brethren so ill provided of all things, & told them they should want for nothing whilst I was with them; & I tooke my sword I had by my side & gave it unto him from whom I took the peece of Iron; also I caus'd some bundles of litle knives to bee brought from my canoo, which I distributed amongst them. I made them smoke, & gave them to eate, & whilst they were eating, I set forth the presents I brought them, amongst the rest a fowling-peece, with some powder & shot for their chief commander. I told him, in presenting him with it, I took him for my Father; hee in like mannor took me to bee his sonn in covering me with his gowne. I gave him my blanket, which I desired him to carry unto his wife as a token from me, intending shee should bee my mother. Hee thanked me, as also did the rest, to the number of 26, who in testimony of their gratitude cast their garments at my feete & went to their canoos & brought all the furr Skins they had; after which ceremonys wee parted. They promised before noone they would send me 3 of their canoos, wherein they failed not. They put my Beavors in them, & wee went towards the place where I left my Brother-in-Law. I arrived the 12th of 7ber, to the great satisfaction of all our people, having inform'd them the happy success of my Journey by meeting with the Natives.

The very day I return'd from this litle Journey wee were alarm'd by the noise of some Great Gunns. The Indians that came along with us heard them, & I told them that these Gunns were from some of our shipps that were in the great River called Kawirinagaw, 3 or 4 leagues' distance from that wher wee were setled; but being desirous to bee sattisfyed what it should meane, I went in a Canoo unto the mouth of our River, & seeing nothing, I suppos'd wee were all mistaken, & I sent my nephew with another french man of my crew back with the salvages unto the Indians; but the same evening they heard the Gunns so plaine that ther was no farther cause of doubt but that ther was a shipp; upon which they return'd back to tell me of it, wherupon I presently went myself with 3 men to make the discovery. Having crossed over this great River Kawirinagaw, which signifies the dangerous, on the 16th, in the morning, wee discovered a Tent upon an Island. I sent one of my men privatly to see what it was. He came back soon after & told me they were building a House & that there was a shipp; wherupon I approached as neere as I could without being discover'd, & set myself with my men as it were in ambush, to surprize some of thos that were there & to make them prisoners to know what or who they might bee. I was as wary as might bee, & spent the whole night very neere the place where the Hous stood, without seeing anybody stirr or speak untill about noon next day, & then I see they were English, & drawing neerer them the better to observe them, I return'd to my canoo with my men. Wee shewed ourselves a Cannon-shott off & stayed as if wee had ben salvages that wonder'd to see anybody there building a House. It was not long before wee were discover'd, & they hollowed unto us, inviting us to goe unto them, pronouncing some words in the Indian tongue, which they Read in a Book. But seeing wee did not come unto them, they came unto us along the shoare, & standing right opposit unto us, I spoke unto them in the Indian tongue & in French, but they understood me not; but at last asking them in English who they were & what they intended to do there, they answer'd they were English men come hether to trade for Beaver. Afterwards I asked them who gave them permission, & what commission they had for it. They told me they had no commission, & that they were of New England. I told them I was setled in the country before them for the French Company, & that I had strength sufficient to hinder them from Trading to my prejudice; that I had a Fort 7 leagues off, but that the noise of their Gunns made me come to see them, thinking that it might bee a french shipp that I expected, which was to come to a River farther North then this where they were, that had put in there by some accident contrary to my directions; that I had 2 other shipps lately arriv'd from Canada, commanded by myself & my Brother, & therefore I advised them not to make any longer stay there, & that they were best bee gon & take along with them on board what they had landed.

In speaking I caus'd my canoo to draw as neer the shoare as could bee, that I might the better discern thos I talked with; & finding it was young Guillem that comanded the shipp, I was very glad of it, for I was intimately acquainted with him. As soon as hee knew mee hee invited me ashore. I came accordingly, & wee imbraced each other. Hee invited me on board his shipp to treat me. I would not seem to have any distrust, but having precaution'd myself went along with him. I caus'd my 3 men to come out of my canoo & to stay ashore with 2 Englishmen whilest I went on board with the Captain. I see on board a New England man that I knew very well. Before I enter'd the shipp the Captain caused English coullers to bee set up, & as soon as I came on board some great Gunns to bee fir'd. I told him it was not needfull to shoot any more, fearing least our men might bee allarm'd & might doe him some mischief. Hee proposed that wee might Traffick together. I told him I would acquaint our other officers of it, & that I would use my endeavor to get their consent that hee should pass the winter wher hee was without receaving any prejudice, the season being too far past to bee gon away. I told him hee might continue to build his House without any need of fortifications, telling him I would secure him from any danger on the part of the Indians, over whom I had an absolute sway, & to secure him from any surprize on my part. I would before our parting let him know with what number of men I would bee attended when I came to visit him, giving him to understand that if I came with more then what was agreed betwixt us, it would bee a sure signe our officers would not consent unto the proposal of our trading together. I also advised him hee should not fier any Gunns, & that hee should not suffer his men to goe out of the Island, fearing they might bee met by the french men that I had in the woods, that hee might not blame me for any accident that might ensue if hee did not follow my advice. I told him also the salvages advised mee my shipp was arrived to the Northwards, & promiss'd that I would come visit him againe in 15 days & would tell him farther. Wherof hee was very thankfull, & desired me to bee mindfull of him; after which wee seperated very well sattisfy'd with each other, hee verily beleeving I had the strenght I spake of, & I resolving always to hold him in this opinion, desiring to have him bee gon, or if hee persisted to interrupt me in my trade, to wait some opportunity of seizing his shipp, which was a lawfull Prize, having no Commission from England nor france to trade. But I would not attempt anything rashly, for fear of missing my ayme; especially I would avoide spilling blood.

Being returned with my men on board my Canoo, wee fell down the River with what hast wee could; but wee were scarce gon three Leagues from the Island where the new England shipp lay, but that wee discovered another shipp under saile coming into the River. Wee got ashore to the southwards, & being gon out of the Canoo to stay for the shipp that was sailing towards us, I caused a Fier to bee made; & the shipp being over against us, shee came to Anchor & sent not her Boat ashore that night untill next morning. Wee watched all night to observe what was don, & in the morning, seeing the long boat rowing towards us, I caused my 3 men, well armed, to stand at the entrance into the wood 20 paces from me, & I came alone to the water side. Mr Bridgar, whom the Company sent Governor into that country, was in the Boate, with 6 of the crew belonging unto the shipp wherof Capt Guillam was Commander, who was father, as I understood afterwards, unto him that Comanded the New England shipp that I had discover'd the day before. Seeing the shallopp come towards me, I spake a kinde of jargon like that of the salvages, which signify'd nothing, only to amuse those in the boat or to make them speake, the better to observe them, & to see if there might bee any that had frequented the Indians & that spak their Languadge. All were silent; & the boat coming a ground 10 or 12 paces from me, seeing one of the seamen leap in the water to come a shore, I showed him my wepons, forbidding him to stirr, telling him that none in the Boate should come a shore untill I knew who they were; & observing by the make of the shipp & the habit of the saylors that they were English, I spake in their Languadge, & I understood that the seamen that leapt in the water which I hinder'd to proceed any farther said aloud, "Governor, it is English they spake unto you;" & upon my continuing to ask who they were who comanded the shipp, & what they sought there, some body answer'd, "What has any body to doe to inquire? Wee are English." Unto which I reply'd, "And I am French, and require you to bee gon;" & at the same instant making signe unto my men to appeare, they shewed themselves at the entrance of the wood. Those of the shallop thinking in all likelyhood wee were more in number, were about to have answer'd me in mild terms & to tell me they were of London, that the shipp belong'd unto the Hudson Bay Company, & was Comanded by Capt Guillem. I inform'd them also who I was; that they came too late, & that I had taken possession of those parts in the name & behalf of the King of ffrance.

There was severall other things said, which is not needfull heere to relate, the English asserting they had right to come into thos parts, & I saying the contrary; but at last Mr Bridgar saying hee desired to come ashore with 3 of his crew to embrace me, I told him that I should bee very well sattisfy'd. Hee came a shore, & after mutuall salutations, hee asked of me if this was not the River Kakiwakionay. I answer'd it was not, & that it was farther to the Southward; that this was called Kawirinagau, or the dangerous. Hee asked of me if it was not the River where Sir Thomas Button, that comanded an English shipp, had formerly winter'd. I told him it was, & shew'd him the place, to the northwards. Then hee invited me to goe aboard. My crew being come up, disswaded me, especially my Nephew; yet, taking 2 hostages which I left ashore with my men, for I suspected Capt Guillem, having declared himself my Ennemy at London, being of the faction of those which were the cause that I deserted the English Intrest, I went aboard, & I did well to use this precaution, otherwise Capt Guillem would have stop't me, as I was since inform'd; but all things past very well. Wee din'd together. I discoursed of my Establishment in the country; that I had good numbers of ffrench men in the woods with the Indians; that I had 2 shipps & expected another; that I was building a Fort; to conclude, all that I said unto young Guillem, Master of the New England shipp, I said the same unto Mr Bridgar, & more too. He took all for currant, & it was well for me hee was so credulous, for would hee have ben at the troble I was of travelling 40 leagues through woods & Brakes, & lye on the could ground to make my Discoverys, hee wold soon have perceaved my weakness. I had reason to hide it & to doe what I did. Morover, not having men suffitient to resist with open force, it was necessary to use pollicy. It's true I had a great advantage in having the natives on my side, which was a great strength, & that indeed wherupon I most of all depended.

Having stay'd a good while on board I desir'd to go ashore, which being don, I made a signe to my men to bring the hostages, which they had carry'd into the woods. They brought them to the water side, & I sent them aboard their shipp. I confess I repented more then once of my going aboard. It was too rashly don, & it was happy for me that I got off as I did. Before I came ashore I promised Mr. Bridgar & the Captain that in 15 Dayes I would visit them againe. In the mean time, the better to bee assured of their proceedings, I stay'd 2 dayes in the Woods to observe their actions; and having upon the matter seen their dessigne, that they intended to build a Fort, I passed the River to the Southwards to return to my Brother-in-Law, who might well bee in some feare for me. But coming unto him, hee was very glad of what had past, & of the good condition I had sett matters. Wee consulted together what mesures to take not to be surpriz'd & to maintaine ourselves the best wee could in our setlement for carrying on our Treaty. Wee endeavor'd to secure the Indians, who promis'd to loose their Lives for us; & the more to oblidge them to our side I granted them my nephew & another frenchman to goe along with them into the country to make the severall sorts of Indians to come traffick with us, & the more, to incourage them I sent presents unto the chiefest of them.

During my voyage of Discovering 2 English shipps, there happned an Ill accident for us. Our Company had kill'd 60 Deere, which had ben a great help towards our winter provisions; but by an Inundation of waters caused by great Rains they were all carry'd away. Such great floods are common in those parts. The loss was very great unto us, for wee had but 4 Barrells of Pork & 2 of Beef; but our men repair'd this Losse, having kill'd some more Deere and 4,000 white Partridges, somewhat bigger than thos of Europ. The Indians also brought us Provisions they had kill'd from severall parts at a great distance off. Ten dayes after my return from Discovering the English, I took 5 other men to observe what they did. I had forseen that wee should bee forced to stay for faire weather to crosse the mouth of the dangerous River of Kauvirinagaw, which also proved accordingly, for the season began to be boisterous; but having stay'd some time, at last wee got safe over, although it was in the night, & 14 dayes after our departure wee gained neere the place where Mr Bridgar lay. Wee presently see the shipp lay aground on the ooze, a mile from the place where they built their House. Being come neere the shipp, wee hailed severall times & no body answered, which oblig'd us to goe towards land, wondring at their silence. At length a man called us & beckn'd to us to come back. Going towards him & asking how all did, hee said something better, but that all were asleep. I would not disturb them & went alone unto the Governor's house, whom I found just getting up. After the common ceremonys were past, I consider'd the posture of things, & finding there was no great danger, & that I need not feare calling my people, wee went in all together. I made one of my men pass for Captain of the shipp that I said was lately arrived. Mr Bridgar beleev'd it was so, & all that I thought good to say unto him, endeavoring all along that hee should know nothing of the New England Interloper. Wee shot off severall Musquets in drinking healths, those of the vessell never being concern'd, wherby I judg'd they were careless & stood not well on their gard, & might bee easily surpriz'd. I resolved to vew them. Therefore, takeing leave of Mr. Bridgar, I went with my people towards the vessell. Wee went on board to rights without opposition. The Captain was somthing startled at first to see us, but I bid him not feare; I was not there with any dessigne to harme him; on the contrary, was ready to assist & help him wherin hee should comand me, advising him to use more Diligence than hee did to preserve himselfe & shipps from the Danger

I see hee was in of being lost, which afterwards happned. But hee was displeas'd at my Counsill, saying hee knew better what to doe than I could tell him. That might bee, said I, but not in the Indians' country, where I had ben more frequent than he. However, hee desired me to send him som refreshments from time to time during the winter season, espetially some oyle & candles, of which hee stood in great want, which I promis'd to doe, & perform'd accordingly. Hee made me present of a peece of Beeff & a few Bisketts. Being fully inform'd of what I desired to know, & that I need not feare any harm these Gentlemen could doe me in regard of my trade, I took leave of the Captain, to goe see what passed on behalf of the new England Interloper.

I arrived there next day in the afternoon, & found they had employ'd the time better than the others had don, having built a Fort, well fortifyed with 6 great Gunns mounted. I fired a musket to give notice unto those in the Fort of my coming, & I landed on a litle beach under the Gunns. The lieutenant came out with another man well arm'd to see what wee were. When hee see me hee congratulated my safe return, & asked what news. I told him I had found, though with great difficulty, what I sought after, & that I came to visit them, having taken other men than those I had before; that one of those with me was captain of the shipp lately arrived, & the other 4 were of Cannada. The Licutenant answer'd me very briskly. "Were they 40 Devills wee will not feare. Wee have built a Fort, & doe fear nothing." Yet hee invited mee into his Fort to treat me, provided I would go in alone, which I refused, intimating hee might have spoke with more modesty, coming to visit him in friendship & good will, & not in a hostile manner. I told him also I desired to discours with his Captain, who doubtless would have more moderation. Wherupon he sent to inform the Captain, who came unto me well armed, & told me that I need not bee jealous of the Fort hee had caused to bee built, that 'twas no prejudice to me, & that I should at any time comand it, adding withall that hee feared me not so much as hee did the English of London, & that hee built this fort to defend himself against the Salvages, & all thos that would attack him. I thank'd him for his civillitys unto me, & assur'd him I came not thither to shew any displesure for his building a fort, but to offer him 20 of my men to assist him, & to tell him that thos hee so much feared were arrived, offering my servis to defend him, telling him if hee would follow my consill I would defend him from all danger, knowing very well the Orders these new comers had, & also what condition they were in. I also told him that as to the difference which was betwixt us about the trade, it was referr'd unto the arbitrement of both our Kings; that for good luck to him, his father comanded the shipp newly arrived; that he brought a Governor for the English Company, whom I intended to hinder from assuming that Title in the Countrys wherin I was established for the french company, & as for his part, I would make him pass for a french man, therby to keep him from receaving any dammadge.

Having said thes things to the Captain of the fort, I made him call his men together, unto whom I gave a charge in his presence that they should not goe out of their fort, nor fire any Gunns, nor shew their cullers; that they should cover the head & stern of their shipp; & that they should suffer neither ffrench nor English to come near their fort, neither by land nor by Water, & that they should fier on any of my people as would offer to approach without my orders. The Captain promis'd all should bee observ'd that I had said, & comanded his men in my presence so to doe, desiring me to spare him 2 of my men as soon as I could, to guard them. I told him that his father, Captain of the Company's shipp, was sick, wherat hee seem'd to bee much trobled, & desired me to put him in a way to see him without any damadge. I told him the danger & difficulty of it; nevertheless, having privat reasons that this enterview of Father & Sonn might be procur'd by my means, I told him I would use my best endeavor to give him this satisfaction, & that I hop'd to effect it, provided hee would follow my directions. Hee agreed to doe what I advised, & after some litle studdy wee agreed that hee should come along with me disguis'd like one that lived in the woods, & that I wold make him passe for a french man. This being concluded, I sent my men next morning early to kill some fowle. They returned by 10 o'clocke with 30 or 40 Partridge, which I took into my canoo, with a Barrill of Oyle & some candles that I had promis'd the old Captain Guillem. I left one of my men hostage in the fort, and imbarked with young Guillem to goe shew him his father. The tyde being low, wee were forced to stop a mile short of the shipp, & goe ashore & walk up towards the shipp with our provisions. I left one of my men to keepe the Canoo, with orders to keep off, & coming neere the shipp I placed 2 of my best men betwixt the House Mr. Bridgar caus'd to bee built & the water side, comanding them not to shew themselves, & to suffer the Governor to goe to the vessell, but to seize him if they see him come back before I was got out of the shipp.

Having ordered things in this manner, I went with one of my men & young Guillem aboard the shipp, where wee againe entered without any opposition. I presented unto Captain Guillem the Provisions I had brought him, for which hee gave me thanks. Afterwards, I made my 2 men go into his cabbin, one of which was his son, though unknown to him. I desired Captain Guillem to bid 2 of his servants to withdraw, having a thing of consequence to inform him of, which being don, I told him the secret was that I had brought his sonn to give him a visit, having earnestly desired it of me; & having told him how necessary it was to keep it privat, to prevent the damadge might befall them both if it shold bee known, I presented the son unto his father, who Imbraced each other very tenderly & with great joy; yet hee told him hee exposed him unto a great deale of danger. They had some priviat discours togather, after which hee desired me to save my new French man. I told him I would discharge myself of that trust, & againe advised him to bee carefull of preserving his shipp, & that nothing should bee capable of making any difference betwixt us, but the Treaty hee might make with the Indians. Hee told me the shipp belonged to the Company; that as to the Trade, I had no cause to bee afraid on his account, & that though hee got not one skin, it would nothing troble him; hee was assured of his wages. I warned him that he should not suffer his men to scatter abroad, espetially that they should not goe towards his sonn's fort, which hee promis'd should bee observ'd. Whilst wee were in this discours, the Governor, hearing I was come, came unto the Shipp & told me that my Fort must needs bee neerer unto him than hee expected, seeing I return'd so speedily. I told him, smiling, that I did fly when there was need to serve my friends, & that knowing his people were sick & wanted refreshments, I would not loose time in supplying them, assuring him of giving him part what our men did kill at all times. Some prying a litle too narrowly, young Guillem thought hee had ben discovered, wherat the Father & son were not a litle concern'd. I took upon me, & said it was not civill so narrowly to examine my people; they excus'd it, & the tyde being com in, I took leave to be gon. The Governor & Captain divided my provisions, & having made a signe unto my 2 men to rise out of their ambush, I came out of the shipp, & wee march'd all of us unto the place where wee left our Canoo. Wee got into it, & the young Captain admired to see a litle thing made of the rhind of a Tree resist so many knocks of Ice as wee met withall in returning.

Next day wee arrived at the Fort, & very seasonably for us; for had wee stayed a litle longer on the water, wee had ben surprized with a terrible storm at N. W., with snow & haile, which doubtless would have sunk us. The storm held 2 days, & hinder'd us from going to our pretended fort up the river; but the weather being setled, I took leave of the Captain. The Lieut. would faine have accompanyed us unto our habitation, but I sav'd him that Labour for good reasons, & to conceall the way. Parting from the fort, wee went to the upper part of the Island; but towards evening wee returned back, & next day were in sight of the sea, wherin wee were to goe to double the point to enter the River where our habitation was; but all was so frozen that it was almost impossible to pass any farther. Wee were also so hem'd in on all sides with Ice, that wee could neither go forward nor get to Land, yet wee must get over the Ice or perrish. Wee continued 4 hours in this condition, without being able to get backwards or forwards, being in great danger of our lifes. Our cloaths were frozen on our backs, & wee could not stirr but with great paine; but at length with much adoe wee got ashore, our canoo being broke to peeces. Each of us trussed up our cloaths & arms, & marched along the shoare towards our habitation, not having eat anything in 3 days, but some crows & Birds of prey that last of all retire from these parts. There was no other fowle all along that coast, which was all covered with Ice & snow. At length wee arrived opposite unto our habitation, which was the other side of the River, not knowing how to get over, being cover'd with Ice; but 4 of our men ventur'd in a Boat to come unto us. They had like to have ben staved by the Ice. Wee also were in very great danger, but wee surmounted all these difficultys & got unto our habitation, for which wee had very great cause to give God thanks of seeing one another after having run through so great Dangers.

During my travelling abroad, my brother-in-Law had put our House into pretty good order. Wee were secure, fearing nothing from the Indians, being our allies; & as for our neighbours, their disorder, & the litle care they took of informing themselves of us, set us safe from fearing them. But as it might well happen that the Governor Bridgar might have notice that the New England Interloper was in the same river hee was, & that in long running hee might discover the truth of all that I had discoursed & concealed from him, & also that hee might come to understand that wee had not the strength that I boasted of, I thought it fit to prevent Danger; & the best way was to assure my self of the New England shipp in making myself master of her; for had Mr. Bridgar ben beforehand with mee, hee would have ben too strong for me, & I had ben utterly unable to resist him; but the question was how to effect this businesse, wherin I see manifest difficultys; but they must bee surmounted, or wee must perrish. Therefore I made it my business wholy to follow this Enterprise, referring the care of our House & of the Traffick unto my brother-in-Law.

Seeing the River quite froze over, every other day for a fortnight I sent my men through the woods to see in what state the Company's shipp lay. At length they told me shee lay a ground neer the shoare, the creek wherin shee was to have layn the Winter being frozen up, which made me conjecture shee would infallibly bee lost. I also sent 2 of my men unto Young Captain Guillem into the Island, which hee had desired of me for his safegard; but I was told by my people that hee intended to deceave me, having, contrary unto his promise of not receaving any into his Fort but such as should come by my Orders, had sent his Boat to receave 2 men from the Company's shipp, which Mr. Bridgar had sent to discover what they could the way that I tould him our fort was, & also to see if they could find any wreck of their shipp; but these 2 men, seeing thos of the fort begin to stir & to Lanch out their Boat, they thought they would fier on them, as I had comanded. They were affrighted & run away. Being come to Mr. Bridgar, they told him there was a Fort & a french shipp neerer unto them than I had said. Upon this information, Mr. Bridgar sent 2 men to pass from north to south, to know if it were true that wee had 2 Shipps besides that which was at the Island. Wherof being advised by my people, I sent out 3 severall ways to endeavor to take the 2 men Mr. Bridgar had sent to make this discovery, having ordered my people not to doe them any violence. My people succeded, for they found the 2 poore men within 5 leagues of our House, allmost dead with cold & hunger, so that it was no hard matter to take them. They yeelded, & were brought unto my habitation, where having refreshed them with such provision as wee had, they seemed nothing displeas'd at falling into our hands. I understood by them the orders Mr. Bridgar had given them for making the Discovery, which made me stand the more close on my Gard, & to use fresh means to hinder that the Governor Bridgar should not have knowledge of the New-England Interlopers.

About this time I sent some provisions unto Mr. Bridgar, who was in great want, although hee strove to keep it from my knowledge. Hee thanked mee by his Letters, & assur'd me hee would not interrupt my trade, & that hee would not any more suffer his men to come neere the forts, which hee thought had ben ours. I also sent to visit young Guillem to observe his proceedings, & to see in what condition hee was, to make my best advantage of it. The 2 Englishmen which my people brought, told me the Company's shipp was stay'd to peeces, & the captain, Leftenant, & 4 seamen drown'd; but 18 of the company being ashore escaped that danger. Upon this advice I went to visit Mr. Bridgar, to observe his actions. I brought him 100 Partridges, & gave him some Powder to kill fowle, & offer'd him my servis. I asked where his shipp was, but hee would not owne shee was lost, but said shee was 4 leagues lower in the River. I would not press him any farther in the businesse, but civilly took our leave of each other.

From thence I went unto the Fort in the Island also, to see what past there, & to endeavor to compasse the dessigne I had laid of taking the Shipp & fort, having since discovered by letters intercepted, that young Guillim intended to shew me a trick & destroy me. Being come to the fort in the Island, I made no shew of knowing the losse of his father, nor of the Company's shipp, only I told young Guillim his father continued ill, & did not think safe to write him, fearing to discover him. Afterwards I desired hee would come unto our habitation; & so I returned without effecting any more that day. Eight days after, I returned to see Mr. Bridgar, unto whom I said that hee did not take sufficient care to preserve his men; that I had 2 of them at my Fort, who told me of the losse of his shipp, which hee owned. I told him I would assist him, & would send him his 2 men & what else hee desired. I also offer'd him one of our Barques, with provisions requisit to convey him in the Spring unto the bottom of the Bay, which hee refused. I assured him of all the servis that lay in my power, treating him with all civillity could bee for the Esteeme that I ever bore unto the English nation. As for Mr. Bridgar, I had no great caus to bee over well pleased with him, being advised that hee spake ill of mee in my absence, & had said publickly unto his people that hee would destroy my Trade, should hee give 6 axes & proportionably of other Goods unto the Indians for a Bevor Skin. [Footnote: The Company's early standard for trading was: "For 1 Gun, one with another, 10 good Skins, that is, winter beavor; 12 Skins for the biggest sort, 10 for the mean, and 8 for the smallest. Powder, a beaver for 1/2 a lb. A beaver for 4 lb. of shot. A beaver for a great and little hatchet. A beaver for

6 great knives or 8 jack-knives. Beads, a beaver for 1/2 a lb. Six beavers for one good laced coat. Five beavers for one red plain coat. Coats for women, laced, two yards, six beavers. Coats for women, plain, Five beavers. Tobacco, a beaver for 1 lb. Powder-horns, a beaver for a large one and two small ones. Kettles, a beaver for one lb. of Kettle. Looking-glasses and combs, 2 skins."] I have an attestation heerof to shew. I stayed 2 dayes on this voyadge with Mr. Bridgar, having then a reall intent to serve him, seeing hee was not in a condition to hurt me; & returning unto my habitation, I called at Young Gwillim's fort in the Island, where I intended to execute my dessigne, it being now time.

When I arrived at the fort, I told young Gwillim his father continued ill, & that hee referr'd all unto me, upon which I said unto him touching his father & of his resolution, hee earnestly desired I would goe back with him & take him along with me, disguised as before, that hee might see him; but I disswaded him from this, & put in his head rather to come see our habitation, & how wee lived. I knew hee had a desire to doe soe, therefore I would sattisfy his curiosity. Having, therefore, perswaded him to this, wee parted next morning betimes. Hee took his Carpenter along with him, & wee arrived at our habitation, Young Gwillim & his man being sufficiently tired. I thought it not convenient that young Gwillim should see the 2 Englishmen that was at our House. I kept them privat, & fitted them to bee gon next morning, with 2 of my men, to goe athwart the woods unto their habitation, having promis'd Mr. Bridgar to send them unto him. I gave them Tobacco, Cloaths, & severall other things Mr. Bridgar desired; but when they were to depart, one of the Englishmen fell at my feet & earnestly desired that I would not send him away. I would not have granted his request but that my Brother-in-Law desired me to do it, & that it would also ease Mr. Bridgar's charge, who wanted provisions; so I sufferred the other to depart along with my 2 men, having given them directions. I caused young Gwillem to see them going, telling him I sent them unto our Fort up the river.

I continued a whole moneth at quiet, treating young Guillem, my new guest, with all civillity, which hee abused in severall particulars; for having probably discovered that wee had not the strength that I made him beleeve wee had, hee unadvisedly speak threatning words of me behind my back, calling me Pyrate, & saying hee would trade with the Indians in the Spring in spight of me. Hee had also the confidence to strike one of my men, but I connived at it. But one day discoursing of the privilledges of new England, he had the confidence to speak slightly of the best of Kings, wherupon I called him pittyfull Dogg for talking after that manner, & told him that for my part, having had the honour to have ben in his majesty's servis, I would pray for his majesty as long as I lived. Hee answered mee with harsh words that hee would return back to his fort, & when hee was there, that would not dare talk to him as I did. I could not have a fairer opportunity to begin what I dessigned. Upon which I told the young foole that I brought him from his fort & would carry him thither againe when I pleas'd, not when hee liked. Hee spake severall other impertinencys, that made me tell him that I would lay him up safe enough if hee behaved not himself wiser. Hee asked me if hee was a prisoner. I told him I would consider of it, & that I would secure my Trade, seeing hee threatened to hinder it. After which I retired & gave him leave to bee inform'd by the Englishman how that his father & the company's shipp were lost, & the bad condition Mr. Bridgar was in. I left a french man with them that understood English, but they knew it not. When I went out, young Gwillim bid the Englishman make his escape & goe tell his master that hee would give him 6 Barrills of Powder

& other provisions if hee would attempt to deliver him out of my hands. The Englishman made no reply, neither did hee tell me of what had ben proposed unto him. I understood it by my frenchman, that heard the whole matter, & I found it was high time to act for my owne safety.

That evning I made no shew of any thing, but going to bed I asked our men if the fier Locks that wee placed at night round our fort to defend us from thos that would attack us were in order. At this word of fire Locks young Gwillim, who knew not the meaning of it, was suddenly startled & would have run away, thinking wee intended to kill him. I caused him to bee stay'd, & freed him of his feare. But next morning I made him an unwelcom compliment; I told him that I was going to take his shipp & fort. Hee answered very angrily that if I had 100 men I could not effect it, & that his men would kill 40 before they could come neere the pallissade. I was nothing discouradged at his bravado, knowing very well that I should compasse my dessigne. I made account that 2 of my men would have stay'd in the fort for hostages, but having what libberty they would, one of them returned to our habitation without my order. I was angry at it, but I made no shew of it, having laid my dessigne so as to make more use of skill & pollicy than of open force; seeing therefore the haughty answer young Gwillem made me, that I could not take his fort with 100 men, I asked of him how many men hee had in it. Hee said nyne. I desired him to choose the like number of myne, I being one of the number, telling him I would desire no more, & that in 2 dayes I would give him a good account of his fort & of his shipp, & that I would not have him to have the shame of being present to see what I should doe. Hee chose & named such of my men as hee pleas'd, & I would not choose any others. I sufferr'd him to come with me to the water side, & I made the ninth man that went upon this

Expedition, with an Englishman of Mr. Bridgar's to bee a wittness of the busenesse.

Being arriv'd within half a league of the fort, I left the Englishman with one frenchman, ordering they should not stirr without farther order; at the same time I sent 2 of my men directly to the fort to the Southward of the Island, & I planted myself with my other 5 men at the North point of the same Island to observe what they did that I sent to the fort. They were stop't by 3 Englishmen armed, that asked if they had any letters from their master. My people answer'd, according to my Instructions, that hee was coming along with mee; that being weary, wee stay'd behind; that they came a litle before for some brandy which they offerr'd to carry. The Englishmen would needs doe the office, & my 2 men stay'd in the fort. Hee that was hostage had orders to seize on the Court of Gard Dore, one of them newly come to seize the Dore of the House, & the 3 was to goe in & out, that in case the dessigne was discover'd hee might stopp the passage of the Dore with Blocks of wood, to hinder it from being shutt & to give me freedom to enter unto their assistance; but there needed not so much adoe, for I enter'd into the fort before thos that were appointed to defend it were aware. The Lieutenant was startled at seeing me, & asked "wher his master was; it was high time to appear & act." I answered the Lieutenant "it matter'd not where his master was, but to tell me what men hee had & to call them out;" & my men being enter'd the fort & all together, I told thos that were present the cause of my coming, that I intended to bee Master of the place, & that 'twas too late to dispute. I commanded them to bring me the Keys of the Fort & all their Arms, & to tell mee if they had any Powder in their chests, & how much, referring myself unto what they should say. They made no resistance, but brought me their Arms, & as for Powder, they said they had none. I took possession of the Fort in the name of the King of ffrance, & from thence was conducted by the Lieutenant to take possession of the shipp also in the same name, which I did without any resistance; & whilst I was doing all this, young Guillem's men seemed to rejoyce at it rather then to bee troubled, complaining of him for their Ill usage, & that hee had kill'd his Supercargo. But a Scotchman, one of the crew, to shew his zeale, made his Escape & run through the woods towards Mr. Bridgar's House to give him notice of what pas't. I sent 2 of my nimblest men to run after him, but they could not overtake him, being gon 4 hours before them. Hee arrived at Mr. Bridgar's house, who upon the relation of the Scotchman resolved to come surprise me.

In the meane while I gave my Brother notice of all that past, & that I feared a Scotchman might occasion me some troble that had got away unto Mr. Bridgar, & that I feared I might bee too deeply ingadg'd unless hee presently gave me the assistance of 4 men, having more English prisoners to keep than I had french men with me. I was not deceiv'd in my conjecture. At midnight one of our Doggs alarm'd our sentinell, who told me hee heard a noise on board the shipp. I caus'd my People to handle their armes, & shut up the English in the cabins under the Gard of 2 of my men. I with 4 others went out to goe to the shipp. I found men armed on board, & required them to lay downe their arms & to yeeld. There was 4 that submitted & some others got away in the dark. My men would have fired, but I hinder'd them, for which they murmur'd against me. I led the prisoners away to the fort & examin'd them one after another. I found they were of Mr. Bridgar's people, & that hee was to have ben of the number, but hee stay'd half a League behind to see the success of the businesse. The last of the Prisoners I examin'd was the Scotch man that had made his escape when I took the fort; & knowing hee was the only cause that Mr. Bridgar ingadg'd in the businesse, I would revenge me in making him afraid.

I caus'd him to bee ty'd to a stake & told that hee should bee hang'd next day. I caus'd the other prisoners, his comrades, to bee very kindly treated; & having no farther dessigne but to make the Scotch man afraide, I made one advise him to desire the Lewtenant of the fort to begg me to spare his life, which hee did, & easily obtain'd his request, although hee was something startled, not knowing what I meant to doe with him. The 4 men I desired of my Brother-in-Law arrived during these transactions, & by this supply finding myself strong enough to resist whatever Mr. Bridgar could doe against me, I wrote unto him & desired to know if hee did avow what his men had don, whom I detain'd Prisoners, who had Broke the 2 Dores & the deck of the shipp to take away the Powder. Hee made me a very dubious answer, complaining against me that I had not ben true unto him, having concealed this matter from him. Hee writ me also that having suffitient orders for taking all vessells that came into those parts to Trade, hee would have joyned with me in seizing of this; but seeing the purchas was fal'n into my hands, hee hoped hee should share with mee in it.

I sent back his 3 men with some Tobacco & other provisions, but kept their arms, bidding them tell Mr. Bridgar on my behalf that had I known hee would have come himself on this Expedition, I would have taken my mesures to have receav'd him ere he could have had the time to get back; but I heard of it a litle too late, & that in some short time I would goe visit him to know what hee would bee at, & that seeing hee pretended to bee so ignorant in what quallity I liv'd in that country, I would goe and inform him. Before these men's departure to Mr. Bridgar's I was inform'd that some English men had hidden Powder without the fort. I examin'd them all. Not one would owne it; but at last I made them confess it, & 5 or 6 pound was found that had ben hid. Then I took care to secure the fort. I sent 4 of the English men of the fort unto my Brother-in-Law, & I prepar'd to goe discover what Mr. Bridgar was doing. I came to his House & went in before hee had notice of my coming. Hee appeared much surpris'd; but I spoke to him in such a manner as shewed that I had no intent to hurt him, & I told him that by his late acting hee had so disoblidged all the ffrench that I could not well tell how to assist him. I told him hee had much better gon a milder way to work, in the condition hee was in, and that seeing hee was not as good as his word to me, I knew very well how to deall with him; but I had no intention at that time to act any thing against Mr. Bridgar. I only did it to frighten him, that hee should live kindly by me; & in supplying him from time to time with what he wanted, my chief ayme was to disable him from Trading, & to reduce him to a necessity of going away in the Spring.

Seeing Mr. Bridgar astonish'd at my being there with 12 men, & in a condition of ruining him if I had desire to it, I thought fit to setle his mynd by sending away 6 of my men unto my Brother-in-Law, & kept but 6 with me, 4 of which I sent out into the woods to kill some provisions for Mr. Bridgar. About this time I receaved a letter from my Brother wherin hee blam'd me for acting after this manner with persons that but 2 days agoe endeavor'd to surprise me; that if I did so, hee would forsake all, that I had better disarm them for our greater security, & that I should not charge myself with any of them. It was also the judgment of the other french men, who were all exasperated against Mr. Bridgar. Not to displease my owne people, instead of 4 English men that I promis'd Mr. Bridgar to take along with me that hee might the better preserve the rest, I took but 2, one of which I put in the Fort at the Island, & the other I brought unto our habitation. I promiss'd Mr. Bridgar before I left him to supply him with Powder & anything else that was in my power, & demanding what store of musquets hee had remaining, hee told me hee had Ten, & of them 8 were broken. I tooke the 8 that were spoyl'd, & left him myne that was well fixt, promising to get his mended. Hee also offer'd me a pocket Pistoll, saying hee knew well enough that I intended to disarm him. I told him it was not to disarm him, to take away his bad arms & to give him good in stead of them. I offerr'd him my Pistolls, but hee would not accept of them. In this state I left him, & went to our habitation to give my Brother-in-Law an account of what I had don.

Some dayes after, I went to the Fort in the Island to see if all was well there, & having given all necessary directions I return'd unto our place, taking the Lieutenant of the Fort along with me, unto whom I gave my owne chamber & all manner of libberty; taking him to bee wiser than his captain, whom they were forc'd to confine in my absence. Hee thanked mee for my civillityes, & desiring hee might goe to his Captain, I consented. About this time I had advise, by one of the men that I left to guard the fort in the Island, that Mr. Bridgar, contrary to his promis, went thether with 2 of his men, & that our men having suffer'd them to enter into the fort, they retain'd Mr. Bridgar & sent the other 2 away, having given them some Bread & Brandy. This man also told me that Mr. Bridgar seemed very much trobl'd at his being stopt, & acted like a mad man. This made me presently goe to the fort to hinder any attempts might be made against me. Being arrived, I found Mr. Bridgar in a sad condition, having drank to excess. Him that comanded in the fort had much adoe to hinder him from killing the Englishman that desired to stay with us. Hee spoke a thousand things against me in my hearing, threatning to kill me if I did not doe him right. But having a long time born it, I was at length constraint to bid him bee quiet; & desirous to know his dessignes, I asked him if any of his People were to come, because I see smoake & fiers in crossing the River. Hee Said Yes, & that hee would shortly shew me what hee could doe, looking for 14 men which hee expected, besides the 2 my people return'd back. I told him I knew very well hee had not soe many men, having let many of his men perish for want of meate, for whom hee was to bee accountable; & morover I was not afraid of his threats. Nevertheless, no body appear'd, & next dayly I order'd matters so as Mr. Bridgar should come along with me unto our habitation, wherunto hee see it was in vaine to resist. I assured him that neither I nor any of my People shold goe to his House in his absence, & that when hee had recreated himself 10 or 15 Days with mee at our habitation, hee might return with all freedom againe unto his House.

Mr. Bridgar was a fortnight at our House without being overtired, & it appeared by his looks that hee had not ben Ill treated; but I not having leasure allways to keep him company, my affairs calling me abroad, I left him with my Brother-in-Law whilst I went unto the Fort in the Island to see how matters went there; & at my going away I told Mr. Bridgar that if hee pleas'd hee might dispose himself for his departure home next morning, to rectify some disorders committed by his people in his absence, to get victualls, & I told him I would meet him by the way to goe along with him. Having dispatcht my business at the fort of the Island, I went away betimes to bee at Mr. Bridgar's house before him, to hinder him from abusing his men. The badness of the weather made me goe into the House before hee came. As Soon as I was enter'd, the men beseech'd me to have compassion on them. I blam'd them for what they had don, & for the future advised them to bee more obedient unto their master, telling them I would desire him to pardon them, & that in the Spring I would give passage unto those that would goe home by the way of ffrance. Mr. Bridgar arrived soon after me. I beg'd his pardon for going into his House before hee came, assuring him that I had still the dessigne of serving him & assisting him, as hee should find when hee pleas'd to make use of me, for Powder & anything else hee needed; which also I performed when it was desir'd of me, or that I knew Mr. Bridgar stood in need of any thing I had. I parted from Mr. Bridgar's habitation to return unto our own. I passed by the fort in the Island, & put another frenchman to comand in the place of him was there before, whom I intended to take with me to work uppon our shipps.

The Spring now drawing on, the English of the fort of the Island murmur'd because of one of Mr. Bridgar's men that I had brought thether to live with them. I was forst to send him back to give them content, not daring to send him to our habitation, our french men opposing it, wee having too many allready. Arriving at our habitation, I was inform'd that the English captain very grossly abused one of his men that I kept with him. Hee was his carpenter. I was an eye witness myself of his outrageous usage of this poore man, though hee did not see me. I blamed the Captain for it, & sent the man to the fort of the Island, to look after the vessell to keep her in good condition. My nephew arrived about this time, with the french men that went with him to invite downe the Indians, & 2 days after there came severall that brought provisions. They admired to see the English that wee had in our House, & they offer'd us 200 Bevor skins to suffer them to goe kill the rest of them; but I declar'd unto them I was far from consenting therunto, & charged them on the contrary not to doe them any harm; & Mr. Bridgar coming at instant with one of his men unto our habitation, I advised him not to hazard himself any more without having some of my men with him, & desir'd him, whilst hee was at my House, not to speak to the Indians. Yet hee did, & I could not forbeare telling him my mynde, which made him goe away of a suddain. I attended him with 7 or 8 of my men, fearing least the Indians who went away but the Day before might doe him a mischief. I came back next day, being inform'd that a good company of Indians, our old Allies, were to come; & I found they were come with a dessigne to warr against the English, by the perswasion of some Indians that I see about 8ber last, & with whom I had renew'd an alliance. I thanked the Indians for their good will in being ready to make warr against our Ennemys; but I also told them that I had no intent to doe them any harm, & that having hindred them from hurting me I was sattisfy'd, & that therefore they would oblidge me to say nothing of it, having promis'd me they would bee gon in the Spring, but if they came againe I would suffer them to destroy them. The Indians made great complaints unto me of the English in the bottom of the Bay, which I will heere omitt, desiring to speak only of what concerns myself; but I ought not omit this. Amongst other things, they alleadg'd to have my consent that they might warr against the English. They said thus: "Thou hast made us make presents to make thine Ennemys become ours, & ours to bee thyne. Wee will not bee found lyers." By this may bee seen what dependance is to bee laid on the friendship of this people when once they have promis'd. I told them also that I lov'd them as my own Brethren the French, & that I would deal better by them than the English of the Bay did, & that if any of my men did them the least injury I would kill him with my own hands; adding withall that I was very sorry I was not better stor'd with Goods, to give them greater tokens of my friendship; that I came this voyage unprovided, not knowing if I should meet them, but I promis'd to come another time better stor'd of all things they wanted, & in a condition to help them to destroy their Ennemys & to send them away very well sattisfy'd. The English admir'd to see with what freedom I lived with these salvages. This pas't in the beginning of Aprill, 1683. Being faire wether, I caused my nephew to prepare himself, with 3 men, to carry Provisions & Brandy unto our french men & to the English men at the fort of the Island. The Ice began to bee dangerous, & I see that it was not safe hazarding to goe over it after this time; therefore I said to my nephew that hee would doe well to proceed farther unto the Indians, unto whom hee promis'd to give an account how wee did, & to inform them also that wee had conquer'd our Ennemys.

After my nephew's departure on this voyadge, there hapned an unlookt-for accident the 22 or 23rd of Aprill, at night. Having haled our vessells as far as wee could into a litle slip in a wood, wee thought them very secure, lying under a litle Hill about 10 fathom high, our Houses being about the same distance off from the River side; yet about 10 o'clock at night a hideous great noise rous'd us all out of our sleep, & our sentinill came & told us it was the clattering of much Ice, & that the floods came downe with much violence. Wee hasted unto the river side & see what the sentinell told us, & great flakes of Ice were born by the waters upon the topp of our litle Hill; but the worst was that the Ice having stop't the river's mouth, they gather'd in heaps & were carry'd back with great violence & enter'd with such force into all our Brooks that discharg'd into the River that 'twas impossible our vessells could resist, & they were stay'd all to peeces. There remained only the bottom, which stuck fast in the Ice or in the mudd, & had it held 2 hours longer wee must have ben forst to climbe the trees to save our lives; but by good fortune the flood abated. The river was cleer'd by the going away of the Ice, & 3 days after, wee see the disorder our vessells were in, & the good luck wee had in making so great a voyadge in such bad vessells, for myne was quite Rotten & my Brother's was not trunnel'd. This accident put us into a great feare the like mischief might bee hapned unto the New England shipp; the Indians telling us that the River was more dangerous than ours, & that they beleev'd the vessell could not escape in the place wher shee lay. But mr Bridgar having heertofore related unto me alike accident hapned in the River Kechechewan in the Bottom of the Bay, that a vessell was preserv'd by cutting the Ice round about her, I took the same cours, & order'd the Ice should bee cut round this vessell quite to the keele, & I have reason to thank mr Bridgar for this advice; it sav'd the vessell. Shee was only driven ashore by the violence of the Ice, & there lay without much dammadge. Whilst the waters decreas'd wee consulted upon which of the 2 bottoms wee should build us a shipp, & it was at last resolv'd it shold bee on myne. Upon which wee wrought day & night without intermission, intending this vessell should carry the English into the Bay, as I had promis'd mr Bridgar.

I went down 2 or 3 times to the River's mouth to see what the floods & Ice had don there, & if I could pass the point into the other River, wher mr Bridgar & the English vessell was at the fort of the Island, for was impossible to pass through the woods, all being cover'd with water. I adventur'd to pass, & I doubled the point in a canoo of bark, though the Ice was so thick that wee drew our canoo over it. Being enter'd the River, I march'd along the South Shore & got safe to the fort of the Island with great difficulty. I found the shipp lying dry, as I mention'd before, in a bad condition, but easily remedy'd, the stern being only a litle broke. I gave directions to have her fitted, & I incouradged the English to work, which they did perform better than the french. Having given these directions, I took the shipp's Boat & went down to Mr. Bridgar's habitation, & looking in what condition it was, I found that 4 of his men were dead for lack of food, & two that had ben poyson'd a litle before by drinking some liquer they found in the Doctor's chest, not knowing what it was.

Another of Mr. Bridgar's men had his Arm broke by an accident abroad a hunting.

Seeing all these disorders, I passed as soon as I could to the South side of the river to recover unto our Houses, from whence I promis'd Mr. Bridgar I would send his English Curiorgion that was with us some Brandy, vinegar, Lynnen, & what provisions I could spare out of the small store wee had left. Being got a shore, I sent back the Boat to the fort of the Isle, with orders unto my 2 men I left there to bring my canoo & to use it for fowling. In returning I went a shore with one of Mr. Bridgar's men that I took along with me to carry back the provisions I had promis'd, although hee did not seeme to be very thankfull for it, continueing his threatnings, & boasted that hee expected shipps would come unto him with which hee would take us all. I was nothing daunted at this, but kept on my cours, knowing very well Mr. Bridgar was not in a capacity of doing us any harm; but it being impossible but that his being present on the place should hinder me, I order'd my business so as to bee gon with what skins I had, & sent away Mr. Bridgar after having secured our Trade.

I made severall journeys to the Fort of the Island about repairing of the shipp; also I went severall times to Mr. Bridgar's house to carry him provisions, & to assist him & also his men with all things that I could procure, which they can testify; & had it not ben for me they had suffred much more misery. I had like to bee lost severall times in these journeys by reason of great stores of Ice; & the passage of the entrance of the River to Double the point to enter into that where Mr. Bridgar & the new England shipp lay was allways dangerous.

I will not here insist upon the perrills I expos'd my self unto in coming & going to prepare things for our departure when the season would permitt; but I cannot omit telling that amongst other kindnesses I did Mr. Bridgar I gave him stuff suffitient to sheath his shallup, which was quite out of order, as also cordage & all things else necessary; but hee did not well by me, for contrary to his word which he had given me not to goe to the fort in the Island, hee attempted to goe thether with his people in his shallup, & being come within musket-shott under a pretence of desiring some Powder, the comander would not suffer him to come any neerer, & made him cast anker farther off. Hee sent his boats for Mr. Bridgar, who came alone into the fort, though hee earnestly desired one of his men might bee admitted along with him, but was deny'd. His men were order'd to lodge themselves ashore the North side of the River in hutts, & provisions was sent unto them. Mr. Bridgar spent that night in the Fort, went away the next day. The day before I see the shallup going full salle towards the fort, whether I was also going myself by land with one Englishman in whom I put a great deale of confidence, having no body else with me. I did suspect that Mr. Bridgar had a dessign to make some surprise, but I was not much afraid by reason of the care & good order I had taken to prevent him.

Nevertheless I feared that things went not well; for when I came neer the fort, seeing the boate coming for me, & that the comander did not make the signall that was agreed upon betwixt us, this startled me very much, & I appeared as a man that had cause to feare the worst; which one of our frenchmen that steered the boat wherin ther was 4 Englishmen perceiving, cry'd out all was well, & made the signall. I blamed him & the comander for putting me in feare in not making the usuall signes.

When I came to the fort I was told Mr. Bridgar was there, & that hee was receayed, as has been recited. I was also tould hee had privat discours with the carpenter of the new England shipp that I had formerly ingadged in a friendly manner to attend & serve him. This discours made the comander the more narrowly to inspect Mr. Bridgar. & to stand better upon his gard, the Scotch man telling him hee was not come thither with any good intention; so that the comander of the Fort sent him away in the morning, having given him some Pork, Pease, & Powder. Having given Orders at the fort, I went to Mr. Bridgar. Being come to his House, I taxed him of breach of promise, & I tould him ther should bee no quarter if hee offered to doe soe any more, & that therefore hee should prepare himself to goe for the Bay (as soone as ever the Ice did permitt) in the vessell that wee had left, it being so agreed on by our french men, assuring him I would furnish him with all things necessary for the voyadge. Hee appear'd much amaz'd at the compliment I made him, & hee told me in plaine terms that it must bee one of thes 3 things that must make him quit the place,— his master's orders, force, or hunger. Hee desired me afterwards that if the captain of the salvages of the river of new Severn came, that hee might see him by my means, which I promis'd to doe.

Having thus disposed Mr. Bridgar for his departure, I continued to assist him & his people with all that I could to enable them to work to sit ourselves to bee gon. I left Mr. Bridgar in his house & I went unto ours, & having consulted my Brother-in-Law, wee resolved that 'twas best to burn the fort in the Island & secure Mr. Bridgar, thereby to draw back our men & to ease us of the care of defending the fort & of the trouble of so many other precautions of securing ourselves from being surprized by Mr. Bridgar. The crew of both our vessells made an agreement amongst themselves to oppose our dessigne of giving our shipp unto the English for their transportation. It was necessary at the first to seeme to yeeld, knowing that in time wee should master the factions. It was the master of my Bark that began the mutiny. The chief reason that made me seem to yeeld was that I would not have the English come to know of our Divisions, who happly might have taken some advantage of it. Wee had 4 amongst us unto whom I granted libberty upon their parole; but to make sure of those of new England, wee caus'd a Lodge to bee built in a litle Island over against our House where they were at a distance off us. Wee sent from time to time to visit them to see what they did. Wee gave them a fowling-peece to divert them, but one day abusing my nephew, wee took away the Gun from them.

Going afterwards unto the fort of the Island, I sent a boate unto Mr. Bridgar, advising him the captain hee desired to see was come, & that hee might come with one of his men; which hee did, & as soon as hee was come I told him that to assure our Trade I was obliged to secure him & would commit him into the custody of my nephew, unto whom I would give orders to treat him kindly & with all manner of respect, telling him withall that when I had put all things on board the vessell that was in the fort, I would go & set it on Fier. I told him hee might send his man with me to his House with what Orders hee thought fit. I went thither the same day. I told Mr. Bridgar's people that not being able to supply them any longer but with Powder only, & being redy for my departure to Cannada, it was necessary that those that intended to stay should speak their minds, & that those that desired to go should have their passage. I demanded their names, which they all told me except 2. I ordered them to have a great care of all things in the House. I left one frenchman to observe them & to goe fowling, Mr. Bridgar's men not being us'd to it. These Orders being given, I left Mr. Bridgar's house & cross'd over to the South side, where I met 2 of our french men a hunting. I sent them with what fowle they had kill'd to the fort of the

Island, where they might bee servisable unto the rest in carrying down the shipp & in bringing her to an anker right against Mr. Bridgar's house, to take on board his goods, which was accordingly don. I came by land unto the other river, & met at the entrance of it severall Indians that waited impatiently for me, how wee might adjust & setle our Trade.

They would have had my Brother-in-Law to have rated the Goods at the same prizes as the English did in the bottom of the Bay, & they expected also I would bee more kind unto them. But this would have ruined our trade; therefore I resolved to stand firm in this occasion, becaus what wee now concluded upon with these Salvages touching comers would have ben a Rule for the future. The Indians being assembled presently after my arrivall, & having laid out their presents before me, being Beavors' tailes, caribou tongues dry'd, Greas of Bears, Deere, & of Elks, one of the Indians spake to my Brother-in-Law & mee in this wife: "You men that pretend to give us our Lifes, will not you let us live? You know what Beavor is worth, & the paines wee take to get it. You stile your selves our brethren, & yet you will not give us what those that are not our brethren will give. Accept our presents, or wee will come see you no more, but will goe unto others." I was a good while silent without answering the compliment of this Salvage, which made one of his companions urge me to give my answer; and it being that wheron our wellfare depended, & that wee must appear resolute in this occasion, I said to the Indian that pressed me to answer, "To whom will thou have me answer? I heard a dogg bark; let a man speak & hee shall see I know to defend myself; that wee Love our Brothers & deserve to bee loved by them, being come hither a purpose to save your lives." Having said these words, I rose & drew my dagger. I took the chief of thes Indians by the haire, who had adopted me for his sonn, & I demanded of him who hee was. Hee answered, "Thy father." "Well," said I, "if thou art my father & dost love me, & if thou art the chief, speak for me. Thou art master of my Goods; this Dogg that spoke but now, what doth hee heare? Let him begon to his brethren, the English in the Bay; but I mistake, hee need not goe so farr, hee may see them in the Island," intimating unto them that I had overcom the English. "I know very well," said I, continueing my discours to my Indian father, "what woods are, & what 'tis to leave one's wife & run the danger of dying with hunger or to bee kill'd by one's Ennemys. You avoide all these dangers in coming unto us. So that I see plainly 'tis better for you to trade with us than with the others; yet I will have pitty on this wretch, & will spare his life, though hee has a desire to goe unto our Ennemys." I caused a sword-blade to bee brought me, & I said unto him that spake, "Heere, take this, & begon to your brethren, the English; tell them my name, & that I will goe take them." There was a necessity I should speak after this rate in this juncture, or else our trade had ben ruin'd for ever. Submit once unto the Salvages, & they are never to bee recalled.

Having said what I had a mind to say unto the Indian, I went to withdraw with my Brother-in-Law; but wee were both stop't by the chief of the Indians, who incouraged us, saying, Wee are men; wee force nobody; every one was free, & that hee & his Nation would hold true unto us, that hee would goe perswade the Nations to come unto us, as hee had alredy don, by the presents wee had sent them by him; desiring wee would accept of his, & that wee would trade at our own discretion. Therupon the Indian that spake, unto whom I had presented the sword, being highly displeas'd, said hee would kill the Assempoits if they came downe unto us. I answer'd him I would march into his country & eate Sagamite in the head of the head of his grandmother, which is a great threat amongst the Salvages,

271

& the greatest distast can bee given them. At the same instant I caus'd the presents to be taken up & distributed, 3 fathom of black tobacco, among the Salvages that were content to bee our friends; saying, by way of disgrace to him that appear'd opposit to us, that hee should goe smoak in the country of the tame woolfe women's tobacco. I invited the others to a feast; after which the salvages traded with us for their Beavors, & wee dismissed them all very well sattisfy'd.

Having ended my business with the Indians, I imbark'd without delay to goe back, & I found the new England shipp at anchor over against Mr. Bridgar's House, as I had order'd. I went into the House & caus'd an Inventory to be taken of all that was there. Then I went to the fort of the Island, having sent order to my nephew to burn it. I found him there with Mr. Bridgar, who would himself bee the first in setting the Fort a fire, of which I was glad. There being no more to doe there, I went down to the shipp, & found they had put everything abord. I gave Order to my Nephew at my coming away that the next day hee should bring Mr. Bridgar along with him unto our House, where being arriv'd, my Brother-in-Law, not knowing him as well as I did, made him bee sent into the Island with the Captain of the new England shipp & his folks; of which Mr. Bridgar complain'd unto me next day, desiring that I would release him from thence, saying hee could not endure to bee with those people; which I promis'd to doe, & in a few days after brought him unto a place I caus'd to bee fitted on a point on the North side of our River, where hee found his own men in a very good Condition. I not being yet able to overcome our Men's obstinacy in not yeelding that I should give our vessell unto the English, Mr. Bridgar propos'd that hee would build a Deck upon the Shallup if I would but furnish him with materialls necessary for it; saying that if the shallup were but well decked & fitted, he would willingly venture to goe in her unto the Bay, rather then to accept of his passage for france in one of our vessells. I offerr'd him all that hee desir'd to that purpos, & stay'd with him till the shipp that I caus'd to bee fitted was arriv'd. When shee was come, I see a smoak on the other side of the River. I crossed over, & found that it was my Indian father. I told him how glad I was to see him, & invited him to goe aboard, saying that going at my request, my nephew would use him civilly; that they would fier a Great Gun at his arrivall, would give him something to eate, would make him a present of Bisketts, & of 2 fathom of Tobacco. Hee said I was a foole to think my people would doe all this without order. I wrote with a coale on the rind of a Tree, & gave it to him to carry aboard. Hee, seeing that All I said unto him was punctually perform'd, was much surpris'd, saying wee were Divells; so they call thos that doe any thing that is strange unto them. I return'd back to our houses, having don with Mr. Bridgar.

I had sounded the Captain of the Shipp that was in the Island right against our house, to know of him that, being an English man, whether hee would give a writing under his hand to consent that Mr. Bridgar should bee put in posession of his shipp, or if hee had rather I should carry her to Quebeck; but hee & his men intreated mee very earnestly not to deliver them unto Mr. Bridgar, beleeving they should receave better usage of the french than of the English. I told my Brother-in-Law what the Captain said, & that hee refer'd himself wholy unto our discretion.

Whilst wee were busy in fitting things for our departure, I found myself necessitated to compose a great feude that hapined betwixt my Indian father's familly & another great familly of the country. I had notice of it by a child, some of my Indian father's, who playing with his comrades, who quarrelling with him, one told him that hee should bee kill'd, & all his Familly, in revenge of one of the family of the Martins, that his father had kill'd; for the famillys of the Indians are distinguis'd by the names of Sundry Beasts; & death being very affrighting unto thos people, this child came to my House weeping bitterly, & after much adoe I had to make him speak, hee told me how his comrade had threatned him. I thought at first of somthing else, & that the salvages had quarrel'd amongst themselves. Desiring, therefore, to concern my self in keeping peace amongst them, I presently sent for this chief of the Indians, my adopted father, who being come according to my order, I told him the cause of my feare, & what his child had told me. I had no sooner don speaking, but hee leaning against a pillar and covering his face with his hands, hee cryed more than his child had don before; & having asked what was the matter, after having a litle dry'd up his teares, hee told me that an Indian of another familly, intending to have surpris'd his wife, whom hee loved very tenderly, hee kill'd him, & the salvages that sided to revenge the other's cause having chased him, hee was forc'd to fly, & that was it that made him meet mee about 8ber last; that hee continued the feare of his Ennemys' displeasure, that they would come kill him.

I tould him hee should not fear any thing, the frenchmen being his fathers & I his sonn; that our king that had sent mee thither cover'd him with his hand, expecting they should all live in Peace; that I was there to setle him, & that I would doe it or dye; that I would require all the Indians to come in that day [that they] might know me & that hee should know my intentions. Having thus spoke unto him, I caus'd a fowling-peece & 2 ketles, 3 coats, 4 sword-blades, 4 tranches, 6 graters, 6 dozen of knives, 10 axes, 10 fathom of tobacco, 2 coverlets for women, 3 capps, some Powder & shott, & said unto the salvage my adopted father, in presence of his allies that were ther present, "Heere is that will cure the wound & dry away tears, which will make men live. I will have my brethren love one another; let 2 of you presently goe and invite the family of the Martins to the feast of amity, and make them accept my presents. If they refute it & seek for blood, it is just I should sacrifice my life for my father, whom I love as I doe all the rest of the Indians our allies, more than I doe my owne selfe, So that I am redy to lay down my head to bee cutt off in case my presents did not serv turn, but I would stirr up all the frenchmen my brethren to carry Gunns to assist me to make warr against that familly."

The salvages went to goe unto the familly that was ennemy unto my adopted father to make them offer of my presents, & in my name to invite them unto the feast of unity. I stay'd so litle a while in the country afterwards that I could not quite determine this differrence. In due time I will relate what upon Inquiry I farther heard of it in my last voyadge.

This businesse being upon a matter ended, I was inform'd that Mr. Bridgar, contrary to his promise of not speaking with the Indians, yet enter'd into discours with them & said that wee were Ill people, & told them hee would come & kill us; that hee would traffick with them more to their advantage then wee did; that hee would give them 6 axes for a Bever Skin & a fowling-peece for 5 skins. I taxed Mr. Bridgar with it, also I ratted the salvages, who promis'd they would go neere him no more, & that I should feare nothing. Being desirous to make all things redy for my departure, I againe crossed over the dangerous river to goe burn Mr. Bridgar's House, there being nothing left remaining in it, having caused evry thing to bee put on board the New England shipp & taken a full Inventary of it before. I had along with me 3 English men & one frenchman, relying more on the English, who loved me because I used them kindly, than I did on the ffrenchmen.

What I did at this time doth shew the great confidence I put in the English; for had I in the least distrusted them, I would not have ventur'd to have gon 11 Leagues from my habitation with 3 English & but one of my owne french men to have fired Mr. Bridgar's House. Wee were very like to bee lost in returning home. I never was in so great danger in all my life. Wee were surpris'd with a suddain storm of wind neere the flats, & there was such a great mist that wee knew not where wee were.

Being return'd unto our Habitation, I found our Men had brought the shipp to anker neere our House, & seeing the weather beginning to come favorable, I gave my Nephew Instructions to carry on the Trade in my absence untill our Return. I left 7 men with him & the absolute comand & disposall of all things; which being don I caused our ffurrs to bee put on board & the shipp to fall down to the mouth of the river to set saile the first faire wind. It was where I left Mr. Bridgar. His shallup being well provided & furnish'd with all things, hee was ready to saile; but having made some tripps from one river unto the other, the sight of such vast quantitys of Ice as was in those seas made him afraide to venture himselfe in so small a vessell to saile unto the Bay. So that wee fitting things to bee gon the 20 July, having sent for Mr. Bridgar to come receave his Provisions, hee told me hee thought it too rash an action for him to venture himself so great a voyadge in so small a vessell, & desired I would give him passage in our shipp, supposing all along that I would compell him to imbark for ffrance. I told him hee should bee very welcom, & that I intended not to force him to anything but only to quitt the place. It was concluded that hee should imbark with my Brother-in-Law in the small vessell. Hee said hee had rather goe in the other shipp; but it was but just that the Captain should continue on board, & wee could not with great reason take Mr. Bridgar on board, having allredy more English to keep then wee were french.

The 27th of July wee weighed Ankor & passed the flatts; but next day, having as yet sailed but 8 or 9 Leagues, wee were forced to enter into the Ice & used all our Endevor not to bee farr from each other. The Bark, tacking to come, cast her Grapers on the same Ice as wee fastned unto. Shee split to peeces, so that wee were forced to fend presently to their help & to take out all the goods was on board her, & to lay them on the Ice, to careen, which wee did with much difficulty. Wee continued in this danger till the 24 of August. Wee visitted one another with all freedom; yet wee stood on our gard, for the Englishman that wee found the beginning of the winter in the snow, remembring how kindly hee was used by me, gave mee notice of a dessigne the Englishmen had that were in the Bark, of cutting all the Frenchmen's throats, & that they only waited a fit opportunity to doe it. This hint made us watch them the more narrowly. At night time wee secured them under lock & key, & in the day time they enjoy'd their full liberty.

When wee were got to the southward in the 56 Degree, Mr. Bridgar desired me to let him have the Bark to goe to the Bay along with his men. I tould him I would speak to my Brother-in-Law about it, who was not much against it. Ther was only the master & some other obstinat fellows that opposed; but at length I got all to consent, and having taken the things out, wee delivered the Bark unto Mr. Bridgar, taking his receipt. It was in good will that I mannadg'd all this for him, and I thought hee would have gon in the Bark, for hee knows that I offerrd it unto him; but having made the Englishman that belong'd unto him, and since chosen to stay with us, and in whom wee put much confidence, to desire leave of me to goe along with Mr. Bridgar, wee presently supposed, and wee were not deceived, that 'twas by his perswasion this seaman desired to bee gon, & wee had some apprehension that Mr. Bridgar might have some dessigne to trepan us by returning unto port Nelson before us to surprise our people, wherunto the English seaman that understood our business might have ben very servicable unto him. Having therefore conferr'd amongst ourselves upon this Demand, wee resolv'd to keep Mr. Bridgar and to take him along with us unto Quebeck. Wee caus'd him to come out of the Bark and told him our resolution; wherat hee flew into great passion, espetially against me, who was not much concerned at it. Wee caus'd him to come into our vessell, and wee tould his people that they may proceed on their voyage without him, and hee should come along with us; after which wee took in our graple Irons from off the Ice, seeing the sea open to the westward and the way free'd to saile. Wee were distant about 120 leagues from the bottom of the Bay when wee parted from the Bark, who might easily have got ther in 8 days, and they had Provisions on board for above a month, vizt, a Barrill of Oatmealle, 42 double peeces of Beeff, 8 or 10 salt gees, 2 peeces of Pork, a powder Barrell full of Bisket, 8 or 10 pounds of powder, & 50 pounds of short. I gave over & above, unknown to my Brother-in-Law, 2 horns full of Powder & a Bottle of Brandy, besides a Barrill they drank the evening before wee parted. I made one of the new England seamen to goe on board the Bark to strengthen the crew, many of them being sickly.

Being got out of the Ice, having a favorable wind, wee soon got into the straights, where through the negligence or the ignorance of one of our French pilots and seamen, the English being confin'd in the night, a storm of wind & snow drove us into a Bay from whence wee could not get out. Wee were driven a shoare without any hopes of getting off; but when wee expected evry moment to be lost, God was pleased to deliver us out of this Danger, finding amongst the Rocks wherin wee were ingadg'd the finest Harbour that could bee; 50 shipps could have layn there & ben preserv'd without Anchor or cable in the highest storms. Wee lay there 2 days, & having refitted our shipp wee set saile & had the wether pretty favorable untill wee arriv'd at Quebeck, which was the end of 8ber. As soon as ever wee arriv'd wee went unto Monr La Barre, Governor of Cannada, to give him an Account of what wee had don. Hee thought fit wee should restore the shipp unto the new England Merchants, in warning them they should goe no more unto the place from whence shee came. [Footnote: This restoration did not meet with the approval of Monsr. de Seignelay, for he wrote to Govr. De la Barre, 10th April, 1684: "It is impossible to imagine what you meant, when of your own authority, without calling on the Intendant, and without carrying the affair before the Sovereign council, you caused to be given up to one Guillin, a vessel captured by the men named Radisson and des Grozelliers, and in truth you ought to prevent the appearance before his Majesty's eyes of this kind of proceeding, in which there is not a shadow of reason, and whereby you have furnished the English with matter of which they will take advantage; for by your ordinance you have caused a vessel to be restored that according to law ought to be considered a Pirate, having no commission, and the English will not fail to say that you had so fully acknowledged the vessel to have been provided with requisite papers, that you had it surrendered to the owners; and will thence pretend to establish their legitimate possession of Nelson's river, before the said Radisson and des Grozeliers had been there." New York Colonial MSS., Vol. IX. p. 221.] Mr. Bridgar imbark'd himself on her with young Guillem for New England against my mynde, for I advis'd him as a friend to imbark himself on the ffrench shipps, which were ready to saile for Rocheil. I foretold him what came to pass, that hee would lye a long while in New England for passage. Wee parted good ffriends, & hee can beare me witnesse that I intimated unto him at that time my affection for the English Intrest, & that I was still of the same mynde of serving the King & the nation as fully & affectionately as I had now serv'd the ffrench.

Eight or tenn days after my arrivall, Monsr. La Barre sent for me, to shew me a letter hee had receaved from Monsr. Colbert by a man-of-warr that had brought over some soldiers, by which hee writ him that those which parted last yeare to make discoverys in the Northern parts of America being either returned or would soon return, hee desired one of them to give the court an account of what they had don, & of what setlements might bee made in those parts; & the Governour told me that I must forthwith prepare myself to goe sattisfy Monsr. Colbert in the business. I willingly accepted the motion, & left my business in the hands of Monsr. De La Chenay, although I had not any very good opinion of him, having dealt very ill by me; but thinking I could not bee a looser by satisfying the prime Minister of state, although I neglected my owne privat affaires, I took leave of Monsr. La Barre, & imbark'd for france with my Brother-in-Law, the 11 9ber, 1683, in the frigat that brought the soldiers, and arrived at Rochell the 18 of Xber, where I heard of the death of Monsr. Colbert; yet I continued my jorney to Paris, to give the Court an account of my proceedings. I arriv'd at Paris with my Brother-in-Law the 15th January, wher I understood ther was great complaints made against me in the King's Councill by my Lord Preston, his Majesty's Envoy Extrordinary, concerning what had past in the River and Port Nelson, and that I was accus'd of having cruelly abused the English, Robbed, stoln, and burnt their habitation; for all which my Lord Preston demanded satisfaction, and that exemplary punishment might bee inflicted on the offenders, to content his majesty. This advice did not discourage me from presenting myself before the Marquiss De Signalay, & to inform him of all that had past betwixt the English and me during my voyadge. Hee found nothing amiss in all my proceedings, wherof I made him a true relation; and so farr was it from being blamed in the Court of france, that I may say, without flattering my self, it was well approved, & was comended. [Footnote: Louis XIV. to De la Barre, to April, 1684: "The King of England has authorized his ambassador to speak to me respecting what occurred in the river Nelson between the English and Radisson and des Grozelliers, whereupon I am happy to inform you that, as I am unwilling to afford the King of England any cause of complaint, & as I think it important, nevertheless, to prevent the English establishing themselves on that river, it would be well for you to have a proposal made to the commandant at Hudson's Bay that neither the French nor the English should have power to make any new establishments; to which I am persuaded he will give his consent the more readily, as he is not in a position to prevent those which my subjects wish to form in said Nelson's river."] I doe not say that I deserv'd it, only that I endeavor'd, in all my proceedings, to discharge the part of an honnest man, and that I think I did no other. I referr it to bee judged by what is contain'd in this narrative, which I protest is faithfull & sincere; and if I have deserved the accusations made against me in the Court of ffrance, I think it needlesse to say aught else in my justification; which is fully to bee seen in the Relation of the voyadge I made by his Majesty's order last year, 1684, for the Royal Company of Hudson's Bay; the successe and profitable returns whereof has destroyed, unto the shame of my Ennemys, all the evell impressions they would have given of my actions.

THE VOYAGE ANNO 1684

I have treated at length the narrative of my voyage in the years 1682 and 1683, in Hudson's Bay, to the North of Canada. Up to my arrival in the city of Paris, all things were prepared for the fitting out of the ships with which I should make my return to the North of Canada, pending the negotiations at Court for the return to me of every fourth beaver skin that the very Christian King took for the customs duty, which had been promised to me in consideration of my discoveries, voyages, and Services; by which I hoped to profit over & above my share during the first years of that establishment. It was also at the same time that my Lord Viscount Preston, Minister Extraordinary from the King at the Court of France, continued to pursue me concerning the things of which I was accused by the account against me of the gentlemen of the Royal Hudson's Bay Company; my enemies having taken due care to publish the enormous crimes of which I was charged, & my friends taking the pains to support me under it, & to give me advice of all that passed. Although at last no longer able to suffer any one to tax my conduct, I considered myself obliged to undeceive each one. I resolved at length within myself to speak, to the effect of making it appear as if my dissatisfaction had passed away. For that effect I made choice of persons who did me the honor of loving me, and this was done in the conversations that I had with them upon the subject. That my heart, little given to dissimulation, had avowed to them, on different occasions, the sorrow that I had felt at being obliged to abandon the service of England because of the bad treatment that I had received from them, & that I should not be sorry of returning to it, being more in a condition than I had been for it, of rendering service to the king and the nation, if they were disposed to render me justice and to remember my services. I spoke also several times to the English Government. I had left my nephew, son of Sieur des Groseilliers, my brother-in-law, with other Frenchmen, near Port Nelson, who were there the sole masters of the beaver trade, which ought to be considerable at that port, and that it depended upon me to make it profitable for the English. All these things having been reported by one of my particular friends to the persons who are in the interest of the Government, they judged correctly that a man who spoke freely in that manner, & who made no difficulty in letting his sentiments be known, & who shewed by them that it was possible to be easily led back, by rendering justice to him, to a party that he had only abandoned through dissatisfaction, I was requested to have some conferences with these same persons. I took in this matter the first step without repugnance, & upon the report that was made to my Lord Preston of things that we had treated upon in the interviews, & of that of which I claimed to be capable of doing, I was exhorted from his side of re-entering into my first engagements with the English; assuring me that if I could execute that which I had proposed, I should receive from His majesty in England, & from His Royal Highness of the Hudson's Bay Company, & from the Government, all kinds of good treatment & an entire satisfaction; that, moreover, I need not make myself uneasy of that which regarded my interests, this minister being willing himself to be charged with the care of me, to preserve them, & of procuring me other advantages after that I should be put in a position of rendering service to the King his master. They represented to me again that His Royal Highness honoring the Hudson's Bay Company with his protection, it would pass even on to me if I would employ upon it my credit, my attentions, & the experience that I had in the country of the North, for the utility & the benefit of the affairs of that Company, in which His Royal Highness took great interest.

At the same time I received some letters at Paris from the Sieur Ecuyer Young, one of those interested in the Hudson's Bay Company, in which he solicited me on his part, & in the name of the Company, to return into England, giving me some assurances of a good reception, & that I should have reason to be satisfied on my part in regard to my particular interests, as well as for some advantages that they would make me. These letters, joined to those in which my Lord Preston continued his urgencies against me to the very Christian King, decided me to determine, by the counsel of one of my friends, to yield myself at last to all their solicitations of passing over to England for good, & of engaging myself so strongly to the service of His Majesty, & to the interests of the Nation, that any other consideration was never able to detach me from it. There was only my Lord Preston, some of his household, & the friend who had counselled me to come into England, who knew of my design. I took care to save appearances from suspicion by the danger in which I exposed myself, & up to the evening of my departure I had some conferences with the ministers of the Court of France, & the persons who there have the departments of the marine & commerce, upon some propositions of armament, & the Equipment of the Ships destined for my 2nd voyage. They wished to bind me to make them upon the same footing as the proceeding, which has made since then the talk of the two nations.

The day of my departure was fixed for the 24th of April, 1684; but at last, that those with whom I was obliged to confer daily by order of the Ministers of France never doubted in the least of my discontinuing to see them, I told them that I was obliged to make a little journey into the country for some family business, & I could be useful to them during that time by going to London, where I arrived the 10th of May.

At the moment of my arrival I had the honor of going to see the gentlemen, Ecuyer Young and the Chevalier Hayes, both of whom were interested in the Hudson's Bay Company, who gave me a good reception in showing me the joy that they felt at my return, & in giving me such assurances that I should receive on their part & on that of their company all manner of satisfaction. I then explained fully to them the nature of the service that I expected to render to His Majesty, to the Company, & to the Nation, in establishing the Beaver trade in Canada & making those to profit by it who were interested, to the extent of 15 or 20,000 Beaver skins that I hoped to find already in the hands of the French that I had left there, that would cost to them only the Interest that I had in the thing, & the just satisfaction that was owing to the French who had made the trade for them.

These gentlemen having received in an agreeable manner my proposition, & wishing to give me some marks of their satisfaction, did me the honour of presenting me to His Majesty & to His Royal Highness, to whom I made my submission, the offer of my very humble services, a sincere protestation that I would do my duty, that even to the peril of my life I would employ all my care & attention for the advantage of the affairs of the Company, & that I would seek all occasions of giving proof of my zeal & inviolable fidelity for the service of the King, of all which His Majesty & His Royal Highness appeared satisfied, & did me the favour of honouring me with some evidences of their satisfaction upon my return, & of giving me some marks of their protection.

After that I had several conferences in the assembled body, & in particular with the gentlemen interested in the Hudson's Bay Company, in which I made them acquainted in what manner it was necessary for them to proceed there for establishing to the best advantage the Beaver trade in the Northern country, the means of properly sustaining it, & of ruining in a short time the trade with foreigners, & to that end I would commence by becoming master of both the fort & the settlement of the French, as well as of all the furs that they had traded for since my departure, on the condition that my influence would serve to convert them, & that my nephew whom I had left commandant in that fort & the other French would be paid what would be to them their legitimate due. These gentlemen, satisfied with what I had said to them, believed with justice that they would be able to have entire confidence in me. As for that, having resolved to entrust me with their orders for going with their shipps, equipped & furnished with everything to found that establishment in putting into execution my projects, they gave the power of settling in my own mind & conscience the claims of my nephew & the other French, assuring me that they would be satisfied with the account that I would present to them. I accepted that commission with the greatest pleasure in the world, and I hurried with so much diligence the necessary things for my departure, that in less than eight days I was in a condition to embark myself. This was done even without any precaution on my part for my own interests, for I did not wish to make any composition with these gentlemen. I said to them that since they had confidence in me, I wished also on my part to make use of it generously with them and remit everything to the success of my voyage, and on my return, in the hope that I had that they would satisfy my honesty of purpose, and that after having given to them some marks of my sincerity in executing the things to perform which I had engaged myself for their service, they would render me all the justice that I had cause for hoping from gentlemen of honour and probity. The ships destined for Hudson's Bay and the execution of my design were ready to make sail, &

myself being all prepared for embarking, I took leave of the gentlemen of the Company in giving them fresh assurances of the good success of my voyage if God did me the favour of preserving me from the dangers to which I went to expose myself; of which they appeared so well satisfied that the Chevalier Hayes dared not flatter himself of the advantage that I promised to him, that they should get from 15 to 20,000 Beavers that I hoped to find in the hands of the French, said, in embracing me, that the company would be satisfied if I had only 5,000 of them there.

The event has justified that which I predicted, and these gentlemen have not been deceived in the hopes that I have given to them. I departed from the port of Gravesend the 17th of the same month of May, in the ship called "The Happy Return," in the company of 2 others that these gentlemen sent also to Port Nelson for the same reason. The winds having been favourable for us, we arrived in a few days upon the western side of Buttons Bay without anything happening to us worth mentioning, but the winds and the currents. We having been made to drift to the South of Port Nelson about 40 leagues, and the ice having separated the ship in which I was from the 2 others in Hudson's Straits, I began to doubt of succeeding in my enterprise by the apprehension that I had that the 2 ships having arrived sooner than ours the men who were inside would not hazard themselves to take any step which could at all do them any damage. Under this anxiety, knowing the necessity that there was that I should arrive the first, I resolved to embark myself in a shallop that we had brought to be employed in any service that might be necessary. I ordered the captain to equip it, and although but little more than 20 leagues from Port Nelson, I put myself on board with 7 men, and after 48 hours of fatigue, without having been able to take any rest because of the danger that there was to us, we found by the breadth of Hayes river, which having recognized, at last we touched land at a point north of the river, where we landed with an Englishman who spoke good french, whom I wished to make accompany me in order that he might be the witness of all that I did.

After having come to land I recognized by certain marks that my nephew, having heard the noise of the cannon of the English ships, had come to the place where we landed to know if his father or myself were arrived, and that he had himself returned after having recognized that they were English shipps. These same marks gave me also to know that he had left me further away from those that I had given him since I had established him for Governor in my absence. The which should inform me of his condition and the place where he was with his men; but I did not find it to the purpose of going as far as that place, that I had not learned truly the condition of the English who had arrived in the country since I had departed from it. I resolved then to embark myself afresh in the shallop to go and learn some news. I encouraged for that purpose the 7 men who were with me, who were so diligent that in spite of a contrary wind and tide we arrived in a very little time at the mouth of that great and frightful river of Port Nelson, where I had wished to see myself with such impatience that I had not dreamed a moment of the danger to which we had exposed ourselves. That pleasure was soon followed by another; for I saw at anchor in this same place 2 ships, of which one had the glorious flag of His Majesty hoisted upon his main mast, that I recognized to be the one that was commanded by Captain Outlaw when the one in which I was passed had been separated from the 2 others. At the same time I made the shallop approach & I perceived the new Governor with all his men under arms upon the deck, who demanded of us where our shallop came from, and who we were. Upon that I made myself known, & I went on board the ship, where I learned that the one which was alongside was an English frigate that had wintered in the Port of Nelson with the Governor, which port they had abandoned to retire themselves for fear of being insulted by the French & the savages; but that having been met with by Capt Outlaw going out of the bay, he had returned, having learned that I had thrown myself into the service of England, and that I came into the country to re-establish there everything to the advantage of the nation.

My first care after that was of making myself informed of what had passed between the English & the French since my departure & their arrival. By what the English told me I judged that it was proper to risque everything to try to join my nephew as soon as possible, & the men that I had left with him; in fine, of endeavouring to reach them by kindness, or to intercept them by cunning, before they received the shock upon what design I came, for that was of extreme consequence. Thus without waiting for the arrival of the ship in which I had come, I resolved to embark myself upon the same shallop, which was named "The Little Adventure;" which I did not, nevertheless, on the same day, because the Governor found it proper to delay the party until the following day, & of giving me other men in the place of those that I had brought, who sound themselves fatigued. I embarked myself on the morrow, early in the morning, with Captain Gazer; but the wind being found contrary, I had myself landed on the coast, with Captain Gazer & the Englishman who spoke French, & after having sent back the shallop with the other men, I resolved to go by land as far as the place where I should find the marks of my nephew, which should make me recognise the place where he was & his condition. We marched, all three, until the morrow morning; but being arrived at the place where I had told my nephew to leave me some marks, which having taken up, I learned that he & his men had left our old houses & that they had built themselves another of them upon an island above the rapids of the river Hayes. After that we continued our route until opposite to the houses which had been abandoned, where I hoped that we should discover something, or at least that we should make ourselves seen or heard by firing some reports of the gun & making of smoke; in which my attempt was not altogether vain, for after having rested some time in that place we perceived 10 canoes of savages, who descended the river. I believed at first that it would be probable they had there some French with them; that my nephew would be able to send to discover who were the people newly arrived, which obliged me to tell Captain Gazer that I should go down to the bank of the river to speak to them; that I prayed him to await me upon the heights without any apprehension, & that in a little while he would be able to render evidence of my fidelity for the service of the Company. I was at the same moment met by the savages, & from the bank of the river I made them the accustomed signal, to the end of obliging them to come towards me; but having perceived that they did not put themselves to the trouble of doing it, I spoke to them in their language, for to make myself known; which done, they approached the bank, & not recognising me, they demanded of me to see the marks that I had; which having shown them, they gave evidence, by their cries & postures of diversion, the pleasure that they had of my arrival. I learned then from them that my nephew & the other Frenchmen were above the rapids of the river, distant about 4 leagues from the place where I was, & that they had told them that my brother-in-law, des Groisille, should also come with me; which obliged me telling them that he was arrived, & that they would see him in a few days. Then I told them that we had always loved them as our brothers, & that I would give them some marks of my amity, for which they thanked me in begging me to not be angry for that which, by counsel, they had been trading with the English, nor of that when I found them going to meet their captain, who had gone across some woods, with 20 men, to the English ships, to procure some powder & guns, which they did; that their laying over for a month, in awaiting for me, had compelled them, but that since I had arrived they would not go on farther, & that their chief, whom they went to inform of my arrival, would speak more of it to me. As I had occasion for some one among them to inform my nephew that I was in the country, I asked of all of them if they loved the son of des Groisille, & if he had not some relation among them; upon which there was one of them who said to me, "He is my Son; I am ready to do that which thou wishest;" & at that moment, he having landed, I made him throw his Beaver skin on the ground, & after having called Captain Gazer, I spoke in these terms to this savage in the presence of all the others: "I have made peace with the English for love of you. They & I from henceforth shall be but one. Embrace this captain & myself in token of peace. He is thy new brother, & this one thy son. Go at once to him to carry this news, with the token of peace, & tell him to come to see me in this place here, whilst the savages of the Company go to attend me to the mouth of the river."

This savage did not fail to go & inform his son, my nephew, of my arrival, & of carrying to him the news of peace between the French & the English, during which we awaited with impatience his descent towards the place where we were; whom, nevertheless, did not arrive until the morrow, about 9 o'clock in the morning. I saw at first appear my nephew, in a canoe with 3 other Frenchmen, accompanied by another canoe of the savages that I had sent, & which came in advance to inform me of the arrival of my nephew. I promised to this savage & his comrade each one a watch-coat, & returned to them their Beaver skins, with the order of going to join those of their nation,

& to wait for me at the mouth of the river. After that, Captain Gazer, the Englishman who spoke French, & myself waded into the water half-leg deep to land upon a little island where my nephew, with his men, would come on shore. He had arrived there before us, & he came to meet us, saluting me, greatly surprised at the union that I had made with the English. We then proceeded all together in his canoe as far as our old houses, where I had the English and French to enter, & whilst they entertained each other with the recital of their mutual hardships, I spoke privately to my nephew in these terms:—

"It is within your recollection, without doubt, of having heard your father relate how many pains & fatigues we have had in serving France during several years. You have also been informed by him that the recompense we had reason to hope for from her was a black ingratitude on the part of the Court as well as on the part of the company of Canada; & that they having reduced us to the necessity of seeking to serve elsewhere, the English received us with evidences of pleasure & of satisfaction. You know also the motives that have obliged your father & myself, after 13 years of service, to leave the English. The necessity of subsisting, the refusal that showed the bad intention of the Hudson's Bay Company to satisfy us, have given occasion to our separation, & to the establishment that we have made, & for which I left you in possession in parting for France. But you ignore, without doubt, that the Prince who reigns in England had disavowed the proceedings of the Company in regard to us, & that he had caused us to be recalled to his service, to receive the benefits of his Royal protection, & a complete satisfying of our own discontents. I have left your father in England, happier than we in this, that he is assured of his subsistance, and that he commences to taste some repose; whilst I come to inform you that we are now Englishmen, & that we have preferred the goodness & kindness of a clement & easy king, in following our inclinations, which are to serve people of heart & honour in preference to the offers that the King of France caused to be made to us by his ministers, to oblige us to work indirectly for his glory. I received an order, before leaving London, of taking care of you, & of obliging you to serve the English nation. You are young, & in a condition to work profitably for your fortune. If you are resolved to follow my sentiments I never will abandon you. You will receive the same treatment as myself. I will participate even at the expense of my interests for your satisfaction. I will have a care also of those who remain under my control in this place with you, & I shall leave nothing undone that will be able to contribute to your advancement. I love you; you are of my blood. I know that you have courage & resolution; decide for yourself promptly, & make me see by your response, that I wait for, that you are worthy of the goodness of the clement prince that I serve; but do not forget, above all things, the injuries that the French have inflicted upon one who has given his life to you, & that you are in my power."

When my nephew had heard all that I had to say to him, he protested to me that he had no other sentiments but mine, & that he would do all that I would wish of him, but that he begged me to have care of his mother; to which I answered that I had not forgotten that she was my sister, & that the confidence that he gave me evidence of had on that occasion imposed upon me a double engagement, which obliged me of having care of her & of him; with which, having been satisfied, he remitted to me the power of commandant that I had left to him, & having embraced him, I said to him that he should appear in the assembly of the English & French as satisfied as he should be, & leave the rest to my management. After which we re-entered into the house, & I commanded one of the Frenchmen to go out immediately & inform his comrades that all would go well if they should have an entire confidence in me & obey all my orders, which doing, they should want nothing. I ordered also this same Frenchman to inform the savages to come to me & work immediately with their comrades to bring back into the house newly built the Beaver skins buried in the wood; & to that end, to be able to work with more diligence, I told them I would double their rations. Then I told my nephew to cross the river with the Frenchman who served him as interpreter, & go by land to the north side at the rendezvous that I had given to the savages the preceding day, whilst I would make my way by water to the same meeting-place with Captain Gazer & 2 other men who remained with me; the which having embarked in my nephew's canoe, I descended the river as far as the mouth, where I found the savages, who awaited me with impatience, they having been joined the following day by 30 other canoes of savages that I had had warned to descend, by their captain who had come towards me. We were all together in the canoes of the savages & boarded some ships which were stranded upon Nelson's River.

This was in that strait that the chief of the savages spoke to me of many things, & who after having received from my hands one of the presents designed for the chief of these nations, he told me that he & his people would speak of my name to all the nations, to invite them to come to me to smoke the pipe of peace; but he blamed strongly the English Governor for telling him that my brother had been made to die, that I was a prisoner, & that he had come to destroy the rest of the French. The chief of the savages added to the blame his complaint also. He said haughtily that the Governor was unworthy of his friendship & of those of their old brothers who commenced to establish it amongst them, in telling them such falsehoods. Grumbling & passion had a share in his indignation. He offered several times to inflict injuries upon the governor, who endeavoured to justify himself for these things that he had said to them through imprudence against the truth. But the chief savage would not hear anything in his defense, neither of those of the other Englishmen there; all of them were become under suspicion. Nevertheless I appeased this difference by the authority that I have upon the spirit of these nations; & after having made the governor & the chief embrace, & having myself embraced both of them, giving the savage to understand that it was a sign of peace, I said to him also that I wished to make a feast for this same peace, & that I had given orders what they should have to eat.

On such similar occasions the savages have the custom of making a speech precede the feast, which consists in recognising for their brothers those with whom they make peace, & praise their strength. After having informed the chief of the savages of the experience, strength, valour of the English nation, he acquitted himself with much judgment in that action, for which he was applauded by our and his own people. I said afterwards in presence of his people that the French were not good seamen, that they were afraid of the icebergs which they would have to pass across to bring any merchandise, besides that their ships were weak & incapable of resistance in the northern seas; but as to those of the English, they were strong, hardy, & enterprising, that they had the knowledge of all seas, & an infinite number of large & strong ships which carried for them merchandises in all weathers & without stoppage. Of which this chief, having full evidence, was satisfied.

He came to dine with us whilst his people were eating together of that which I had ordered to be given them. The repast being finished, it was a question with me whether I should commence to open a trade; & as I had formed the design of abolishing the custom which the English had introduced since I had left their service, which was of giving some presents to the savages to draw them to our side, which was opposed to that that I had practised, for in place of giving some presents I had myself made, I said then to the chief of the savages in the presence of those of his nation, "that he should make me presents that I ordinarily received on similar occasions." Upon that they spoke between themselves, & at length they presented me with 60 skins of Beaver, in asking me to accept them as a sign of our ancient friendship, & of considering that they were poor & far removed from their country; that they had fasted several days in coming, & that they were obliged to fast also in returning; that the French of Canada made them presents to oblige them to open their parcels; & that the English at the bottom of the bay gave to all the nations 3 hatchets for a Beaver skin. They added to that, that the Beaver was very difficult to kill, & that their misery was worthy of pity.

I replied to them that I had compassion for their condition, & that I would do all that was in my power to relieve them; but that it was much more reasonable that they made me some presents rather than I to them, because that I came from a country very far more removed than they to carry to them excellent merchandise; that I spared them the trouble of going to Quebec; & as to the difference in the trade of the English at the bottom of the Bay with ours, I told them that each was the master of that which belonged to him, & at liberty to dispose of it according to his pleasure; that it mattered very little of trading with them, since I had for my friends all the other nations; that those there were the masters of my merchandises who yielded themselves to my generosity for it; that there were 30 years that I had been their brother, & that I would be in the future their father if they continued to love me, but that if they were of other sentiments, I was very easy about the future; that I would cause all the nations around to be called, to carry to them my merchandises; that the gain that they would receive by the succour rendered them powerful & placed them in a condition to dispute the passage to all the savages who dwelt in the lands; that by this means they would reduce themselves to lead a languishing life, & to see their wives & children die by war or by famine, of which their allies, although powerful, could not guarantee them of it, because I was informed that they had neither knives nor guns.

This discourse obliged these savages to submit themselves to all that I wished; so that seeing them disposed to trade, I said to them that as they had an extreme need of knives & guns, I would give them 10 knives for one Beaver, although the master of the earth, the King, my sovereign, had given me orders to not give but 5 of them, & that as for the guns, I would give them one of them for 12 Beavers; which they went to accept, when the Governor, through fear or imprudence, told them that we demanded of them but 7 & up to 10 Beavers for each gun, which was the reason that it was made necessary to give them to the savages at that price. The trade was then made with all manner of tranquillity & good friendship. After which these people took their leave of us very well satisfied according to all appearances, as much in general as in particular of our proceeding, & the chief as well as the other savages promised us to return in token of their satisfaction. But at the moment that they went to leave, my nephew having learned from a chief of a neighbouring nation who was with them that they would not return, he drew aside the savage chief & told him that he had been informed that he did not love us, & that he would return no more. At which this chief seemed very much surprised in demanding who had told him that. My nephew said to him, "It is the savage called Bear's Grease;" which having heard, he made at the same time all his people range themselves in arms, speaking to one & to the other; in fine, obligeing the one who was accused to declare himself with the firmness of a man of courage, without which they could do nothing with him, but Bear's Grease could say nothing in reply. Jealousy, which prevails as much also among these nations as among Christians, had given place to this report, in which my nephew had placed belief because he knew that the conduct of the Governor towards them had given to them as much of discontent against us all as he had caused loss to the Company; the genius of these people being that one should never demand whatever is just, that is to say, that which one wishes to have for each thing that one trades for, & that when one retracts, he is not a man. That makes it clear that there are, properly, only the people who have knowledge of the manners & customs of these nations who are capable of trading with them, to whom firmness & resolution are also extremely necessary. I myself again attended on this occasion, to the end of appeasing this little difference between the savages, & I effected their reconciliation, which was the reason that their chief protested to me afresh in calling me "Porcupine's Head,", which is the name that they have given me among them, that he would always come to me to trade, & that whereas I had seen him but with a hundred of his young men, he would bring with him 13 different nations, & that he wanted nothing in his country, neither men nor beaver skins, for my service; after which they left us, & we dispersed ourselves to go and take possession of the house of my nephew in the manner that I had arranged with him for it.

With this in view I parted with the Governor, Captain Gazer, & our people to go by land as far as the place where we had left one of our canoes upon the river Hayes, whilst the other party went by sea with the shallop, "the Adventure," to round the point. We had the pleasure of contemplating at our ease the beauty of the country & of its shores, with which the Governor was charmed by the difference that there was in the places that he had seen upon Nelson's river.

We embarked ourselves then in the canoe just at the place where the French had built their new house, where we found those who were left much advanced in the work that I had ordered them to do, but, however, very inquiet on account of having no news from my nephew, their commandant, nor of me. They had carried all the beaver skins from the wood into the house & punctually executed all my other orders.

Having then seen myself master of all things without having been obliged to come to any extremity for it, the French being in the disposition of continueing their allegiance to me, I made them take an Inventory of all that was in the house, where I found 239 packages of beaver skins, to the number of 12,000 skins, and some merchandise for trading yet for 7 or 8,000 more, which gave me much satisfaction. Then I told my nephew to give a command in my name to these same Frenchmen to bring down the beaver skins as far as the place where they should be embarked to transport them to the ships, which was executed with so much diligence that in 6 days eight or ten men did (in spite of difficulties which hindered them that we could go in that place but by canoes because of the rapidity & want of water that they had in the river) what others would have had trouble in doing in 6 months, without any exaggeration.

My nephew had in my absence chosen this place where he built the new house that was, so to speak, inaccessible, to the end of guaranteeing himself from the attacks that they would be able to make against him; & it was that same thing which restrained the liberty of going & coming there freely & easily. The savages with whom we had made the trading, not having made so much diligence on their route as we, for returning themselves into their country, having found out that I was in our house, came to me there to demand some tobacco, because that I had not given them any of that which was in the ships, because that it was not good, making as an excuse that it was at the bottom of the cellar. I made them a present of some that my nephew had to spare, of which they were satisfied; but I was surprised on seeing upon the sands, in my walk around the house with the governor, rejected quantities of an other tobacco, which had been, according to appearances, thus thrown away through indignation. I turned over in my mind what could have possibly given occasion for this, when the great chief & captain of the savages came to tell me that some young men of the band, irritated by the recollection of that which the English had said to them, that my brother, des Groseilliers, was dead, that I was a prisoner, & that they were come to make all the other Frenchmen perish, as well as some reports of cannon that they had fired with ball in the wood the day that I was arrived, had thus thrown away this tobacco which had come from the English by mistake, not wishing to smoke any of it. He assured me also that the young men had wicked designs upon the English; that he had diverted them from it by hindering them from going out of the house. The Governor, who had difficulty in believing that this tobacco thrown upon the sands was the omen of some grievous enterprise, was nevertheless convinced of it by the discourse of the savage. I begged him to come with me into the house, & to go out from it no more, with the other English, for some time; assuring them, nevertheless, that they had nothing to fear, & that all the French & myself would perish rather than suffer that one of them should be in the least insulted. After which I ordered my nephew to make all those savages imbark immediately, so as to continue their journey as far as their own country, which was done. Thus we were delivered from all kinds of apprehension, & free to work at our business.

In the mean while I could not admire enough the constancy of my nephew & of his men in that in which they themselves laboured to dispossess themselves of any but good in favour of the English, their old enemies, for whom they had just pretensions, without having any other assurances of their satisfaction but the confidence that they had in my promises. Besides, I could not prevent myself from showing the pleasure that I experienced in having succeeded in my enterprise, & of seeing that in commencing to give some proofs of my zeal for the service of the English Company I made it profit them by an advantage very considerable; which gave them for the future assurances of my fidelity, & obliged them to have care of my interests in giving me that which belonged to me legitimately, & acquitting me towards my nephew & the other French of that which I had promised them, & that a long & laborious work had gained for them. After that, that is to say, during the 3 days that we rested in that house, I wished to inform myself exactly, from my nephew, in the presence of the Englishmen, of all that which had passed between them since that I had departed from the country, & know in what manner he had killed two Englishmen there; upon which my nephew began to speak in these words:—

"Some days after your departure, in the year 1683, the 27th of July, the number of reports of cannon-shots that we heard fired on the side of the great river made us believe that they came from some English ship that had arrived. In fact, having sent 3 of my men to know, & endeavour to understand their design, I learned from them on their return that it was 2 English ships, & that they had encountered 3 men of that nation a league from these vessels, but that they had not spoken to them, having contented themselves with saluting both. As my principal design was to discover the English ones, & that my men had done nothing in it, I sent back 3 others of them to inform themselves of all that passed. These 3 last, having arrived at the point which is between the 2 Rivers of Nelson & Hayes, they met 14 or 15 savages loaded with merchandise, to whom, having demanded from whence they were & from whence they had come, they had replied that their nation lived along the river called Nenosavern, which was at the South of that of Hayes, & that they came to trade with their brothers, who were established at the bottom of the Bay; after which my men told them who they were and where they lived, in begging them to come smoke with them some tobacco the most esteemed in the country; to which they freely consented, in making it appear to them that they were much chagrined in not having known sooner that we were established near them, giving evidence that they would have been well pleased to have made their trade with us.

"In continueing to converse upon several things touching trade, they arrived together in our house, reserving each time that but one of them should enter at once; which under a pretext of having forgotten something, one had returned upon his steps, saying to his comrades that they had leave to wait for him at the house of the French, where he arrived 2 days after, to be the witness of the good reception that I made to his brothers, whom I made also participants in giving to him some tobacco; but I discovered that this savage had had quite another design than of going to seek that which he had lost, having learned that he had been heard telling the other savages that he had been to find the English, & that he was charged by them of making some enterprise against us. In fact, this villain, having seen me alone & without any defence, must set himself to execute his wicked design. He seized me by the hand, & in telling me that I was of no value since I loved not the English, &

that I had not paid him by a present for the possession of the country that I lived in to him who was the chief of all the nations, & the friend of the English at the bottom of the Bay, he let fall the robe which covered him, & standing all naked he struck me a blow with his poniard, which I luckily parried with the hand, where I received a light wound, which did not hinder me from seizing him by a necklace that he had around his neck, & of throwing him to the ground; which having given me the leisure of taking my sword & looking about, I perceived that the other savages had also poniards in their hands, with the exception of one, who cried out, 'Do not kill the French; for their death will be avenged, by all the nations from above, upon all our families.'

"The movement that I had made to take my sword did not prevent me from holding my foot upon the throat of my enemy, & knew that that posture on my sword had frightened the other conspirators. There was none of them there who dared approach; on the contrary, they all went out of the house armed with their poniards. But some Frenchmen who were near to us, having perceived things thus, they ran in a fury right to the house, where having entered, the savages threw their poniards upon the ground in saying to us that the English had promised to their chief a barrel of powder & other merchandise to kill all the French; but that their chief being dead, for they believed in fact that he was so, we had nothing more to fear, because that they were men of courage, abhorring wicked actions. My people, having seen that I was wounded, put themselves into a state to lay violent hands on the savages; but I prevented any disturbance, wishing by that generousity, & in sparing his life to the chief, to give some proofs of my courage, & that I did not fear neither the English there nor themselves. After which they left us, & we resolved to put ourselves better upon our guard in the future, & of making come to our relief the savages our allies.

"Some days after, these savages, by the smoke of our fires, which were our ordinary signals, arrived at our house. According to their custom, they having been apprised of my adventure, without saying anything to us, marched upon the track of the other savages, & having overtaken them, they invited them to a feast, in order to know from them the truth of the things; of which having been informed, the one among them who was my adopted brother-in-law spoke to the chief who had wished to assassinate me thus, as has been reported to me by him: 'Thou art not a man, because that, having about thee 15 of thy people thou hast tried to accomplish the end of killing a single man.' To which the other replied haughtily, & with impudence, 'It is true; but if I have missed him this autumn with the fifteen men, he shall not escape in the Spring by my own hand alone.' 'It is necessary,' then replied my adopted brother-in-law, 'that thou makest me die first; for without that I shall hinder thy wicked design.' Upon which, having come within reach, the chief whose life I had spared received a blow of a bayonet in the stomach, & another of a hatchet upon the head, upon which he fell dead upon the spot. In respect to the others, they did not retaliate with any kind of bad treatment, & they allowed them to retire with all liberty, in saying to them that if they were in the design of revenging the death of their chief, they had only to speak, & they would declare war upon them.

"After that expedition these same savages our allies divided into two parties, & without telling us their design descended to the place where the English made their establishment; they attacked them & killed some of them, of which they then came to inform me, in telling me that they had killed a great number of my enemies to avenge me of the conspiracy that they had done me & my brother, and that they were ready to sacrifice their lives for my service; in recognition of which I thanked them & made them a feast, begging them not to kill any more of them, & to await the return of my father & my uncle, who would revenge upon the English the insult which they had made me, without their tarnishing the glory that they had merited in chastising the English & the savages, their friends, of their perfidy. We were nevertheless always upon the defensive, & we apprehended being surprised at the place where we were as much on the part of the English, as of those of the savages, their friends; that is why we resolved of coming to establish ourselves in the place where we are at present, & which is, as you see, difficult enough of access for all those who have not been enslaved as we are amongst the savages. We built there this house in a few days with the assistance of the savages, & for still greater security we obliged several among them to pass the winter with us on the condition of our feeding them, which was the reason that our young men parted in the summer, having almost consumed all our provisions. During the winter nothing worthy of mention passed, except that some savages made several juggles to know from our Manitou, who is their familiar spirit among them, if my father and my uncle would return in the spring; who answered them that they would not be missing there, and that they would bring with them all kinds of merchandise and of that which would avenge them on their enemies.

"At the beginning of April, 1684, some savages from the South coast arrived at our new house to trade for guns; but as we had none of them they went to the English, who had, as I afterwards learned, made them Some presents & promised them many other things if they would undertake to kill me with the one of my men whom you saw still wounded, who spoke plainly the language of the country.

These savages, encouraged by the hope of gain, accepted the proposition and promised to execute it. For that means they found an opportunity of gaining over one of the savages who was among us, who served them as a spy, and informed them of all that we did. Nevertheless they dared not attack us with open force, because they feared us, & that was the reason why they proceeded otherwise in it; and this is how it was to be done.

"The Frenchman that you saw wounded, having gone by my orders with one of his comrades to the place where these savages, our friends, made some smoked stag meat that they had killed, to tell them to bring me some of it, fell, in chasing a stag, upon the barrel of his gun, and bent it in such a manner that he could not kill anything with it without before having straightened it; which having done, after having arrived at the place where the savages were, he wished to make a test of it, firing blank at some distance from their cabin; but whilst he disposed himself to that, one of the savages who had promised to the English his death & mine, who was unknown to several of his comrades amongst the others, fired a shot at him with his gun, which pierced his shoulder with a ball. He cried out directly that they had killed him, & that it was for the men who loved the French to avenge his death; which the Savages who were our friends having heard, went out of their cabins & followed the culprit without his adherents daring to declare themselves. But the pursuit was useless, for he saved himself in the wood after having thrown away his gun & taken in its place his bow & his quiver. This behaviour surprised our allies, the savages, exceedingly, & obliged them to swear, in their manner, vengeance for it, as much against that savage nation as against the English; but not having enough guns for that enterprise, they resolved to wait until my father and uncle had arrived. In the mean time they sent to entreat all the nations who had sworn friendship to my father & my uncle to come to make war upon the English & the savages on the southern coast, representing to them that they were obliged to take our side because that they had at other times accepted our presents in token of peace & of goodwill; that as to the rest, we were always men of courage, & their brothers.

"As soon as these other nations had received intelligence of the condition in which we were, they resolved to assist us with all their forces, & in waiting the return of my father or my uncle to send hostages for it to give a token of their courage, in the persons of two of their young men. One of the most considerable chiefs among these nations was deputed to conduct them. I received them as I ought. This chief was the adopted father of my uncle, & one of the best friends of the French, whom I found adapted to serve me to procure an interview with the English, to the end of knowing what could possibly be their resolution. For that purpose I deputed this chief savage towards the English, to persuade them to allow that I should visit them & take their word that they would not make me any insult, neither whilst with them nor along the route there, for which this chief stood security. The English accepted the proposition. I made them a visit with one of the French who carried the present that I had seat to make them, in the manner of the savages, & who received it on their part for me according to custom. We traded nothing in that interview regarding our business, because I remembered that the English attributed directly that which had been done against them to the savages. All the advantage that I received in that step was of making a trade for the savages, my friends, of guns which I wanted; although they cost me dear by the gratuity which I was obliged to make to those who I employed there; but it was important that I had in fact hindered the savages from it who came down from the country to trade, of passing on as far as the English. The end of that invitation and that visit, was that I promised to the solicitation of the Governor of the English of visiting there once again with my chief; after which we retired to our house, where I was informed by some discontented savages not to go any more to see the English, because that they had resolved either to arrest me prisoner or of killing me. Which my chief having also learned, he told me that he wished no more to be security with his word with a nation who had none of it; which obliged us to remain at home, keeping up a very strict guard. At the same time the river Hayes having become free, several detachments of the nations who were our allies arrived to assist us. The Asenipoetes [Footnote: Asenipoetes, Assinipoueles, Assenipoulacs, and, according to Dr. O'Callaghan, Assiniboins, or "Sioux of the Rocks."] alone made more than 400 men. They were the descendants of the great Christionaux of the old acquaintance of my uncle, & all ready to make war with the English; but I did not find it desirable to interest them in it directly nor indirectly, because I did not wish to be held on the defensive in awaiting the return of my father or of my uncle, & that besides I knew that several other nations who loved the French, more particularly those who would come to our relief at the least signal. In the mean time the chief of the Asenipoetes did not wish us to leave his camp around our house, resolved to await up to the last moment the return of my uncle, of whom he always spoke, making himself break forth with the joy that he would have in seeing him by a thousand postures; & he often repeated that he wished to make it appear that he had been worthy of the presents that the Governor of Canada had made to him formerly in giving tokens of his zeal to serve the French.

"The necessity for stores which should arrive in their camp partly hindered the effects of that praiseworthy resolution, & obliged the chief of the Asenipoetes to send back into his country 40 canoes in which he embarked 200 men of the most feeble & of the least resolute. He kept with him a like number of them more robust, & those who were able to endure fatigue & hunger, and determined having them to content themselves with certain small fruits, which commenced to ripen, for their subsistence, in order to await the new moon, in which the spirit of the other savages had predicted the arrival of my uncle, which they believed infallible, because their superstitious custom is of giving faith to all which their Manitou predicts. They remained in that state until the end of the first quarter of the moon, during which their oracles had assured them that my uncle would arrive; but the time having expired, they believed their Manitou had deceived them, & it was determined between them to join themselves with us & of separating in 2 bodys, so as to go attack the English & the savages at the south; resolved in case that the enterprise had the success that they expected, of passing the winter with us, to burn the English ships in order to remove the means of defending themselves in the Spring & of effecting their return. That which contributed much to that deliberation was some information which was given to them that the English had formed a design of coming to seek the French to attack them, which they wished to prevent.

"These menaces on the part of the English were capable of producing bad effects, the genius of the savages being of never awaiting their enemies, but on the contrary of going to seek them. In this design the chief of the Asenipoetes disposed himself to march against the English with a party of his people; when 10 or 12 persons were seen on the northern side of the Hayes river seeking for these same fruits on which the savages had lived for some time, he believed that they were the advance guard of the English & of the savages from the South, whom he supposed united, who came to attack us; which obliged him to make all his men take their bows and arrows, after which he ranged them in order of battle & made this address in our presence: 'My design is to pass the river with 2 of the most courageous among you to go attack the enemy, & of disposing of you in a manner that you may be in a condition of relieving me or of receiving me, whilst the French will form the corps of reserve; that our women will load in our canoes all our effects, which they are to throw over in case necessity requires it But before undertaking this expedition I wish that you make choice of a chief to command you in my absence or in case of my death.' Which having been done at the moment, this brave chief addressing us said: 'We camp ourselves upon the edge of the wood with our guns, so as to hinder the approach of the enemy; & then it would be necessary to march the men upon the edge of the water, to the end that they should be in a condition to pass to support or to receive him, according to the necessity.'

"After that he passes the river with 2 men of the most hardihood of his troops, who had greased themselves, like himself, from the feet up to the head. Having each only 2 poniards for arms, their design was to go right to the chief of the English, present to him a pipe of tobacco as a mark of union, & then, if he refused it, endeavour to kill him & make for themselves a passage through his people with their poniards as far as the place where they would be able to pass the river to be supported by their men. But after having marched as far as the place where the persons were who they had seen, they recognized that it was some women; to whom having spoken, they returned upon their steps, & said to us that there was nothing to fear, & that it was a false alarm. This general proceeding on their part gave us proofs of their courage & of their amity in a manner that the confidence that we had placed in their help had put us in a condition of fearing nothing on the part of the English nor of those there of the savages of the South; and we were in that state when God, who is the author of all things, & who disposes of them according to his good pleasure, gave me the grace of my uncle's arrival in this country to arrest the course of the disorders, who could come & work for our reconciliation. That work so much desired on both sides is accomplished. It depends not upon me that it may not be permanent. Live henceforth like brothers in good union & without jealousy. As to myself, I am resolved, if the time should arrive, of sacrificing my life for the glory of the King of Great Britain, for the interest of the nation & the advantage of the Hudson's Bay Company, & of obeying in all thirds my uncle."

I found this with regard to repeating the recital that my nephew made us concerning what had passed between him & the English & the savages, their allies, that although he had apprised me of the true state in which the 2 parties were at the time of my arrival, yet I also saw plainly the need that the English had of being succoured, & the necessity that the French had for provisions, of merchandise, and especially of guns, which could not come to them but by my means.

But it is time to resume the care of our affairs, & to continue to render an account of our conduct. Our people worked always with great application to transport the beaver skins a half league across the wood, for it was the road that it was necessary to make from the house as far as the place where the shallops were, & they carried them to the little frigate, which discharged them upon the ships. I was always present at the work, for the purpose of animating all our men, who gave themselves in this work no rest until it was done, & that against the experience of the Captains of our ships, whom some had made believe that the business would drag at length; but having gone to them I assured them that if they were ready to do so they could raise the anchor to-morrow.

There things thus disposed of, it only disturbed me yet more to execute a secret order that the company had given me, leaving it, however, to my prudence and discretion. It was of retaining in its service my nephew and some other Frenchmen, & above all the one who spoke the savage dialect, who was the wounded one, to remain in the country in my absence, which I dared not promise myself. In the meantime I resolved to make the proposition to my nephew, believing that after gaining him I should be able easily to add the others also. I caused to assemble for that end 5 or 6 of the savages of the most consideration in the country with the Governor, & in their presence I said to him, that for the glory of the King & for the advantage of the company it was necessary that he should remain in the country. To which he was averse at first; but the Governor having assured him that he would trust him as his own nephew, & that he would divide the authority that he had with him, & myself on my part having reproached him that he was not loyal to the oath of allegiance that he had sworn to me, these reasons obliged him to determine, & he assured me that he was ready to do all that I wished of him. What contributed much was the discourse that the savages made to him, telling him that I left him amongst them to receive in my absence the marks of amity that they had sworn to me, & that they regarded him as the nephew of the one who had brought peace to the nations & made the union of the English & French in making by the same means the brothers of both.

This last success in my affairs was proof to me of the authority that I had over the French & the savages; for my nephew had no sooner declared that he submitted himself to do what I wished, than all the other Frenchmen offered themselves to risk the ennui of remaining in the country, although my design was only to leave but two of them; & the savages on their part burst out in cries of joy in such a manner that I no more considered after that but to put an end to all things.

All our beaver skins having been embarked, I resolved, after having put everything into tranquil & assured state for my return into England, where my presence was absolutely necessary, to make known to the Company in what manner it was necessary to act to profit advantageously the solid establishment that I came to do & the things which were of indispensible necessity in the country to facilitate the trade with the savages & hindering them from making any of it with foreigners, that is to say, with the French of Canada.

I was then for the last time with my nephew at the house of our Frenchmen, to the end of leaving there some Englishmen. I found there a number of savages arrived to visit me, who called my nephew & myself into one of their cabins, where a venerable old man spoke to me in these terms: "Porcupine's head, thy heart is good & thou hast great courage, having made peace with the English for the love of us. Behold, we have come towards thee, old & young, wives & daughters & little children, to thank thee for it, & to recognise thee for our father. We wish to be the children & adopt for our son thy nephew that thou lovest so much, & in fine to give thee an eternal mark of the obligation that we have to thee. We weep no more henceforth except for the memory of those of whom thou bearest the name." After which, having told one of the young people to speak, he fell like as if in a swoon, & the other spoke after that same manner: "Men & women, young men & children, even those who are at the breast, remember this one here for your father. He is better than the sun who warms you. You will find always in him a protector who will help you in your needs & console you in your afflictions. Men, remember that he gave you guns during the course of the year for you to defend yourselves against your Enemies, & to kill the beasts who nourish you & your families. Wives, consider that he gave you hatchets & knives with which you banish hunger from your country; daughters & children, fear nothing more, since the one who is your father loves you always, & that he gave you from time to time all that is necessary for you to have your subsistance. We all together weep no more, on the contrary give evidence by cries of our mirth that we have beheld the man of courage;" & at the same time they set themselves to cry with all their might, weeping bitterly for the last time, in saying, "We have lost our father; [Footnote: "But here is one that you adopt for your father." Note by Radisson,] we have lost our children." [Footnote: "Here is the nephew of your father, who will be your son; he remains with you & he will have care of his mothers." Note by Radisson,]

After that piteful music they all came to be acknowledged. To be acknowledged by our adoption with some presents, & covering us with robes of white beaver skins, giving us quantities of beavers' tails, Some bladders of stag's marrow, several tongues of the same animal smoked, that which is the most exquisite to eat among them. They also presented us two great copper boilers full of smoked & boiled flesh, of which we ate all together, they, the English, & ourselves, & it is what is called a feast among these nations. After that I said adieu to them, & having given charge in the house what should be embarked in the ship, I went down to the mouth of the River, where Captain Gazer worked to build a fort in the same place where the preceding year Sieur Bridger had made to be constructed his shallop. It was the most advantageous situation that he had been able to find, & I advised that he should make all the diligence possible; but he had some men who by their delicacy were incapable of responding to his vigilence. I made this observation because I hold it for a maxim that one should only employ men robust, skilful, & capable of serving, & that those who are of a complexion feeble, or who flatter themselves of having protection & favour, ought to be dismissed.

Then we passed to the place where the ships were, because my design was to oblige by my presence the captains to return to their ships ready to make sail; but I was no sooner arrived there than a savage came to inform me that my adopted father, whom I had not seen because that he was at the wars, waited for me at the place where Captain Gazer was building the Fort of which I came to speak. That is why I resolved to go there, & I expressed the same hope to the savage whom I sent back to give information to my father that the Governor would come with me to make some friendship to him & protect him in my absence. It was with the consent of the Governor & upon his parole that I had told him that; nevertheless he did not wish to come, & I was for the first time found a liar among the savages, which is of a dangerous consequence, for these nations have in abomination this vice. He came to me, however, in no wise angry in that interview, & I received not even a reproach from him.

When I was at the rendezvous they told me that my adopted father was gone away from it because I had annoyed a savage, for he had been informed that I had arrived to see him. This savage having remembered the obligation to return, although very sad on account of some news that he had learned upon the road, which was that the chief of the nation who inhabited the height above the river Neosaverne, named "the bearded," & one of his sons, who were his relations, had been killed in going to insult those among the savages who were set to the duty of taking care of the Frenchman who had been wounded by a savage gained over by the English, after that he had embraced me, & that he had informed me of the circumstance of that affaire, & the number of people he had as followers, I wrote to the Governor to come to me in the place where we were, to make him know in effect that he must after my departure prevent the continuation of these disorders in virtue of the treaty of peace & of union that I had made in presence of the savages between the French & the English.

The Governor having arrived, I presented to him my adopted father, & said to him that as it was the chief who commanded the nation that inhabited in the place where they built the fort, I had made him some little presents by Captain Gazer, & that it was also desirable that he make some to him, because I had promised some the preceeding year that I had not given; which the Governor found very bad, & he became irritated even against this chief without any cause for it; except that it might be because he was my adopted father, & I have learned since that he was angry that when I had arrived I had not given any present to a simple savage who served as a spy, who was the son of that chief called "the bearded." That was a horrible extravagence; for this Governor was inferior to me, & I was not under any obligation to recognize his favor; besides, I had never made any presents but to the chiefs of the nations. Moreover, it was not for our Governor to censure my conduct. I had received some independent orders, which had been given me on account of the outrage that he had committed; but acting for the service of my King and for those of the Company, I passed it over in silence. I saw that it would be imprudent if I should speak my sentiments openly to a man who after my departure should command all those who remained in the country.[Footnote: "That would have perhaps drawn upon him some contempt." Note by Radisson.] I contented myself then with letting him know the inconveniences which would happen from the indifference that he affected to have for the chief of the savage nations, & I exhorted him also to change at once his policy in regard to my adopted father; not by that consideration, but because that he was, as I said to him, the chief of the nations which inhabited the place where they built the fort, which he promised me of undoing. After that I went on board our ship.

My nephew, who remained in the fort with the Governor, having learned that the ships were ready to leave, kept himself near me with the French whom I had resolved to leave in Canada, to say adieu to me, & it was in the company of this Governor that they made the journey, during which, as I have since learned from my nephew, he showed to them more good will than he had yet done, assuring them that they should never want anything, & in consideration of me they would receive the same treatment as himself. The behaviour that my nephew & the other Frenchmen had shown gave no reason for doubting the sincerity of their protestations. They no longer believed that any one could have any mistrust of them. My nephew & his interpreter had been solicited to remain in the country to serve the company, & they had consented to it without a murmur because I had charged myself with the care of their interests in England. All that passed in the presence and by the persuasions of the Governor. Nevertheless, behold a surprising change which came to pass by the inconstancy, the caprice, & the wicked behaviour of this same Governor.

I disposed myself to part with the other Frenchmen, when the Governor, having come aboard of the little frigate, caused a signal to be made to hold a council of war. Upon this the Captains of the ships & myself rendered ourselves on board, where my nephew followed us, remaining upon the poop, whilst the officers & myself were in the room where this Governor demanded of us, at first, if we had any valid reasons why he should not send back in the ships all the Frenchmen who were in the country; to all which the others having said nothing, I was obliged to speak in these terms: "At my departure from England I received a verbal order from the company, in particular from Sir James Hayes, to leave in the country where we are as many of the Frenchmen as I should find desirable for the good & advantage of the company. I have upon that resolved to engage my nephew & his interpreter to remain in it, & I have come for that end, by my attendance, for the consent of the Governor, who demands to-day that they may be sent back as people who apparently are known to him as suspected. I have always believed, & I believe it still, that their presence is useful in this Country and also necessary to the Company, and it was difficult to be able to overlook two, because they are known to all the nations. It is also upon them that I have relied for the Security of the merchandises which are left behind at the houses of the French, because without their assistance or their presence they would be exposed to pillage. Nevertheless I do not pretend to oppose my self to the design that the Governor has put in execution & the proposition that he proposes making. He is free to undo what he pleases, but he cannot make me subscribe to his resolutions, because I see that they are directly opposed to those of the Company, to my instructions, and to my experience. On the contrary, I will protest before God and before men against all that he does, because, after what he has said to you, he is incapable of doing what is advantageous for his masters. It is in vain that one should give him good councels, for he has not the spirit to understand them, that he may again deal a blow to which he would wish I opposed nothing."

This declaration had without doubt made some impression upon a spirit not anticipated in an imaginary capacity of governor; but this one here, on the contrary, fortified himself in his resolution, & begged me to tell the French to embark themselves, without considering that my nephew had not time enough to go seek his clothes, nor several bonds that were due to him in Canada, which remained in the house of the French, and that I had abandoned to him, to yield whatever I was in a condition of giving satisfaction to him, & that in the hope that the Company would set up for him the way exclusively.

The Council after that broke up; but the Governor, apprehending that the Frenchmen would not obey, wished to give an order to the Captains to seize upon them and put them on board. He had even the insolence of putting me first on the lists, as if I was suspected or guilty of something, for which Captain Bond having perceived, said to him that he should not make a charge of that kind, as I must be excepted from it, because he remembered nothing in me but much of attachment for the service of his masters, & that they should take care of the establishment that we had made, & of the advantages that would accrue to the Company. They obliged the Governor to make another list, and thus finished a council of war held against the interests of those who had given power to assemble them. The persons who had any knowledge of these savages of the north would be able to judge of the prejudice which the conduct of this imprudent Governor would without contradiction have caused the Company. Many would attribute his proceeding to his little experience, or to some particular hatred that he had conceived against the French. Be it as it may, I was not of his way of thinking; and I believed that his timidity & want of courage had prompted him to do all that he had done, by the apprehension that he had of the French undertaking something against him; & what confirmed me in that thought was the precaution that he had taken for preventing the French from speaking to any person since the day of council, for he put them away from the moment that we went away from them. I made out also that he had wanted but the occasion of putting to the sword my nephew if he had had the least pretext; but knowing his wicked designs, I made him understand, as well as the other Frenchmen, that we were to go to England, & that he must not leave the ship, because we were at any moment ready to depart.

Although this change surprised my nephew & his interpreter, nevertheless they appeared not discontented with it, especially when I had assured them, as well as the other Frenchmen, that they would receive all kinds of good treatment in England, and that it would do them no harm in their persons nor in their pretensions. I left them then in the ship, and having embarked myself in the frigate, we were put ashore two leagues from the place where they were at anchor, to take on board some goods that remained on the shore, with more diligence than we had been able to make with the ships; which having succeeded in happily doing, we went to rejoin the ships at the place where they were at anchor, in one of which my nephew and the other Frenchmen were staying during this time without having taken the least step, although they were in a condition for any enterprise, because they could easily render themselves masters of the two ships and burn them, having there for both but two men and one boy in each; after which they could also, without danger, go on shore on the south side with the canoes of the savages, who were from the north, and then make themselves masters of their houses and their merchandise, which were guarded but by two men; but to go there to them, he made doubts of all that I had told him, and that it would be ill intentioned to the service of the company, as it was to the Governor. That is why they were not capable, neither those nor the others, after having submitted themselves & having taken the oath of fidelity as they had done.

At length, after having suffered in my honour and in my probity many things on the part of the Governor, [Footnote: "Before Radisson's arrival, Capt. John Abraham had been to Port Nelson with supplies of stores, & finding Mr Bridgar was gone, he staid himself, & was continued Governor by the Company in 1684." Oldmixon.] and much fatigue and indisposition of trouble and of care in my person, to come to the end of my design, having happily succeeded, and all that was to be embarked in the ships being on board, we made sail the 4th day of September, 1684, and we arrived at the Downs, without anything passing worth mentioning, the 23rd of October of the same year.

The impatience that I had of informing the Gentlemen of the Hudson's Bay Company of the happy success of my voyage, and our return, and that I had acquitted myself for the service of the King and their own interest in all the engagements into which I had entered, obliged me to mount a horse the same day, to present myself in London, where I arrived at midnight. All which did not hinder me, so the Sieur Ecuyer Young was informed, who was one of those interested, who having come to me on the morrow morning to take me, did me the honour to present me to His Majesty and to His Royal Highness, to whom I rendered an account of all which had been done; and I had the consolation of receiving some marks of the satisfaction of these great princes, who in token gave order to the Sieur Ecuyer Young to tell the company to have care of my interests, & to remember my services.

Some days after, I went before the Committee of the Hudson's Bay Company, to render to it an account of my conduct, hoping to receive their approbation of my proceeding as the first fruits of the just satisfaction &

recompence which was my due; but in place of that I found the members of the Committee for the most part offended because I had had the honour of making my reverence to the King and to his Royal Highness, & these same persons continued even their bad intention to injure me, and, under pretext of refusing me the justice which is due to me, they oppose themselves also to the solid and useful resolutions that are necessary for the glory of his Majesty and the advantage of the Nation and their own Interest.

FINIS